Katherine Sudor

essential
statistics for
social research

essential statistics for social research

Michael A. Malec
Boston College

J. B. Lippincott Company
PHILADELPHIA
New York   San Jose   Toronto

Copyright © 1977 by J. B. Lippincott Company

This book is fully protected by copyright and,
with the exception of brief excerpts for review,
no part of it may be reproduced in any form by
print, photoprint, microfilm, or by any other
means without the written permission of the
publishers.

ISBN 0-397-47357-5

Library of Congress Catalog Card Number 76-56202

Printed in the United States of America

2 4 6 8 9 7 5 3 1

Library of Congress Cataloging in Publication Data

Malec, Michael A.
    Essential statistics for social research.

    Bibliography: p.
    Includes index.
        1. Social sciences—Statistical methods.
I. Title.
H61.M4224   300'.1'82   76-56202
ISBN 0-397-47357-5

To My Parents with Love and Appreciation

preface

In the past few years there has been a small flood of texts written on statistics in the social sciences. Other than contributing to the author's publication record, his recognition by peers, or his wallet, is there any justification for yet another statistics text? Obviously, I think there is; in fact, there are two reasons which justify this book: practicality and purpose.

As a practical matter, it is my contention that many of today's texts contain much material that is useless to the beginning student and omit much material that the beginning student could well use. This contention is based on an unpublished study of mine in which I examined the use of statistics in four major sociology journals (*American Sociological Review, American Journal of Sociology, Social Forces*, and *Sociometry*) between 1966 and 1973. This study confirmed what I have long suspected—that sociologists actually *use* a very small number of statistics in their published work, that some statistics are not covered at all or are given only superficial mention in many texts (e.g., simple descriptive statistics, or analysis of variance) and that many of the statistics which appear in texts rarely or never appear in sociology journals (e.g., the Mann-Whitney U). This disjunction between what sociologists emphasize in their textbooks and what sociologists actually use as statistical tools has come about for a variety of reasons, not all of which, I suspect, are good. However, this situation is easily remedied by first determining what statistics are used, and then by teaching these to students.

The question of purpose is related to that of practicality. Why do we write statistics texts? What do we hope that students will learn? Why do we want the student to learn a particular subject? I suggest that we do all of these things to help students gain some appreciation of how sociologists do their work. From the beginning course, we tell students about the importance of *method* in sociology (and statistics is a method) but we rarely encourage them to grapple with the statistical method. Consequently, students do not read the current literature, or, if they do, they are not able to fully appreciate it, since the literature today is so heavily dependent on statistics. In other words, we allow students to be literate but not numerate; they may understand words, but not numbers. Thus, my purpose in writing this book is to encourage students to become numerate, to give them the knowledge and understanding of statistics that will enable them to more intelligently read the current sociological literature.

To the Student

This book is written for you, a student just beginning to study statistics. The greater bulk of the text has been used in my classes for four years. My students have pointed out to me the weak spots in earlier drafts, and, if the text has improved in the last few rewritings, it is they who have helped to make it so. I now hope that *you* will continue this helpful process. If, as you use this text, you find sections that are not clear, or if you think a better example or illustration could be developed, please let me know. You may contact me directly or through the publisher.

I wish to give special thanks to three men who introduced me to the art and science of statistics and statistical thinking. They are N. M. Downie, B. J. Winer, and especially Richard J. Hill, a gifted teacher who made exhilarating the study of statistics. Thanks are also due to President J. Donald Monan, S.J., and Dean Charles F. Donovan, S.J., of Boston College who have wisely maintained the leave policy which gave me the time and support to finish this work. Lorraine Bone was, as always, a patient and diligent typist and proofreader; Jeanne Fleming and Kichiro K. Iwamoto carefully corrected the final manuscript, though whatever errors may remain are my sole responsibility. Finally, as the dedication attests, I wish to pay special tribute to my parents, who have given me a lifetime of love.

Michael A. Malec
Boston College 1976

contents

preface vii

1 *introduction* 1

2 *organization and presentation of data* 11

3 *descriptive measures: centrality* 21

4 *measures of dispersion* 42

5 *bases of statistical inference, I: probability and the logic of hypothesis testing* 58

6 *bases of statistical inference, II: sampling and estimation* 75

7 *testing for the difference between means* 90

8 *measuring the association between two nominal level variables* 108

9 *measuring association between two ordinal level variables* 137

10 *measuring association between two interval level variables* 161

11 *analysis of three or more variables* 184

appendix   statistical tables 199
   table A. squares and square roots of numbers from 1 to 1,000 199
   table B. proportions of area under the normal curve 214
   table C. critical values of student's t 217
   table D. critical values of sandler's A 219
   table E. critical values of F 220
   table F. critical values of chi-square 225
   table G. probability that S attains or exceeds a specific value 227
   table H. critical values of rho 228
   table I. critical values of the pearson r 228

references 230

index 233

. . . have you ever noticed that those who have a natural capacity for calculation are, generally speaking, naturally quick at all kinds of study; while men of slow intellect, if they are trained and exercised in arithmetic, if they get nothing else from it, at least all improve and become sharper than they were before?

Plato, **The Republic**

introduction

We need only scan a newspaper or magazine, turn on a news broadcast, or open a sociology text or journal to see that we live in an age that is heavily dependent on statistical information. The extent of this dependency is such that it is rather difficult to be an educated person without having at least a passing acquaintance with basic statistics. More to the point, it is virtually impossible to be a capable social scientist without having a definite, if elementary, understanding of some basic statistics and statistical methods of analysis. But a casual acquaintance with a few simple statistics will not serve the social scientist who attempts to read competently the literature of the field. And if one wishes to do quantitative social research—and most research published today is quantitative—a more thorough knowledge of statistics is imperative. The aspiring sociologist need only examine the books and articles that are being published today for evidence of this claim. For example, a recent study of four major sociology journals showed that four out of every five articles published in the previous six-year period used some form of statistical analysis. Some of these articles, and other works published by sociologists, are incomprehensible without a statistics background; others will simply be read less intelligently or with a lessened sense of appreciation or criticism.

Of course, not all of the subfields of sociology require the same degree of familiarity with statistics. Certain areas of sociology, for example, theory, require little statistical knowledge. However, in other fields, such as demography, a strong competence in quantitative techniques is essential.

In this book, we hope to provide you, the student, with an understanding and appreciation of some of the basic statistics used in sociological work. While we will not focus exclusively on how to compute a certain statistic, we will indicate how such computing can be done. We will also present general ideas about the purpose and nature of statistics, the uses and abuses of statistics, so that you will have a fuller understanding of what you do and what you read. Stated differently, our goal will be to give you a fuller appreciation of the way in which many sociologists do their work. Since much of today's sociology depends on the use and understanding of statistical methods, you must understand not only the words of the English language, but also the numbers of statistical "language." To understand much of contemporary social research, you must be "numerate" as well as literate.

a fear of statistics?

We have written this book for the undergraduate student of sociology who, presumably, has little or no background in statistics, and who, judging from past classroom experience, does not approach this subject with any interest or enthusiasm. Indeed, many students approach it with considerable fear, anxiety, and, if the course is required, with a great deal of resentment and antipathy. We will try to persuade you that such feelings are misplaced.

If you are intelligent enough to have graduated from high school, you are fully capable of handling the mathematics and logical reasoning demanded of you in the following pages. The most complicated thing you will have to do mathematically is to find the square root of a number, which you can do by using published tables (found in the appendix of this book), a slide rule or a small electronic calculator. Other than that, if you can add, subtract, multiply and divide, you can certainly handle all of the mathematics you will encounter here. As you progress, some of this basic arithmetic will get quite cumbersome; for example, the numbers may get very large or very small. In these instances, a slide rule or calculator will be a great timesaver, and will probably insure greater accuracy. But always remember that you still will be performing the simple arithmetic operations of addition, subtraction, multiplication and division. No calculus, advanced algebra or the like is required. You *can* do the work in this book. It will be easier if you put away any fears and anxieties about mathematics.

Another point should be emphasized. At first, do not try to understand what you are doing in a mathematical sense. Rather, *think* about what is happening in a *logical* sense. Do not obey statistical formulas in a rote, unthinking fashion. Ask yourself: What am I doing? Why am I doing this? What does this problem ask for? What does my solution mean? Does it make sense? If you can answer these questions, your understanding of the mathematics involved will be greatly increased. You will be an intelligent consumer of statistical information, not a robot regurgitating gibberish that you do not understand and will immediately forget.

A SMALL EXAMPLE As noted previously, statistics is like a language. It has a vocabulary and a grammar. For our purposes you already know enough of the grammar (the rules for addition, subtraction, multiplication and division) to enable you to hold a simple conversation. You are probably not as familiar with the vocabulary of statistics, the special symbols and terms used by specialists in the field. This lack of familiarity may contribute to whatever uneasiness you may have brought to this course. But be assured that the vocabulary you will have to acquire is used for very good reasons. It enables us to communicate with each other in a precise fashion, and, more important to you now, it saves a great deal of time and work. The statistical vocabulary in this book is simple, and will be introduced slowly and clearly.

Part of this vocabulary is already familiar to you, for example, the arithmetic *mean*. This is the "average" that you learned to compute in the fourth grade: to compute the mean of a series of numbers, we add all of the numbers in the series, then divide that total by the number of figures in the series. Thus, if we have five numbers, 2, 4, 7, 8 and 11, the mean is found by adding, or summing:

$$2 + 4 + 7 + 8 + 11 = 32$$

then dividing this sum by the numer of items in the series:

$$\frac{32}{5} = 6.4$$

We will give a much fuller discussion of the mean and other averages in Chapter 2. Here, we simply wish to illustrate that the ground you are on is not totally unfamiliar.

We can also use the mean to calculate a baseball player's "batting average." This average, technically, is the *mean* number of hits per time at bat. A player who is batting .300 has made, on the average, three tenths of a hit each time he has been officially at bat. (Of course, there is no such thing as three tenths of a hit. Such a hit is only a mathematical construct, or idea or image in our minds. More commonly, we might think of the .300 hitter as one who hits safely three times out of ten, or thirty times per hundred at bats, or *three hundred* per thousand.)

purposes and types of statistics

In general, the kinds of statistics used by sociologists fall into one of two classifications: *descriptive statistics* and *inferential statistics*. The distinction between the two is not always logical, but it does have practical utility. Descriptive statistics, as the term implies, give us at a glance a picture of the data with which we are dealing. These statistics are generally intended to give a reasonably accurate representation of a large mass of data, a representation that is based directly on the raw data. Often, these statistics are used to summarize a body of information. For example, the decennial census of the United States can tell us such things as whether there are more televisions than bathtubs in this country, or how many families own more than two cars. Inferential statistics take us beyond the raw data, to generalizations about even larger units of study. For example, public opinion polls, such as the Harris or Gallup polls, might tell us that 52 percent of the voters prefer Senator Phogghorn, and this might be a reasonably accurate description of the preferences of the 1,500 people who were interviewed. But the pollster, the Senator and the public are not interested in just these 1,500 people; they want to know how *all* of the prospective voters feel. Consequently, the statistician is called upon to draw certain inferences from the responses of the 1,500 and to indicate how all of the voters will behave. Inferential statistics are extremely useful when we are confronted with situations in which it is impossible to assemble all of the data we might need. For example, if you manufacture light bulbs, you might want to tell your consumers about the life expectancy of the bulbs. You could determine this by taking each bulb as it came off the production line and burning it until it gave out. You could then compute some very accurate descriptive information about light bulb life expectancy. Unfortunately, you would have no bulbs to sell, since you destroyed each one in the process of measurement. An alternative procedure would involve sampling your supply of bulbs, say one bulb of every two hundred produced, taking your measuremements of life expectancy on this sample and making an inference about all the bulbs on the basis of your measurements on the sample. Indeed, this is how much industrial quality control is done, and it is how Harris and Gallup make their estimates of voter behavior.

We will now briefly discuss a few of the specific types of descriptive and inferential statistics. In so doing we will also summarize the remaining chapters in this book.

Speaking most generally, the purpose of statistics is to help us interpret information, or data. There are many ways to do this. As noted above, you are probably already familiar with at least one of the several averages which are used to calculate a *typical* measure, or measure of *central tendency* (Chapter 3). We will discuss three of these averages: the mean, the median and the mode. For example, we might note from a census report that the median family income in the (imaginary) town of Jonesville in 1975 was 8,400 dollars. It is certainly far easier to work with this single, simple figure than it would be to handle the hundreds or thousands of particular family income figures for each family in Jonesville. This ease of handling is one of the great advantages of descriptive statistics. (However, by reducing the many particular family income figures to a single average figure, we necessarily lose some of the finer points of information that are contained in the large mass of data. This illustrates a never-ending dilemma for the user of statistics: at what point does the convenience of a summary measure outweigh the utility of having many measures? Or, to state it differently, when does the luxury of having information on each individual unit of measurement— in this case, the family—become too cumbersome to handle? Such questions must be answered according to the purposes of the research and the available resources.)

Taken by itself, a measure of central tendency is, therefore, quite limited. Fortunately, the statistician has additional statistical "tools" with which to work. Thus, although we may know that the median family income in Jonesville is 8,400 dollars, we are also likely to want information about how the total income in the community was distributed among the many families: how many families had incomes of less than 3,500 dollars? What proportion earned over 50,000 dollars? Answers to these questions come from statistical measures of *dispersion*, variability or spread (Chapter 4).

Properly chosen, measures of centrality and dispersion tell us much about a set of data. The measure of centrality gives us a central, focal point, and the measure of dispersion tells us how the various scores in the data set, or distribution, are spread about this focal point.

Another common use of statistics involves the creation and application of measures which enable us to compare different variables, and to relate them to one another. For example, a question such as, "How much is two apples plus three oranges minus one banana?" cannot be answered on its own terms (apples, oranges, bananas). It is either a fool's question, or the wise person can find some common element and answer, "Four pieces of fruit." The statistical analogue comes in the form of *standard scores* (Chapter 4). Standard scores enable the sociologist to look at very different social measures, such as income (measured in dollars) and suicide rate (measured in suicides per 100,000 population), and create the common ground for a meaningful discussion of how the two are related. As with the average, you are already familiar with such standard scores as those you received on the College Board exams. Your performance on various tests (verbal, quantitative and others) were "standardized" so that, for example, your verbal score could be compared with your quantitative score, or with the average verbal score obtained by all high school seniors in 1973.

Statistics which indicate how different variables are related to each other are called measures of *association*, or correlation (Chapters 8–10). We might use such measures to describe, for example, the relationship between family income levels and academic performance of children in elementary school.

Because sociologists are often interested in questions that relate to large numbers of people and because of the high costs (including costs of time, personnel and other resources) of obtaining measures on such large numbers, they often take measures on only a small portion or sample (Chapter 6) of the people in whom they are interested. Then, using their knowledge of *probability* (Chapter 5), they can make certain *estimates* (Chapter 6) of the larger population. These estimates are based on the data gathered from the small sample. From these estimates, certain predictions are often made. Public opinion polls use many of the statistical techniques. Some of these are related to the more general topic of *hypothesis testing* (Chapters 5–7).

In conclusion, we simply note that a variety of other statistical techniques and procedures which will enable us to analyze three or more variables simultaneously will also be discussed (Chapter 11).

measurement and levels of measurement

All statistical work in sociology rests on the fundamental assumption that we can, within reasonable limits, *measure* whatever it is that we are studying, whether it be suicide, crime, religiosity, alienation or any other variable. The problem of measurement is particularly acute for us, because many of our variables cannot be measured precisely. We have no agreed-upon yardstick with which to measure alienation. There is no measuring cup to tell us how much religiosity is in a person. Part of our problem as social scientists is to create our own measuring devices, and to get others to agree that these devices are reasonable, accurate, reliable and valid. The general problem of creating such devices is not a statistical one; it is a problem dealt with in books on research methods or, better yet, in courses dealing with the particular substantive area in which the research is being framed. Yet the statistician cannot be oblivious to the problems of measurement. Indeed, basic decisions about when to use which statistics, as opposed to others, rest upon our knowledge of the type of measurement being used.

Following Stevens (1946:3) we shall define *measurement* as "the assignment of numerals to objects or events according to rules." Stated differently, this definition tells us that we shall take an object or event (or thing or circumstance or quality or quantity), and assign to that entity one or more symbols, 1, 2, 3, . . . , which are called numerals. (Note: a numeral is distinguished from a number by the fact that the numeral does not necessarily have any quantitative value attached to it. Numerals may be numbers, but they are not necessarily numbers.) According to the definition, we must assign numerals according to rules. In the social sciences, we generally have three or four different sets of rules which we can use in our assignment of numerals. These different rules lead us to different *levels of measurement*.

NOMINAL LEVEL

Think for a moment of a basketball team. The five players wear jerseys, and each jersey has an identifying numeral, let us say, 3, 5, 12, 20 and 24. What do these "numbers" mean? Is player 24 twice as good as player 12? Is player 5 taller than player 3? Since $3 + 5 + 12 = 20$, does it follow that player 20 is the equal of the other three combined? Whatever the answers to these questions, they cannot be known from the numbers on the players' jerseys. The numbers are merely identifying signs, which are technically known as numerals. These numerals have no mathematical meaning. So it is with the assignment of numerals to certain types of sociological data.

Many of the variables that the sociologist works with have no real arithmetic qualities: religion, sex, political party and ethnicity are but a few examples. A person is Protestant, Catholic, Jew or "other;" male or female; Democrat, Republican or Independent and so on. Thus we "measure" political affiliation by determining which party a person belongs to. We might, however, have reason to change the symbols used to identify people's party preference. For example, we might say that Democrats will be labeled with numeral 1, Republicans with the numeral 2 and Independents with the numeral 3. Now instead of naming these people Democrat, Republican and Independent we have named them 1, 2 and 3. *But we should not fool ourselves into thinking that these numeral-names are numbers.* We have simply given a new name (the Latin word for name is *nomine*, hence, the nominal level of measurement) to our observation. Having made our nominal classification, we *cannot* now say that $1 + 2 = 3$ (that is, that Democrat plus Republican equals Independent). At this nominal level we must remember that 1, 2 and 3 are not numbers, they are numerals.

The nominal level of measurement is sometimes called the qualitative level. This term emphasizes the fact that at this level we are simply concerned with determining whether various objects are equal in the sense that they possess the same quality. Nothing is implied about the relationships that might exist among different qualities. In our example of political preference, our task is to find all the people who share a certain quality, such as being a Democrat, and to distinguish these people from others who do not possess that quality. Whether we do this by labeling our people as D, R or I, or as 1, 2 or 3 is unimportant. D and 1 are both merely naming devices for the quality of being a Democrat.

The only thing we can say about objects that are measured at the nominal level is that they are either equal to each other or not equal to each other. This level of measurement is thus very simple. We cannot perform even elementary arithmetic operations on such data. But because such measurement is simple does not mean it is of little use. In many instances, nominal level statistics are the only appropriate measures to use. We shall see evidence of this in the following chapters.

My acquaintances who have been to the race track tell me that they are quite uninterested in the time of the winning horse, or in the distance between the first and second horses, the second and third horses and so on. The only important thing to them is the *order* in which the horses finished. In other words, these latent statisticians are interested in ordinal measurement.

ORDINAL MEASUREMENT

Ordinal measurement is concerned with the ranking of objects or events. Ordinal measurement is thus more sophisticated than nominal measurement. At the nominal level, we are only concerned whether two objects, A and B, are equal or unequal in their possession of a certain quality. In ordinal measurement, we are additionally interested in whether A is greater than (larger than, weaker than and so on) B, or whether B is greater than A. (Of course, A and B may be equal.) Ordinal measurement allows us to *rank* objects or events according to some quality. This frequently happens when we lump data together into categories such as low, medium and high. If these terms refer to education, we can then know that all the people in the high category have more education than the people in the other two categories and that the people in the medium category have more education than the people in the low category, but less education than the people in the high category. What we have done is simply ranked our subjects into three categories. Consequently, we know that there is a "distance" between categories, but we do not know what the distance is. We cannot add these categories to each other or perform other mathematical operations on them. But having our categories rank ordered gives us a higher level of measurement than simply naming the categories.

At this point we introduce some mathematical symbols, or notations. These symbols are a kind of shorthand. Suppose we want to express an inequality between two objects, A and B. We might say that A is greater than B or A is less than B. Using mathematical notations, we can say the same thing by $A > B$ and $A < B$. The symbols $>$ and $<$ are inequality signs, just as $=$ is the sign of equality. In the usual sentence which reads from left to right, $<$ means is less than (or smaller than, weaker than and so on), and $>$ means is greater than (or larger than, stronger than and so on). (Occasionally you might also see these symbols: $\leq$ and $\geq$. These mean, respectively, is less than or equal to and is greater than or equal to.)

There is one other point to note about ordinal measurement. If we know that A $<$ B and B $<$ C, it must also be true that A $<$ C. (This is the mathematical property of transitivity.)

Sociologists make frequent use of ordinal level data. Some examples are socioeconomic status, birth order, or ordinal position, and the many attitude scales which range from strongly agree or agree to disagree or strongly disagree.

As with nominal measures, we cannot perform the familiar mathematical operations of addition, subtraction, multiplication or division on ordinal numbers. Ordinal measurement does permit a kind of ranking that cannot be done with nominal level data, but neither of these levels is quantitative or arithmetical in the usual and familiar sense.

INTERVAL AND RATIO MEASUREMENT

We can begin to perform arithmetic operations on data that are at the interval level of measurement. Interval numbers have magnitudes. The reason for this is that they are based on a common unit of measurement, so that the distance from one number to its adjacent number is equal to the distance from any other number in the system to its adjacent number. Thus, such numbers are marked by equal intervals. For example, if we consider a simple series of numbers, 1, 2, 3, 4 and 5, the distance between 2 and 3 is the same as the distance between 4 and 5 and is the same as the distance between 1 and 2. You might also have noticed that the distance between 1 and 3 is the same as the distance between 2 and 4 and between 3 and 5. Because the existence of equal intervals on such a measurement scale gives rise to magnitudes, we can perform arithmetic operations at this level.

The ratio level is distinguished from the interval level in that the ratio scales of measurement have a point of absolute zero. A frequently cited example of the difference between an interval and a ratio scale is found in the various systems we have for measuring heat. The Fahrenheit and Celsius thermometers have equal intervals but their zero points are arbitrarily fixed. The Kelvin thermometer also has equal intervals, but its zero point is set at absolute zero, the point at which there is a complete absence of heat.

In sociological research, the distinction between the interval and ratio levels is usually not important; the same statistics are often used for both levels. Examples of sociological variables used at these levels are income (ratio), IQ (interval), and family size (ratio).

Figure 1.1 summarizes the key points about the various levels.

Level	Nominal	Ordinal	Interval	Ratio
Can two objects be determined to be equal or unequal?	Yes	Yes	Yes	Yes
Can two objects be rank-ordered?	No	Yes	Yes	Yes
Can distances between objects be determined?	No	No	Yes	Yes
Does the scale have an absolute zero point?	No	No	No	Yes

Figure 1.1   *Levels of Measurement*

important terms to know
Descriptive statistics
Inferential statistics
Measurement: nominal, ordinal, interval and ratio

suggested reading
Every student beginning a course in statistics should read Darrel Huff's little book, *How to Lie with Statistics* (1954).

organization and presentation of data

Before statistical analysis of data can begin, we must organize our data in a meaningful, coherent fashion. After statistical analysis is complete, we must present our information to readers in a meaningful, coherent fashion. In this chapter, working with very simple data, we shall examine some of the basic techniques for organizing and presenting data. If there is a single theme in this chapter it is this: any use of data, especially for purposes of comparison, must be *meaningful*. All of the statistical "facts" in the world are useless if they are not meaningfully organized and presented. Let us begin our examination of this theme with a simple example.

rates

In 1973 there were 561 cases of murder or non-negligent manslaughter in the greater Philadelphia area; in that same year, there were 367 such cases in the greater Atlanta area. Examination of these two statistically accurate facts might initially lead us to conclude that, in terms of meeting a violent death, Atlanta is a safer place to be than Philadelphia. But is this comparison meaningful? For example, what would we conclude if we also considered the fact that these two areas differ in population? Greater Philadelphia's population was about 4,878,000, while the population of greater Atlanta was about 1,684,000 (U.S. Bureau of the Census, 1974). If we divide the number of murders in each area by the corresponding population, and multiply by 100,000, we obtain the following

2

murder *rates:* for Philadelphia, 11.5 per 100,000 population, and for Atlanta, 21.8 per 100,000 population. These new statistical facts have been made more meaningful than our original facts because the rates take into consideration the different populations of the two cities. Furthermore, the rates point to a conclusion which is directly opposite to our original conclusion. Our new conclusion is not that Atlanta is safer than Philadelphia, but that it is almost twice as dangerous.

A *rate* is a statistical measure which makes meaningful, direct comparison among two or more unequal data sets. Statistical rates usually consist of three elements. In our example, these elements are (1) the number of murders in the area, (2) the population of the area and (3) the arbitrary value of 100,000. (One hundred thousand is merely a convenient *numerical base.* It is simpler to refer to a murder rate of 21.8 per 100,000 than to a ratio of 0.000218 murders per person.) The number of murders can be called a *criterion variable* and the population a *norming variable.* (Population is the norm, or standard, against which we measure the number of murders.) We can define any rate as

$$\text{Rate} = \frac{\text{Frequency of Criterion Variable}}{\text{Frequency of Norming Variable}} \times \text{Numerical Base}$$

(Formula 2.1)
(Mueller, Schuessler & Costner, 1970: 183)

We can show how we computed Atlanta's murder rate using Formula 2.1. The criterion variable, number of murders, had a frequency of 367; the norming variable, population, was 1,684,000 and the numerical base was 100,000. The murder rate was thus calculated as

$$\frac{367}{1,684,000} \times (100,000) = 21.8.$$

Other examples of commonly used rates in sociology are the birth rate, death rate, marriage rate and divorce rate. Rates can be viewed as percentages or proportions which have been numerically adjusted to facilitate meaningful comprehension.

In addition to rates, data are frequently reported as *percentages, proportions* or *ratios.* A ratio is simply a rate whose numerical base is 1. Some rates are popularly referred to as ratios; for example, the sex ratio is defined as the number of males per one hundred females in a given population.

frequency distribution

A second device which facilitates comprehension and thereby makes data more meaningful is *frequency distribution.* A frequency distribution is a count of the number of cases within well-defined categories of a

table 2.1   **_murder rates for 145 SMSAs, 1973_**

5	10	12	11	10	7	2	15
4	15	6	16	16	5	11	4
13	16	16	2	10	16	5	4
3	11	14	8	17	4	10	12
3	3	14	5	5	6	20	12
5	14	15	19	10	8	2	18
2	18	6	3	17	21	4	1
22	4	16	5	4	20	15	9
12	6	15	3	14	10	8	19
10	5	7	4	13	2	5	16
5	10	12	5	3	4	5	
4	15	8	6	7	12	5	
16	2	4	17	20	8	3	
15	7	5	13	5	8	6	
2	8	14	7	17	9	9	
5	13	3	4	7	7		
4	3	16	17	4	3		
2	9	8	6	3	6		
22	12	13	11	16	13		
18	3	4	4	2	18		

variable. As an example, Table 2.1 lists the 1973 murder rates for 145 SMSAs.* Even a careful examination of this table will leave most readers with an unclear idea of the frequency of murder in American metropolitan areas: there is too much detail and the data are not well organized. But we can present these data in a clearer and more meaningful fashion if we _group_ the 145 murder rates and simply list the frequency for each group. Table 2.2 presents three possible ways of grouping the data into a frequency distribution. Which of these three shall we work with? How shall we decide which distribution is most useful? Let us briefly explore some principles to be observed in the construction of any frequency distribution.

In constructing any frequency distribution we perform two basic operations. We first decide the appropriate number of categories (or classes or intervals) into which we shall group the data; second, we sort and count all of the data into appropriate groups. The second task is purely clerical, so let us devote our attention to the rules for determining the categories. Freund (1973:11) has listed four such rules: (1) _Use at least six and not more than fifteen classes._ Too few classes, as in Table 2.2(c), will result in a homogenization of the data and distinctions

---

*SMSA, or Standard Metropolitan Statistical Area, is a term used by the U.S. Bureau of the Census and other agencies to refer to a city with 50,000 or more inhabitants (or a city of 25,000 plus its contiguous places which total 50,000 inhabitants). In Table 2.1 the SMSAs are those with a population of 200,000 or more.

table 2.2   frequency distributions of 145 murder rates

(a) CLASS INTERVAL = 1		(b) CLASS INTERVAL = 2	
MURDER RATE	FREQUENCY	MURDER RATE	FREQUENCY
1	1	1–2	10
2	9	3–4	28
3	12	5–6	24
4	16	7–8	15
5	16	9–10	12
6	8	11–12	11
7	7	13–14	11
8	8	15–16	17
9	4	17–18	9
10	8	19–20	5
11	4	21–22	3
12	7	TOTAL	145
13	6		
14	5		
15	7		
16	10	(c) CLASS INTERVAL = 6	
17	5	MURDER RATE	FREQUENCY
18	4	1–6	62
19	2	7–12	38
20	3	13–18	37
21	1	19–24	8
22	2	TOTAL	145
TOTAL	145		

between classes will be blurred. Too many classes, as in 2.2(a), will be almost as confusing as the original mass of ungrouped data. (2) *Define classes so that all cases will be included.* There are two points to consider here. First, care must be taken to see that extremely high scores or extremely low scores are included in some class. For example, if we added a 146th area, with a murder rate of thirty-seven, we would have to add fifteen classes to 2.2(a), even though fourteen of them would have a frequency of zero; or we would have to add eight classes to 2.2(b); or we would have to add three classes to 2.2(c). (In certain limited circumstances, it might be permissible to define the last class as twenty-two or more and thereby avoid the need to create extra classes. However, this makes it impossible to perform certain other statistical operations on the data.) Second, there should be no gaps between classes. For example, it would *not* be appropriate to have the following classes: 1–4, 5–9, 12–16, since there would be no place to record scores of 10 or 11. (3) *Each case should fit into only one class.* Simply put, classes should not overlap. For example, if two classes are 5–10 and 10–15, it is unclear where a score of 10 should be recorded. (4) *Whenever possible, the class intervals should be of equal size.* In other words, each class should cover the same range of scores as every other class. The reason for this is that if the width of the class interval changes, comparisons become difficult and, as mentioned above, further statistical manipulation of the data becomes awkward or impossible.

A word should be said about the importance of defining *class boundaries*. The murder rates presented in Table 2.1 were recorded as whole numbers. As such, they conceal the fact that these rates were originally reported as decimal figures. Atlanta's rate of 21.8 was rounded to 22 and Philadelphia's rate of 11.5 was rounded to 12. As a result, the data became easier to read, but some of the precision of measurement was masked. Furthermore, we must now realize that a rate of 22 does not necessarily mean *exactly* 22, for scores such as 21.8, 21.6, 22.1, 22.256, 22.43 and the like are all represented by the single value of 22. In working with frequency distributions, we recognize this fact by utilizing class boundaries (or class limits or true limits). The class boundaries of 22 are, therefore, defined as 21.5 (lower boundary) and 22.5 (upper boundary). Similarly, the class interval of 5–6 has as its lower and upper limits the values 4.5 and 6.5; and the class 13–18 has its true limits defined as 12.5 and 18.5. Figure 2.1 illustrates other classes and their true limits. Note that when we work with decimal figures accurate to *one* place (for example, 9.5, 11.3, 6.6), we define our boundaries by using *two* decimal places. Thus the limits of 9.5 are 9.45 and 9.55; the limits of 6.6 are 6.55 and 6.65. (In general, if the set of values which are to be classed consists of k significant digits, the values which define the limits should have $k + 1$ significant digits.)

pictorial presentation

Even though frequency distributions do a remarkable job of condensing large masses of data, we can still further simplify our task by presenting the data in visual form. One of the most commonly used graphic devices is the *histogram*. A histogram is constructed by drawing rectangles whose widths correspond to class intervals and whose heights correspond to frequencies. For example, Figure 2.2 uses a histogram to present the data on murder rates found in Table 2.2(b). Note that the markings on the horizontal axis of the histogram represent the true class limits, while the markings on the vertical axis represent the class frequencies.

In the previous section we gave four guidelines for the construction of frequency distributions. These same guidelines, especially numbers 2,3 and 4, should be applied to the construction of histograms. Otherwise, distortion of data will most certainly be introduced.

An alternative to the histogram is the frequency polygon. A frequency polygon is constructed by plotting the frequency of a class score at the midpoint of the class interval, and connecting the points with straight lines. Figure 2.3 presents a frequency polygon for Table 2.2(b).

(a) Data Expressed in Units

Class	True Lower Limit	True Upper Limit
0–5	−0.5	5.5
6–10	5.5	10.5
etc.	etc.	etc.

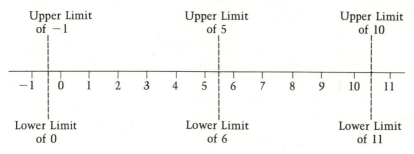

(b) Data Expressed in 1000s

Class	True Lower Limit	True Upper Limit
40,000–49,000	39,500	49,500
50,000–59,000	49,500	59,000
etc.	etc.	etc.

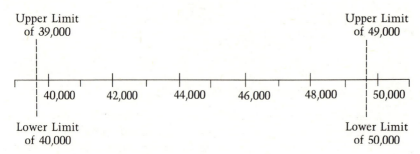

(c) Data Expressed in Decimals

Class	True Lower Limit	True Upper Limit
10.5–19.4	10.45	19.45
19.5–29.4	19.45	29.45
etc.	etc.	etc.

Figure 2.1   *Class Boundaries*

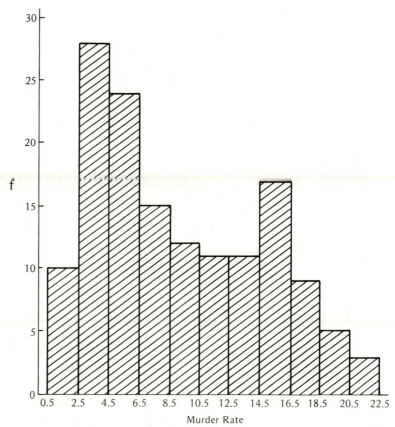

Figure 2.2   *Histogram of the Distribution of 145 Murder Rates*

We can also present these data as a *frequency curve*, which is simply a smoothed version of the frequency polygon (Figure 2.4).

Many other graphic techniques can be used to organize and present data. A few of these are illustrated in Figure 2.5. For a further, more detailed discussion of graphic techniques and other forms of data organization and presentation, see Huff (1954: 60–73), Loether and McTavish (1974a: 69–115), or Mendenhall, Ott and Larson (1974: 43–93).

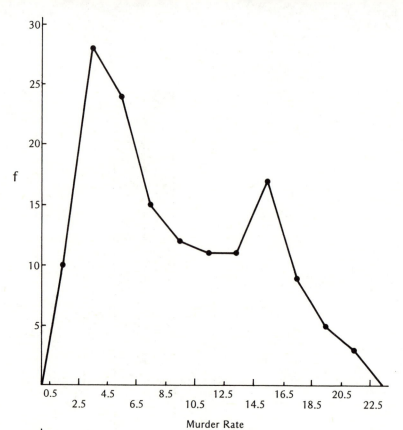

Figure 2.3 *Frequency Polygon.*

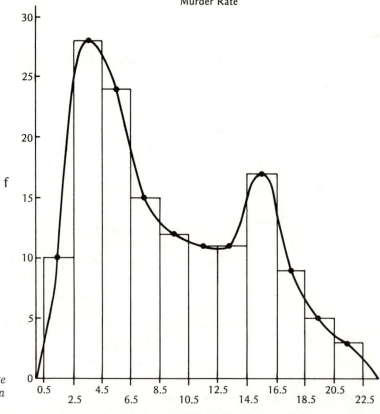

Figure 2.4 *Frequency Curve Superimposed over Histogram*

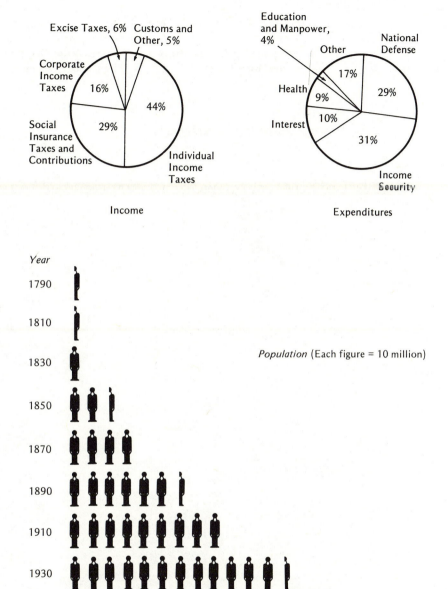

Figure 2.5 *Pictorial Representation of Data. (Top) Pie Chart. The Federal Budget, 1974 (est.). (Bottom) Pictograph. U.S. Population, 1790–1970. Source: U.S. Bureau of the Census (1974:5,220).*

important terms to know

Rate	Histogram
Frequency distribution	Frequency polygon
Class boundary	Frequency curve

suggested readings

Freund (1973: 9–22); Loether and McTavish (1974a: 69–102); Mendenhall, Ott and Larson (1974: 43–93)

descriptive measures: centrality

As we saw in Chapter 2, frequency distributions of large masses of data are useful devices for condensing great quantities of information and, as such, they enable us to convey a large amount of information in a relatively small amount of space or time. However, even this condensation of data can be too detailed and cumbersome for certain purposes. In this chapter we shall examine some of the statistics which are generally known as *measures of location*, and we shall place particular emphasis on measures of central location, or *centrality*. These measures convey a great deal of information in a small amount of space and time, for they reduce a large quantity of data to a single value which, in certain respects, represents the entire mass of data. These measures of centrality are popularly known as averages, but this term is not sufficiently precise for our work, as the following example illustrates.

Suppose that a certain community was being described by three different commentators. (1) In describing the community's financial well-being, the representative of a national businessmen's club states: "Doe City is a thriving, healthy financial community; why, its average family income is 14,500 dollars, far above the national average." (2) Describing the same town, a visiting Marxist comments: "Doe City epitomizes the decadence of capitalism; the average family income is only 3,500 dollars." (3) Finally, a freshman sociology student (who hasn't yet taken a statistics course) writes in a term paper: "Doe City has an average family income of 7,000 dollars." Remember that all three people are speaking about the same city in the same year and their calculations

3

table 3.1   *family incomes in doe city*

$3,500	$10,000
$3,500	$25,000
$3,500	$30,000
$3,500	$30,000
$3,500	$40,000
$7,000	

are based on the same factual information (Table 3.1) and are accurate. All are telling the truth—but not the whole truth. They are all telling the truth because the term average has multiple meanings. All are telling less than the whole truth because they do not specify *which* average they are using when they report their data.

In sociological work, one or more of three common averages are used. These three averages are the mode, the median and the mean. Each is a descriptive measure of central location. Each provides a way of reducing a large mass of data to a single representative value. Most important, each average has a unique meaning which is different from that of the other averages; each represents a different aspect of the data.

the mode

UNGROUPED DATA

The *mode* is perhaps the simplest of all averages, simple in both concept and computation. The mode is defined as *the measure which occurs most frequently* in a distribution. In Table 3.1, for example the family income which occurs most frequently is 3,500 dollars. Therefore, we can state that the modal family income is 3,500 dollars. To use another example, suppose ten students received examination scores of 65, 70, 70, 75, 75, 75, 75, 80, 80 and 90. The mode, or the modal score, is 75 since 75 is the score which occurs most frequently.

It is possible for a distribution to have more than one mode. For example, if one of the exam scores of 75 were changed to 70, there would be three scores of 70 and three scores of 75. Such a distribution can be described as *bi*modal, since there are two modes, 70 and 75.

Because the mode is concerned only with the *frequency* associated with a certain measure, it does not make any arithmetic assumptions about the measurement process. Therefore, it is an especially useful measure for qualitative data; indeed, *the mode is the only appropriate measure of centrality for nominal level data.* (While the other averages discussed below are inappropriate for nominal measurement, the mode can be used to describe ordinal or interval level data.) To illustrate, let us suppose we had twenty persons who reported their ethnic background as follows:

Ethnicity	f
Polish	5
Irish	8
Italian	4
Black	1
Others	2
	20 = N

The mode is Irish. It is important to note that the mode is not 8, which is the *frequency* of the *modal category.* Thus, the mode need not be expressed numerically. It can, and often does, refer to a qualitative variable.

The mode is also called the probability average because, in any distribution of scores, the mode is the score one is most likely to encounter. If you were to randomly select one of the eleven incomes of Table 3.1, you would have five chances in eleven of selecting 3,500 dollars; the probability of selecting any other income would be less than $5/11$. (Taken by itself, however, the mode does not tell us *how* probable its occurrence is.)

GROUPED DATA

The procedure for finding the mode of a set of grouped data is similar to that described above. We simply find the category or interval which has the greatest frequency. We then define the mode as that category (as in the ethnicity example) or, if the data are quantitative, we define the mode as the midpoint of the category. If we refer back to Table 2.2 on page 14, we can see in (b) that the modal frequency is 28, which is associated with the modal category of 3–4. The midpoint of 3–4 is 3.5, so the mode of that distribution is 3.5.

One difficulty with the mode is that it is quite unstable because it is very sensitive to the grouping procedure used. If we had used part (a) of Table 2.2 to determine the modal homicide rate, our answer would have been not 3.5, but 4.5, since 4.5 is the midpoint of the categories 4 and 5, categories with the greatest frequency. You might also note in (a) that if only one of the scores of 14 is changed to 15, the mode changes from 4.5 to 5.0. (Before going on, review Table 2.2 to make certain that you understand what has just been said.) For similar reasons, the mode is usually not very useful for describing small samples or populations, unless there is some overwhelming point of clustering which should not be ignored. Finally, it should be noted that the mode is a dead-end statistic in that it does not lend itself to any further arithmetic manipulation.

*quick quiz
3.1

Calculate the mode of the following distributions:

(A) 16, 17, 21, 16, 18, 21, 16, 24, 25, 17, 16, 20

(B) Eye color	f		(C) IQ Score	f
Blue	4		85–89	3
Brown	15		90–94	9
Gray	7		95–99	15
Green	3		100–104	19
Other	5		105–109	17
			110–114	8
			115–119	4

the median

The *median* is defined as *that point in a distribution which divides an ordered set of scores into two equal parts,* so that one half of the scores fall above and one half below it. Calculation of a median requires that data be at least at the ordinal level of measurement, since it is absurd to talk of above and below (or greater and lesser, and so on) with regard to qualitative data. In Table 3.1, the median family income is 7,000 dollars, since that value, and only that value, has an equal number of scores above and below it. (Unlike the mode, there can be only one median for any set of data.)

UNGROUPED DATA

In the distribution of the scores 1, 3, 4, 7, 8, the median is that point which has one half, or $N/2$, scores above and below it. With five scores, $N/2 = 2.5$. The median is, therefore, the $2\frac{1}{2}$ case, or the midpoint of the middle score. The middle score is 4. If we recall that the true boundaries of 4 are 3.5 and 4.5, the true midpoint is thus 4, and 4 is the median of the distribution. This point is graphically described in Figure 3.1(a).

In another example, we have the following distribution: 1, 2, 4, 7, 8, 10. Here, $N/2 = 3$, so we want to find that point which has three cases above and three cases below. Actually, any value between 4 and 7 could satisfy this condition, but if we follow the convention of true limits, the median point must be 5.5, the midpoint of the distance which separates 4 from 7. Figure 3.1(b) illustrates this.

Remember: if N, the number of cases, is odd, the median score is the middle score in a series of ordered scores. If N is even, the median is the midpoint of the distance between the two midmost scores. In this sense, you can see that the median is a *position* average: it identifies the middle position in a distribution.

*Answers to quick quizzes will be found at the end of each chapter.

(a) Scores: 1, 3, 4, 7, 8.

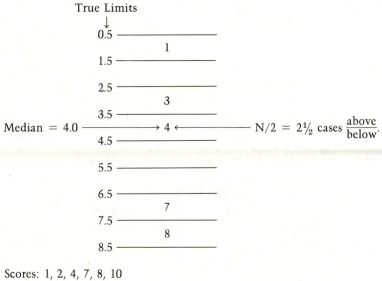

(b) Scores: 1, 2, 4, 7, 8, 10

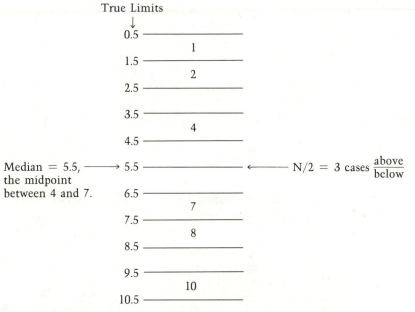

Figure 3.1   *Illustration of the Median as a Position Average*

The same logic of finding the central position governs the computation of the median for grouped data. Let us continue to work with data on homicide rates, as reproduced in Table 3.2. Since N = 145, the median is that point which has N/2 = 72.5 cases above and below it; we are, therefore, seeking the 72.5th case. If we begin to count the number of cases in each class interval, and accumulate our tally, we can hope to find the 72.5th case. The first class interval, 1–2, has ten cases and has brought us to the value of 2.5 (the upper limit of the interval 1–2 and the lower limit of the interval 3–4). Thus, we have accounted for ten of the needed 72.5 cases; we still have a way to go. The second interval, 3–4, adds twenty-eight cases, for a cumulative total of thirty-eight and has moved us to the true limit of 4.5. The third interval, 5–6, adds twenty-four cases, for a cumulative total of sixty-two and has brought us to the true limit of 6.5. Looking ahead to the next interval, 7–8, we see that there are fifteen cases, which is more than we need to reach our goal of 72.5 cases. We need only 10.5 of these fifteen cases (Figure 3.2). In other words, we must go 10.5/15 of the distance into the interval 7–8. Remembering that this interval is two units large, this distance can be expressed as

$$\text{distance} = \frac{10.5}{15}(2) = 1.4$$

The median can now be determined as the value of the last true limit which we fully accounted for, plus the additional distance needed from the median category. The last true limit we accounted for was 6.5, the added value is 1.4, and the median is, therefore,

$$\text{Mdn} = 6.5 + 1.4 = 7.9$$

table 3.2   frequency distribution (with cumulative frequencies) of 145 homicide rates

HOMICIDE RATE	f	CUM.f(↓)	CUM.f(↑)	
1–2	10	10		
3–4	28	38		
5–6	24	62	107	
7–8	15	(77) ←	(83) ←	N/2 = 72.5 case lies
9–10	12	89	68	in this interval.
11–12	11		56	
13–14	11		45	
15–16	17		34	
17–18	9		17	
19–20	5		8	
21–22	3		3	
	145			

essential statistics for social research

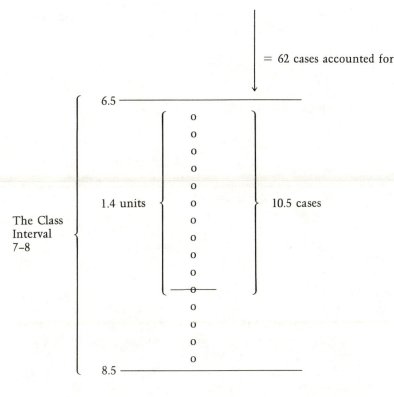

= 62 cases accounted for

6.5

The Class Interval 7–8

1.4 units

10.5 cases

8.5

The fifteen cases, each represented by an o, are assumed to be equally dispersed throughout the interval 7–8.

Figure 3.2   *Location of the Median from Table 3.2*

This procedure can be summarized in the following computational formula:

(*Formula 3.1*)

$$\text{Mdn} = \text{LL} + \frac{N/2 - \text{cum.f}}{f_{\text{Mdn}}}(i)$$

where LL is the true lower limit of the median category; cum.f is the cumulative frequency up to but not including the median category; f_{Mdn} is the frequency of the median category; and i is the size of the median class interval.

In the above example, we started from the smaller class intervals and worked toward the larger; that is, we started with the interval 1–2 and worked up. Alternatively, we could start at the highest interval, 21–22, and work down. If we did so, we would have to adjust the procedure slightly: when we reach the true limit of the median category, we would have to subtract some distance from the true limit. Expressed as a formula, the median can be computed as

$$\text{Mdn} = \text{UL} - \frac{N/2 - \text{cum.f}}{f_{\text{Mdn}}} \ (i) \qquad \qquad (\textit{Formula 3.2})$$

where UL is the true upper limit of the median category. For the data from Table 3.2,

$$\text{Mdn} = 8.5 - \frac{72.5 - 68}{15} \ (2)$$

$$= 8.5 - \frac{4.5}{15} \ (2)$$

$$= 8.5 - 0.6$$

$$= 7.9$$

which is identical to the previously computed value. (Until you become familiar with the procedure for calculating the median, it would be helpful to compute its value twice, once using the lower limit and once using the upper limit; this will provide you with a check on the accuracy of your work.)

Like the mode, the median is a simple concept. It is the central point in a distribution. Fifty percent of the cases are above it, and 50 percent are below it. Also like the mode, the median cannot be manipulated arithmetically. The median is unlike the mode in that it is relatively stable; that is, it is not greatly influenced by grouping procedures. As already mentioned, there is one and only one median for any set of data. Finally, the median cannot be calculated for nominal level data, but can be calculated for ordinal or interval level data.

quick quiz
3.2 | For the data from Quick Quiz 3.1 (A) and (C), compute the median.

RELATED MEASURES

There are frequent occasions when we are interested not in the middle position of a distribution, but in some other position. We might, for example, want to define the top 10 percent of family incomes, or the lowest 25 percent of homicide rates, or the top 16 percent of IQ scores. The procedure for identifying these locations is similar to that of locating the median, except that we are not interested in finding the N/2 case, but the $\frac{9}{10}$ of N case or the N/4 case or the .16N case.

Quartiles are measures of location which divide a distribution into four equal parts (just as the median divides a distribution into two equal parts). The first quartile, Q_1, is that point in a distribution which has 25 percent of the cases below it and 75 percent above it. The third quartile, Q_3, has 75 percent of the cases below it and 25 percent above (Figure 3.3). The second quartile is, of course, the median. For computational purposes, the following formulas may be used:

(*Formula 3.3*)
$$Q_1 = LL + \frac{N/4 - cum.f}{f_{Q_1}}(i) \quad = UL - \frac{3N/4 - cum.f}{f_{Q_1}}(i)$$

(*Formula 3.4*)
$$Q_3 = LL + \frac{3N/4 - cum.f}{f_{Q_3}}(i) = UL - \frac{N/4 - cum.f}{f_{Q_3}}(i)$$

To determine Q_1 for Table 3.2, we must locate the $145/4 = 36\frac{1}{4}$ case. To determine Q_3, we need the 108.75 case. The procedures are

$$Q_1 = 2.5 + \frac{26.25}{28}(2) \qquad Q_3 = 12.5 + \frac{8.75}{11}(2)$$

$$= 2.5 + 1.875 \qquad\qquad = 12.5 + 1.59$$

$$= 4.375 \qquad\qquad\qquad = 14.09$$

(In both cases, we used the lower limit formula. You should verify for yourself the accuracy of this work by using the upper limit formula.) We can interpret these figures by saying that 25 percent of the 145 homicide rates fall below the rate of 4.375 (or that 75 percent fall above 4.375); and, for Q_3, we can say that 75 percent of the homicide rates fall below 14.09 (or that 25 percent fall above 14.09).

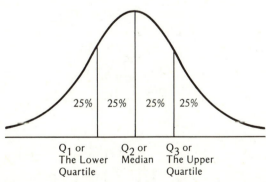

Figure 3.3 *Location of Quartiles in a Symmetric Distribution*

Deciles are measures which divide a distribution into ten equal parts. The first decile, D_1, has 10 percent of the cases below it and 90 percent above. The third decile, D_3, has 30 percent of the cases below it. The fifth decile, D_5, is the median. The ninth decile, D_9, has 90 percent of the cases below it. We will not give specific formulas for each of the deciles, but it should be clear by now that the computational procedure for deciles is the same as that for the median and the quartiles. As illustrations, let us compute D_1 and D_7 from Table 3.2.

$$D_1 = LL + \frac{N/10 - cum.f}{f_{D_1}} \text{(i)} \qquad D_7 = LL + \frac{7N/10 - cum.f}{f_{D_7}} \text{(i)}$$

$$= 2.5 + \frac{14.5 - 10}{28} \text{(2)} \qquad = 12.5 + \frac{101.5 - 100}{11} \text{(2)}$$

$$= 2.5 + .32 \qquad\qquad\quad = 12.5 + .27$$

$$= 2.82 \qquad\qquad\qquad\quad = 12.77$$

Thus, 10 percent of the 145 homicide rates fall below 2.82 and 70 percent of them fall below 12.77.

Centiles (or percentiles) are measures which divide a distribution into one hundred equal parts. The logic and procedures of calculation are as above. For example, we can find the point below which 86 percent of the cases fall as follows:

$$C_{86} = LL + \frac{.86N - cum.f}{f_{C_{86}}} \text{(i)}$$

$$= 14.5 + \frac{124.7 - 111}{17} \text{(2)}$$

$$= 14.5 + 1.61$$

$$= 16.11$$

quick quiz
3.3

From Table 3.2, find
(A) D_9 (B) C_{16}

the mean

The arithmetic mean is the average that most of us think of when we hear the word "average." As we saw in Chapter 1, it is the average we use to determine batting averages in baseball, grade-point averages in college and many other commonly used averages.

CONCEPT OF THE MEAN

A mean can be determined only for data that are at least at the interval level of measurement, because the mean takes into account the value or magnitude of each score which enters into the computation. The mean for a set of ungrouped data is simply computed: sum all scores in a data set and divide by the number of scores. Thus if we have five scores, 3, 8, 0, −5 and 9, we add (or sum) these five values, obtaining a sum of 15 and divide this total by the number of scores, 5. The mean is, therefore, $15/5 = 3$.

Very often a data set will contain a score which appears more than once, for example, 3, 5, 7, 7, 7, 9, 11 and 11. In such instances it is essential that each score be included in the sum *as many times* as it appears in the data set. In our example, the score $X = 7$ must be counted three times, and when $X = 11$ the score must be counted twice. In other words, we must consider the *frequency* with which a score appears.

In statistical notation the mean of a set of scores is usually designated by the symbol $\overline{X}$ (read X-bar) and its simple computational formula is

(*Formula 3.5*)
$$\overline{X} = \frac{\Sigma (fX)}{N}$$

where X is any score; f is the frequency of a score; and Σ (sigma) is the instruction to add. (That is, to add whatever quantity is embraced by the summation command, Σ. In this case, we add all values of X.) Let us use this formula to compute the mean of the set of scores just given.

X (= score)	f (= frequency)	fX
3	1	3
5	1	5
7	3	21
9	1	9
11	2	22
	8 = N	60 = Σ (fX)

$$\overline{X} = \frac{60}{8} = 7.5$$

This example illustrates one of the ways in which the mean is conceptually different from the median or mode: the mean represents the *value* (adjusted for frequency) of the scores. It does not represent position, nor does it represent frequency alone.

This emphasis on value is important to a conceptual understanding of the mean as the true value which represents a set of scores and from which all other scores can be viewed as deviations. Let us return to our simple data set, 3, 8, 0, −5 and 9. We have found the mean of this distribution to be 3. We can now define each score as a *deviation* from the

table 3.3   deviation scores

RAW SCORE X	DEVIATION SCORE $x = X - \overline{X}$
3	0
8	5
0	−3
−5	−8
9	6
	$\overline{0} = \Sigma x$

mean; we symbolize this deviation as $x = (X - \overline{X})$. Table 3.3 presents the data in their deviation score form. The score of $X = 3$ has a deviation score of $x = 0$, since $(X - \overline{X}) = (3 - 3) = 0$; the score of $X = -5$ has a deviation score of $x = -8$, since $(X - \overline{X}) = (-5) -3 = -8$; and so on. Notice in Table 3.3 that the *sum of the deviations from the mean is zero*; if the mean has been correctly computed, this will *always* be so. (This fact can be used to check on the accuracy of your work.)

The mean is analogous to the "center of gravity" of a distribution. If we conceive of our measurements as blocks on a seesaw, the mean is the point of balance (Figure 3.4). If we were to shift the fulcrum to any other point on the scale, the result would be imbalance. Figure 3.5 illustrates the mean as balance point concept for another set of data.

This concept of the mean is very important to more advanced discussions of measurement and sampling. Suppose that we want to know the mean value of some large population, and that we do not have the resources to measure the entire population. We therefore measure only a segment, or sample, of the population. Each of these sample measures deviates from the true population mean. And if our sample is sufficiently large, we can assume that these measurement errors will cancel each

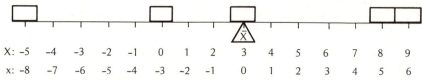

X:	-5	-4	-3	-2	-1	0	1	2	3	4	5	6	7	8	9
x:	-8	-7	-6	-5	-4	-3	-2	-1	0	1	2	3	4	5	6

Figure 3.4   *The Mean as Center of Gravity*

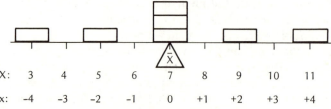

X:	3	4	5	6	7	8	9	10	11
x:	-4	-3	-2	-1	0	+1	+2	+3	+4

Figure 3.5   *The Mean as Center of Gravity*

essential statistics for social research

other out, and the net result, as reflected in the sample mean, will be zero error. Here the mean is the value which would appear if there were no sampling error, no measurement error.

GROUPED DATA   The principle underlying the computation of the mean for grouped data is identical to that for ungrouped data. In practice, one adjustment must be made. When data are grouped the procedure for computing the mean assumes that, within a given class interval, all scores fall at the midpoint of the interval. If we defined this midpoint as M, a computing formula for grouped data would be

(Formula 3.6)
$$\overline{X} = \frac{\Sigma fM}{N}$$

Table 3.4 illustrates this procedure. This procedure is a fairly simple and direct way to compute the mean. However, the values of (fM) can get rather large and cumbersome, and for this reason many people prefer an alternate computing procedure.

The method of the *guessed mean* is based on the center of gravity concept of the mean. It involves guessing where the mean might be, computing the deviations about this guessed mean and making the necessary mathematical adjustment.

To use a very simple example with *un*grouped data, suppose we have again the values 3, 8, 0, −5 and 9. Let us "guess" that the mean of this distribution is 6. If this guessed mean (symbolized as $\overline{X}'$) is correct, the

table 3.4   the mean and formula 3.6

HOMICIDE RATE	M	f	fM
1–2	1.5	10	15.0
3–4	3.5	28	98.0
5–6	5.5	24	132.0
7–8	7.5	15	112.5
9–10	9.5	12	114.0
11–12	11.5	11	126.5
13–14	13.5	11	148.5
15–16	15.5	17	263.5
17–18	17.5	9	157.5
19–20	19.5	5	97.5
21–22	21.5	3	64.5
		145	1329.5

$$\overline{X} = \frac{\Sigma fM}{N}$$

$$= \frac{1329.5}{145}$$

$$= 9.17$$

descriptive measures: centrality

sum of the deviations about the guessed mean (symbolized as x') should be zero. But in fact, $\Sigma x' = -15$ (Table 3.5). Since this sum, -15, is based on five scores, the mean deviation is $-15/5 = -3$. It follows, therefore, that our guessed mean must be adjusted by a value of -3. Thus, the correct value of the mean is our guessed mean *plus* any correction factor. Symbolically,

$$\overline{X} = \overline{X}' + \frac{\Sigma\ fx'}{N}$$

(*Formula 3.7*)

For our data, $\overline{X} = 6 + (-3) = 3$, which is, of course, the true mean of the distribution. It should be noted that this method will work with *any* guess. You may wish to verify for yourself that if the guessed mean were -8 or 145 or 2.917 or any other value, the correction factor of $\Sigma\ fx'/N$ would still lead you to the true mean of 3.

In actual day-to-day practice, procedures for computing the mean often involve *coding* of data. Suppose you were asked to compute the mean of the three scores

CODED DATA

18,984,082   18,984,084   18,984,087

You could simply add the three values, divide this sum by 3, and obtain your answer, $\overline{X} = 18,984,084.33$. With only three values to sum, this is a trivial problem. But if there were many such numbers, the addition task alone would be time-consuming and error-prone. An alternative is to adjust each raw score by some constant. In our example we could subtract 18,984,080 from each score. We could then compute the mean of our coded scores and finally readjust the coded mean by the constant value. Table 3.6 illustrates this procedure. In general, coding can be done by addition, subtraction, multiplication, division or a combination of operations. There are two points to be remembered in any coding of data: (1) every raw score value must be identically coded; and (2) as

table 3.5   **guessed deviations**

RAW SCORE X	GUESSED MEAN $\overline{X}'$	DEVIATION $x' = (X - \overline{X}')$
3	6	-3
8	6	2
0	6	-6
-5	6	-11
9	6	3
		$-15 = \Sigma\ x'$

essential statistics for social research

table 3.6   coding

RAW SCORE X	CODED SCORE $(X - 18,984,080)$
18,984,082	2
18,984,084	4
18,984,087	7
	13

Coded Mean: $\overline{X} = 13/3 = 4.33$
True Mean: Coded Mean + Code Value
$= 4.33 + 18,984,080$
$= 18,984,084.33$

the final step, data must be *decoded*, which means that the original coding procedure must be reversed.

In using coding to compute the mean for grouped data, it is a frequent practice to code the deviations from the mean. It is most common to *divide* each class deviation score by the size of the class interval.* The reason for this is to establish the neat and almost automatic sequence of $0, \pm 1, \pm 2, \pm 3$ and so on, as values representing the *guessed deviations* (x') from the mean (Table 3.7). To compute the mean, each x' value is multiplied by its corresponding frequency; when the values of

table 3.7   the guessed mean and formula 3.8

HOMICIDE RATE	f	x	x'	fx'	
1–2	10	−6	−3	−30	
3–4	28	−4	−2	−56	−110
5–6	24	−2	−1	−24	
7–8	15	0	0	0	
9–10	12	2	1	12	
11–12	11	4	2	22	
13–14	11	6	3	33	
15–16	17	8	4	68	+231
17–18	9	10	5	45	
19–20	5	12	6	30	
21–22	3	14	7	21	
				121 = Σ fx'	

$$\overline{X} = \overline{X}' + \frac{\Sigma\, fx'}{N} \text{(i)}$$

$$= 7.5 + \frac{121}{145} \text{(2)}$$

$$= 7.5 + 1.67$$

$$= 9.17$$

*When using this method, class intervals *must* be of equal size.

fx' are summed, divided by N and then decoded (since the coding involved division by the size of the class interval, the decoding involves multiplication by the size of the class interval), we have a value which corrects the guessed mean. When the correction factor is added to the guessed mean, we have the true mean. In general, this procedure follows the formula

$$\overline{X} = \overline{X}' + \frac{\Sigma\,fx'}{N}\,(i)$$ (*Formula 3.8*)

where $\overline{X}'$, the guessed mean, is the midpoint of the class interval in which the mean is assumed to be; x' is a coded deviation score; and i is the size of the class interval.

In Table 3.7 we guessed the mean to be the midpoint, 7.5, of the category 7-8. (Again, note that *any* guessed midpoint would produce an identical result after coding and correction.) We next computed the deviations from the guessed mean, $x = (X - \overline{X}')$, and coded these values of x by dividing by the size of the class interval (in this case, $i = 2$) obtaining $x' = x/i$.

You will find, as you work with this method, and if you fully understand the logic of what is being done, that it is not necessary to be concerned with the details of deviation scores, for once you have decided on a guessed mean, the x' scores will always follow the 0, ±1, ±2 and so on, sequence.

Table 3.8 illustrates another application of this procedure. Carefully work your way through this and the above examples, until you are certain that you understand both the logic and the procedure.

table 3.8   another application of the guessed mean

X	f	x'	fx'
66–70	3	−3	−9
71–75	11	−2	−22
76–80	18	−1	−18
81–85	30	0	0
86–90	20	1	20
91–95	13	2	26
96–100	5	3	15
	100	0	12

$$\overline{X} = \overline{X}' + \frac{\Sigma\,fx'}{N}\,(i)$$

$$= 83 + \frac{12}{100}\,(5)$$

$$= 83 + 0.6$$

$$= 83.6$$

essential statistics for social research

1. Unlike modes and medians, means can be combined. The procedure for doing so is simple, but caution is required. For example, suppose one group of twenty subjects had a mean score of 74 on a test and another group of twenty had a mean score of 80. Because the Ns are of the same size the *weight* of each mean is equal, and we can compute the grand mean as the *mean of the two submeans.* That is, $\overline{X} = (74 + 80)/2 = 77$.

But suppose that the second group's mean is based on $N = 50$. Here the two groups are not equally weighted, since one mean is based on twenty scores, while the other is based on fifty scores. Since the mean depends on *frequency* as well as *value,* we must take this into account. This is done by multiplying each group mean by its frequency; we then obtain ΣfX for each group, since

(Formula 3.9)

$$\Sigma fX = N\overline{X}$$

For the first group,

$$\Sigma fX = 20(74) = 1,480$$

For the second group,

$$\Sigma fX = 50(80) = 4,000$$

Thus for the two groups combined, the grand sum is $1,480 + 4,000 = 5,480$, and the grand mean is

$$\overline{X} = \frac{\Sigma fX}{N} = \frac{5,480}{70} = 78.3$$

Table 3.9 summarizes this procedure.

table 3.9   *the weighted mean*

	f	$\overline{X}$	$f\overline{X}$
Group 1	20	74	1480
Group 2	50	80	4000

Unweighted Mean $= \dfrac{74 + 80}{2} = 77$ (INCORRECT)

Weighted Mean $= \dfrac{1480 + 4000}{20 + 50} = \dfrac{5480}{70}$

$= 78.3$ (CORRECT)

2. Because it depends on the value of each and every score in a distribution, the mean is strongly influenced by extreme scores. Consider the following distribution:

$$4 \quad 5 \quad 5 \quad 6 \quad 6 \quad 6 \quad 7 \quad 7 \quad 89$$

$$\text{Mode} = 6 \qquad \text{Median} = 6 \qquad \text{Mean} = 15$$

Is the mean a representative value? Probably not, for it has been greatly influenced by the single extreme score of 89, a score which does not seem to be typical of the "usual" scores in the distribution.

From this example we can see that when extreme scores are present, the mean may not be an appropriate measure of central tendency. Figure 3.6 illustrates how the mean is "pulled" in the direction of extreme scores. This figure also locates the approximate position of the mean, median and mode in differently shaped distributions. Depending on the degree of *skewness*, that is, the extent to which the distribution is not symmetric, the mean may or may not be the appropriate measure of centrality.

3. It should also be noted that there are many instances in which a comparison of the same average over two distributions may be misleading. In Figure 3.6(e), for example, we might, upon learning that the two groups have identical means, conclude that the two groups are identical. But this would be an obviously incorrect conclusion. The identical means are simply a reflection of two very differently shaped distributions. In this instance we see the weakness of using only a measure of centrality to describe a distribution. (In Chapter 4 we shall see how distributions can be more completely described by reporting, along with a measure of centrality, a corresponding measure of dispersion.)

4. Choosing an appropriate average to describe a set of data depends not only on the *shape of the distribution* (see above paragraph), but also on the *purpose to be served* by the statistical measures used. It is essential to remember that statistical measures are only tools to aid us in our thinking, and proper use of these tools demands that we know *why* they are being used (not merely *how* to use them). Before we can decide which average to use as an indicator of the average homicide rate, we must have some understanding of why we want that particular piece of information. If we want to estimate the total number of murders, we should use the mean; if we want to know which homicide rate is most common, we should use the mode; if we want to locate our home town's rate relative to all others, we should use the median (or one of its related quantiles). (Can you see why each average answers, in effect, a different question, tells us something different about the data? If not, you should review this chapter.)

In conclusion, Figure 3.7 summarizes the major characteristics of the three averages.

essential statistics for social research

(a) Normal Distribution
(e.g., IQ)

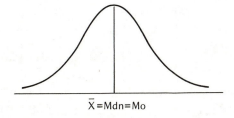

$$\bar{X}=Mdn=Mo$$

(b) Positively Skewed
Distribution (e.g.,
income)

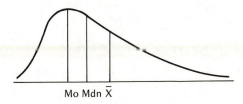

Mo Mdn $\bar{X}$

(c) Negatively Skewed
Distribution (e.g.,
grade-point average)

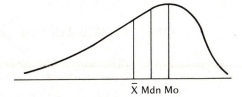

$\bar{X}$ Mdn Mo

(d) Symetric, Bimodal
Distribution

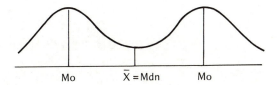

Mo $\bar{X}=Mdn$ Mo

(e) Different Distribu-
tions, Identical
Means

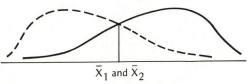

$\bar{X}_1$ and $\bar{X}_2$

Figure 3.6   *Central Locations for Differently Shaped Distributions*

	Mode	*Median*	*Mean*
Chief conceptual characteristic	Most *frequent* value in a distribution	Middle *location* in a distribution	Represents the *value* of every item in a distribution
Number in a distribution	One or more	One and only one	One and only one
Can it be arithmetically manipulated?	No	No	Yes
Applicable to which levels of measurement?	Nominal, ordinal or interval (and ratio)	Ordinal or interval (and ratio)	Interval (and ratio) only

Figure 3.7   *Summary of Characteristics of Mode, Median and Mean*

important terms to know

Mode	Mean
Median	Summation command (Σ)
Quartile	Deviation score (x)
Decile	Guessed mean
Centile	Skewness

suggested readings

Anderson and Zelditch (1975: 65–79); Kolstoe (1973: 62–78); Runyon and Haber (1976: 78–87).

essential statistics for social research

answer section

QUICK QUIZ 3.1   (A)   16   (B)   Brown   (C)   102

QUICK QUIZ 3.2   (A)   17.5

(C) $Mdn = 99.5 + \dfrac{10.5}{19}(5) = 99.5 + 2.76 = 102.26$

QUICK QUIZ 3.3   (A) $D_0 = 18.5 - \dfrac{14.5 - 8}{9}(2)$ (B) $C_{10} = 2.5 + \dfrac{23.2 - 10}{28}(2)$

$= 18.5 - 1.44$ $\qquad\qquad\qquad\qquad\quad = 2.5 + .94$

$= 17.06$ $\qquad\qquad\qquad\qquad\qquad\quad = 3.44$

measures
of
dispersion

At the end of Chapter 3, we stated that, by itself, a measure of central tendency is not sufficient to fully and properly describe a set of data. The reason for this is that such measures focus attention on only one aspect of the data, centrality, and in doing so suppress any information which shows the extent to which the data depart from centrality. An example should help to illustrate the importance of describing data by providing information about both centrality and dispersion. Consider the following sets of data:

$$
\begin{array}{ll}
A: & 93, 93, 93, 93, 93 \\
B: & 92, 93, 93, 93, 94 \\
C: & 91, 92, 93, 94, 95 \\
D: & 89, 91, 93, 95, 97 \\
E: & 73, 83, 93, 103, 113
\end{array}
$$

For each of these sets the mean (and median) is 93. If all we knew about the data sets was these average scores, we might readily conclude that the five groups were quite similar, if not identical. But clearly the groups are *not* identical, and not even similar in the more extreme comparisons (such as A *vs.* E). In group A, each score is identical to every other score; the chosen average is perfectly representative of the entire set; there is no deviation from centrality, no dispersion. In B, there is some variation in scores, but the mean (or median) is still quite representative; the amount of dispersion is slight. But in D, and especially in E, the

4

scores diverge from each other and from the mean to a marked degree, and in these instances we can begin to seriously question how representative our average scores really are.

ranges

The *range* is the simplest of all the measures of dispersion. It is the distance between the highest score and the lowest score in a distribution in which the high and low scores are determined by the true upper and lower limits. (For a review of true limits, see Chapter 2.) Expressed as a formula

(Formula 4.1)   Range = (True Upper Limit) − (True Lower Limit)

For example, using ungrouped data, we can find the range of the scores from group C, above, by determining the true limits of this distribution and subtracting. The true lower limit of 91 is 90.5; the true upper limit of 95 is 95.5. Therefore,

$$\text{Range} = 95.5 - 90.5 = 5.0$$

To say that the range of these scores is 5 is to say that the scores in this distribution all lie within a distance that is five units large. A glance at groups A and E tells us that the range of A is 1 and the range of E is 41. Knowing these ranges, we do not have to examine entire data sets to learn that group E is spread over a greater distance than is C, or that C covers more ground than A.

For grouped data, the computation is the same. As an example, we can use the data from Table 3.2 on page 26. In this table, the true limits are 22.5 and 0.5. Thus,

$$\text{Range} = 22.5 - 0.5 = 22.0$$

This distance of 22 units is the minimal distance required to include all of the homicide rates in the distribution.

The range is easy to compute and comprehend, but it is a very crude measure of dispersion and certain cautions are necessary when using the range. (To a greater or lesser degree, all measures of dispersion are subject to the following deficiencies.)

1. Most important, the range is greatly affected by extreme scores (for it is, after all, defined by the extreme scores). Because of this a set of data whose elements are for the most part quite similar, such as 4, 5, 5, 5, 6, 6, 7, 36, can appear to be quite dissimilar if the range is used as a measure of dispersion. In this example, although most of the scores are actually quite close to one another, the relatively large range of 33 in-

measures of dispersion   **43** dicates a considerable amount of spread in the data; but most of this spread is due to the single score of 36, a score which may or may not be truly representative of the entire data set.

2. In general, ranges cannot be compared with each other unless they are based on a similar number of observations. For example, the range of homicide rates just computed would probably be smaller than 22 if it were computed from a sample of only 15 cities instead of 145. The smaller sample has a smaller probability of including any given score, especially any given extreme score.

3. Like all measures of dispersion, ranges should have some standard of comparison. For example, it is not enough to state that the income range of a group of families is 18,000 dollars, for it probably makes an important difference if we are talking about a group whose incomes lie between 0 dollars and 18,000 dollars or a group whose incomes lie between 65,000 dollars and 83,000 dollars.

4. Ranges do not give us any information about the pattern of variation. Figure 4.1 illustrates several distributions whose ranges are identical. But using only the range as a measure of dispersion does not permit us to distinguish which group has its scores concentrated at one extreme or the other or in the middle.

Because the range is especially subject to influence by extreme scores, many people prefer to use intermediate ranges which, by definition, eliminate from consideration and computation a proportion of the extreme scores. Quite common is the *interdecile* range, the distance between the ninth and first decile points:

$$\text{Interdecile range} = D_9 - D_1 \qquad \qquad (Formula\ 4.2)$$

For example, in the previous chapter we computed D_9 and D_1 for the distribution of homicide rates; the corresponding values were 17.06 and 2.82. Thus, for these data, the interdecile range is $17.06 - 2.82 = 14.24$. (Compare this to the total range of 22.0.)

The interdecile range eliminates from consideration the top 10 percent and the bottom 10 percent of scores, thereby focusing attention on the middle 80 percent of scores in a distribution.

Another commonly used range is the *interquartile range*, the distance between the third and first quartiles of a distribution.

$$\text{Interquartile range} = Q_3 - Q_1 \qquad \qquad (Formula\ 4.3)$$

This range excludes the extreme 50 percent of cases (25 percent from each extreme) and focuses on the middle 50 percent. For the homicide rate data, the interquartile range is

$$Q_3 - Q_1 = 14.09 - 4.38 = 9.71$$

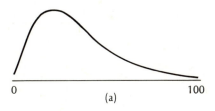

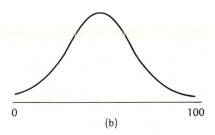

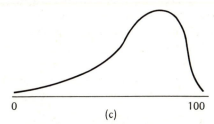

Figure 4.1 *Identical Ranges, Different Patterns of Dispersion*

The great virtue of intermediate ranges is that they reduce the influence of extreme scores. Thus, even though the total range of family incomes in the United States is well over several million dollars, we get a more realistic picture of typical family incomes by noting that the interdecile range is about 10,000 dollars and the interquartile range is about 5,000 dollars. These intermediate ranges display the relative similarities of family incomes, a pattern which is hidden by the total range.

deviation measures

AVERAGE DEVIATION Another way of viewing the concept of dispersion (or spread, deviation, variation) is to ask: Deviation from what? Variation about what? And how much dispersion? For example, let us take the set of scores

table 4.1 **measures of deviation**

X	x	|x|	x²	d	|d|	d²
4	−3	3	9	−2	2	4
5	−2	2	4	−1	1	1
6	−1	1	1	0	0	0
7	0	0	0	1	1	1
13	6	6	36	7	7	49
35	0	12	50	5	11	55

$$\overline{X} = 7 \qquad\qquad Mdn = 6$$

from Table 4.1. If we use the mean ($\overline{X} = 7$) as our measure of centrality we can ask: how much does each score deviate from the mean? The deviation score $x = (X - \overline{X})$ is recorded in column 2. Its sum, as we learned in Chapter 3, is zero. Clearly, since the value of Σx for every distribution is zero, we cannot use the sum of deviations as a measure of dispersion. But suppose we discarded the sign of the deviation (that is, we pay no attention to whether a score is above or below the mean, positive or negative) and consider only the *distance* which separates each score from the mean. This value, *the absolute value* of x, is represented by the symbol $|x|$, and is recorded in column 3. If we sum these absolute deviations from the mean we obtain $\Sigma |x| = 12$, which is a measure of the total amount of deviation from the mean, disregarding signs. Since this value is based, in our example, on five scores we can now define the *average* (mean) *deviation* from the mean ($AD_{\overline{X}}$) as

$$AD_{\overline{X}} = \frac{\Sigma f\,|x|}{N} \qquad\qquad (Formula\ 4.4)$$

For these data, $AD = 12/5 = 2.4$. This can be interpreted by stating that, disregarding direction, the mean distance of each score from the mean is 2.4 units of measurement.

Although average deviation is usually understood to be deviation from the mean, we can also compute the average (mean) deviation from the median, or from any other point. To compute AD_{Mdn} we must first define d as the difference between any score and the median. (Note from column 5 that the sum of these scores is not zero; d will never be zero unless the mean and median are identical.) Again we compute the absolute value, $|d|$, as found in column 6, and sum. We can then define the average (mean) deviation from the median as

$$AD_{Mdn} = \frac{\Sigma f\,|d|}{N} \qquad\qquad (Formula\ 4.5)$$

For these data, $AD_{Mdn} = 11/5 = 2.2$. This can be understood by stating that, disregarding sign, the mean distance of each score from the median is 2.2 units of measurement.

You may note from this example that AD_{Mdn} is smaller than $AD_{\overline{X}}$ ($2.2 < 2.4$). This will always be the case whenever a distribution is skewed. If a distribution is not skewed, that is, if it is symmetric, the mean and median will be identical and $AD_{\overline{X}}$ will equal AD_{Mdn}. This observation leads to the general rule that *whenever a distribution is markedly skewed, the median is the preferred statistic to use as a measure of central tendency* or as the basis for a measure of dispersion. This is so because the median is the point in a distribution which is closest (in terms of absolute value) to all other scores in the distribution.

standard deviation. Since the average deviation is such an easy statistic to compute and understand, you may wonder why we do not make more use of it in sociological work, and why we must move on to an examination of other measures of dispersion. There are several reasons for this. First, for all practical purposes, the AD is a dead-end statistic. Once it is computed, there is little else that can be done with it. There are other measures that lend themselves to further and more useful statistical applications. Second, the interpretation of the AD, while quite clear, does not provide us with as much information about a distribution as do some other measures. Finally, there are certain mathematical properties of the *standard deviation* (that are beyond the scope of this book) which make it by far the preferred measure of dispersion.

Just as the average deviation is based on the concept of absolute deviations from some norm, the standard deviation is based on the concept of *squared deviations* from the mean. A return glance at Table 4.1 will help to clarify the very important *principle of least squares.* Column 4 contains the values of x^2, the squared deviations from the mean; column 7 contains the values of d^2, the squared deviations from the median. Note that $\Sigma x^2 = 50$ is less than $\Sigma d^2 = 55$. This will *always* be so, unless $\overline{X} = Mdn$, for the mean is that point in a distribution which minimizes squared deviations (just as the median is that point which minimizes absolute deviations). This is sometimes called the *least squares principle.*

The value Σx^2 is often referred to as the sum of squares* and is sometimes symbolized as SS. We generally do not use SS as a measure of dispersion, since this measure does not consider the number of cases upon which the sum of squares is based. But if we divide SS by the number of observations, we have an appropriate measure of the mean squared

---

*The sum of squares, SS, will reappear as a crucial concept in our discussion of Analysis of Variance, Chapter 7.

table 4.2 computation of variance and standard deviation

x	x²
4	16
5	25
6	36
7	49
13	169
35	295

$$\Sigma x^2 = \Sigma X^2 - \frac{(\Sigma X)^2}{N}$$

$$\Sigma x^2 = 295 - \frac{35^2}{5}$$

$$= 295 - \frac{1225}{5}$$

$$= 295 - 245$$

$$= 50$$

$$\sigma^2 = \frac{295}{5} - \left(\frac{35}{5}\right)^2$$

$$= 59 - 7^2$$

$$= 59 - 49$$

$$= 10$$

$$\sigma = \sqrt{10}$$

$$= 3.16$$

deviations from the mean, sometimes called the mean square. The technical name for this value is the variance; it is symbolized as σ^2 or s^2[†] and its computational formulas are

$$\sigma^2 = \frac{\Sigma x^2}{N}$$

(Formula 4.6)[‡]

$$s^2 = \frac{\Sigma x^2}{n - 1}$$

(Formula 4.7)[‡]

For the data from Table 4.2 (assuming a population),

$$\sigma^2 = \frac{50}{5} = 10.0$$

The standard deviation, σ or s, is simply the positive square root of the variance. Since the variance was computed by squaring, it is not unreasonable to "unsquare" this value. Thus, the formulas for the standard deviation are

[†]Statisticians usually (but not always) distinguish between values obtained from a *population* and values obtained from a segment or *sample* of a population. In notational terms this distinction is usually symbolized by using Greek letters for population values and Roman letters for sample values. Therefore, the variance is symbolized as σ^2 (the lower case of sigma squared) when it is based on population data, and as s^2 when based on sample data. (Note, too, that N is used for the size of a population, and n for the size of a sample.)

[‡]Because sample statistics often have an error built into them, computational formulas are occasionally adjusted to account for such error. In the cases of the variance and standard deviation, this adjustment is made by using $(n - 1)$ in the denominator, instead of N. This increases slightly the value of the sample statistic, thus making it more accurate. Of course, if n is large, such an adjustment will be negligible, but when samples are relatively small the adjustment should always be made.

essential statistics for social research

(*Formula 4.8*) $$\sigma = \sqrt{\frac{\Sigma\, x^2}{N}}$$

(*Formula 4.9*) $$s = \sqrt{\frac{\Sigma\, x^2}{(n-1)}}$$

For the data from Table 4.1,

$$\sigma = \sqrt{\frac{50}{5}} = \sqrt{10} = 3.16$$

Thus, the standard deviation is somewhat analogous to the average deviation, except that the standard deviation is based on squared deviations whose mean is then unsquared, while the AD is based directly on absolute deviations.

The standard deviation and the variance are obviously closely related, but the relationship is not based simply on a square root sign. It will be shown below that the standard deviation is a linear measure, that is, it measures distance, while the variance measures area.

computing formulas, ungrouped data. The formulas given above for variance and standard deviation are useful to help us remember the conceptual meaning of the statistics in question. However, when the number of cases becomes large, the computation becomes quite cumbersome. In such circumstances it is generally more useful to use the following formulas (even though they have no obvious meaning):

(*Formula 4.10*) $$SS = \Sigma\, x^2 = \Sigma\, X^2 - \frac{(\Sigma\, X)^2}{N}$$

(*Formula 4.11*) $$\sigma^2 = \frac{SS}{N} = \frac{\Sigma\, X^2}{N} - \left(\frac{\Sigma\, X}{N}\right)^2$$

(*Formula 4.12*) $$s^2 = \frac{\Sigma\, X^2 - (\Sigma\, X)^2/n}{n-1}$$

From these formulas the standard deviation can be readily computed simply by extracting the square root of the variance. The great computing advantage of the above formulas is that they operate directly on the raw scores; they do not require the calculations of intermediate values, such as means and deviations. Table 4.2 illustrates the application of the formulas to the data from Table 4.1. In this simple example, the computing formulas may seem overly complicated, but, with a larger or more diverse data set, these formulas will save much time and work.

measures of dispersion

(A) For the following population data set, compute SS, σ^2 and σ.
(B) Assume the same data are obtained from a sample. Compute s^2 and s.

$$-1, 1, 2, 3, 6$$

grouped data. When data are grouped, the procedure for computing these measures of variation is analogous to that used for the mean; that is, we use the same basic formulas, but modify them to account for frequencies and the size of class intervals. Note that in the formulas given below we again assume that the deviations are located at the midpoints of class intervals and are defined as deviations from a guessed mean.

$$SS = \Sigma\, fx^2 = \left[\Sigma\, fx'^2 - \frac{(\Sigma\, fx')^2}{N} \right] i^2 \qquad (Formula\ 4.13)$$

$$\sigma^2 = \frac{\Sigma\, fx^2}{N} = \frac{\Sigma\, fx'^2 - (\Sigma\, fx')^2/N}{N}(i^2) \qquad (Formula\ 4.14)$$

There are several points to note about the above formulas. (1) From Formula 4.14 we can readily compute the standard deviation by extracting the square root of the variance. (2) We have not indicated a separate formula to distinguish sample data from population data. The reason for this is that we assumed that grouped data will always have a sufficiently large N, so that the correction factor of replacing N with (n $-$ 1) is negligible and unnecessary. (3) In computational work, do not confuse the quantity fx'^2 with the quantity $(fx')^2$; remember that the former term refers to the frequency times the squared deviation, while in the latter term the frequency is multiplied by the deviation and the product is squared.

Table 4.3 illustrates the application of these computing formulas to our list of 145 homicide rates.

the standard deviation and the normal distribution. We have now described several measures of variation based on deviation scores. The average deviation has little utility in modern statistical work. The sum of squares and variance are quite important and useful, and we will discuss these further in Chapter 11. In many respects, it is the standard deviation which is *the* most important measure of dispersion. This importance comes from the special relationship with exists between the standard deviation and the normal distribution, a relationship which gives the standard deviation a very elegant and useful interpretation.

table 4.3   *standard deviation, grouped data*

HOMICIDE RATE	f	x'	fx'	(fx')²
1–2	10	−4	−40	160
3–4	28	−3	−84	252
5–6	24	−2	−48	96
7–8	15	−1	−15	15
9–10	12	0	0	0
11–12	11	1	11	11
13–14	11	2	22	44
15–16	17	3	51	153
17–18	9	4	36	144
19–20	5	5	25	125
21–22	3	6	18	108
	145		−24	1108

$$SS = \Sigma fx^2 = \left[\Sigma fx'^2 - \frac{(\Sigma fx')^2}{N} \right] i^2$$

$$= \left[1108 - \left(\frac{24^2}{145} \right) \right] 2^2$$

$$= (1108 - 3.97)4$$

$$= (1104.03)4$$

$$= 4416.12$$

$$s^2 = SS/(n-1)$$

$$= \frac{4416.12}{144}$$

$$= 30.67$$

$$s = \sqrt{30.67}$$

$$= 5.54$$

---

quick quiz
4.2

For the following sample data, compute the standard deviation.

X	f
60–69	4
70–79	11
80–89	18
90–99	30
100–109	20
110–119	13
120–129	5

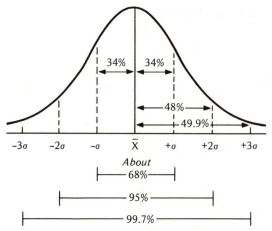

Figure 4.2 *The Normal Distribution and the Standard Deviation*

A normal distribution is one which is based on a theoretically in-finite number of cases. It is unimodal and symmetric. When graphed as a frequency curve, this distribution resembles the familiar bell-shaped curve which can be used as an approximation of the distribution of numerous variables: IQ scores, heights of American males, measurement errors, sampling distributions, and others. What is vitally important about the normal distribution is that *between any two points in a normal distribution we can specify the proportion of the corresponding area which lies under the curve.* This can be best illustrated by using as one point the mean of a distribution and as a second point some standard deviation unit. The normal distribution in Figure 4.2 has a mean of zero and a standard deviation of one. In this, and in any normal distribution, the distance from the mean to $+\sigma$ (or from the mean to $-\sigma$) includes 34.13 percent of the area under the curve.* Therefore, the distance from $+\sigma$ to $-\sigma$ includes 68.26 percent of the area. The distance from the mean to $+2\sigma$ (or from the mean to -2σ) includes 47.72 percent of the area under the curve; therefore, the distance from $+2\sigma$ to -2σ includes 95.44 percent of the area. From the mean to $+3\sigma$ includes 49.85 percent of the area, and from $+3\sigma$ to -3σ includes 99.72 percent. We can similarly define the area corresponding to the distance between any two points when those points are expressed as standard deviation units, which, in this context, are commonly known as *z-scores*.

A z-score is a measure of deviation from the mean, relative to the standard deviation; that is, it is a deviation score expressed in standard

*The precise technical derivation of these figures is beyond the scope of this book, but the curious reader might refer to Blalock (1972: 96–98). For our purposes, we can obtain the necessary figures from Table B of the Appendix.

essential statistics for social research

deviation units. (For this reason, it is also called a standard score.) Symbolically,

(*Formula 4.15*)

$$z = \frac{X - \overline{X}}{\sigma} = \frac{x}{\sigma}$$

A z-score thus expresses any raw score as being so many standard deviations above or below the mean.

For example, suppose we have an approximately normal distribution whose mean is 100 and standard deviation is 10. In this distribution we observe that a certain score is equal to 120. The score of 120 is thus 20 units above the mean. If we divide this deviation score, $x = 20$, by the standard deviation we obtain a z-score of $+2.00$. In other words, the score of 120 lies two standard units above the mean. Since we already know something about the relationship between standard deviation units and the area under a normal curve, we can now determine rather accurately the location of the score of 120 relative to all other scores in the distribution. This location can be expressed as a centile. The exact centile locations are obtained from a table (Appendix Table B). But for the moment we do not need the table, since we know that a z-score of $+2.0$ corresponds to an area of 47.72 percent (from $\overline{X}$ to z). The score of 120 is thus above 48 percent + 50 percent = 98 percent of all scores in the distribution. Figure 4.3 describes this.

Listed below are other z-scores calculated for a distribution whose mean is 100 and standard deviation is 10.

Score	z	Area from $\overline{X}$ to z	Centile
100	0.00	.0000	50.00
105	+0.50	.1915	69.15
90	−1.00	.3413	15.87
87	−1.30	.4032	9.68
123	+2.3	.4893	98.93

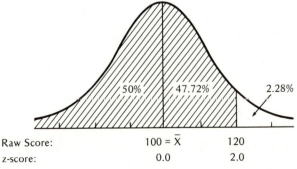

Figure 4.3   *Raw Scores and z-scores, an Example*

Notice that the centile values are found in two different ways, depending on whether the z-score is positive or negative. If the z-score is positive, the area obtained from column B of Table B is *added to* 0.5000; if the z-score is negative, the obtained area is *subtracted from* 0.5000. To convince yourself of this, draw a normal curve, locate each of the above z-scores, and shade in the corresponding areas.

quick quiz
4.3

> Given the data below, compute the appropriate z-score.
> (A) $X = 23, \overline{X} = 20, s = 4$
> (B) $X = 415, \overline{X} = 500, s = 100$
> (C) $X = 100, \overline{X} = 70, s = 12$

Similarly, we can find the area corresponding to the distance between any two points. For example, if we want to know what proportion of scores fall between 105 and 123, we simply subtract the corresponding areas (not z-scores). The area corresponding to a raw score of 123 is .4893 and the area corresponding to a raw score of 105 is .1915. Therefore, the area between 105 and 123 is .4893 − .1915 = .2978 (Figure 4.4). As noted above, it is always useful to draw a figure which illustrates the problem. This will help to clarify where z-scores are in relation to the mean, and whether to add or to subtract areas from each other or from .5000.

For simplicity's sake we have treated the above scores as discrete values. (In other words, we have not considered true limits.)

More frequently, however, we will treat scores as indicators of continuous values. When this is done, it is important to recall that true

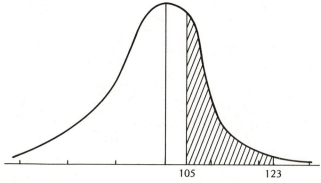

Figure 4.4   *The Area Between Two Scores.*

limits should be observed (see Chapter 2). For example, if the scores of 105 and 123 are assumed to reflect a continous variable, to determine the area corresponding to the distance between these scores, we must deal with the lower limit of 105, which is 104.5 and the upper limit of 123, which is 123.5. The corresponding z-scores and areas are, therefore,

Raw Score	True Limit	z-score	Area
105	104.5	0.45	.1736
123	123.5	2.35	.4906

and the area between 105 (actually 104.5) and 123 (actually 123.5) is .4906 − .1736 = .3170. In other words, nearly 32 percent of all scores fall between 104.5 and 123.5.

quick quiz
4.4   If an IQ test has a mean of 100 and a standard deviation of 15, what proportion of all scores fall between 90 and 120?

important terms to know

Range	Principle of least squares
Interdecile range	Sum of squares
Interquartile range	Variance
Average deviation	z-score
Standard deviation	

suggested reading

Freeman (1965: 59–66); Loether and McTavish (1974a: 143–159); Mueller, Schuessler and Costner (1970: 152–179); Phillips (1973: 22–29).

answer section

QUICK QUIZ 4.1

X	x	x²	X²	
−1	−3	9	1	
1	−1	1	1	
2	0	0	4	$\overline{X} = 2$
3	1	1	9	
5	3	9	25	
10	0	20	40	

(A) SS = 20   Using Formula 4.10:

$$SS = 40 - \frac{10^2}{5} = 40 - 20 = 20$$

$$\sigma^2 = 20/5 = 4 \qquad \sigma = \sqrt{4} = 2$$

(B) $s^2 = 20/(5-1) = 5 \qquad s = \sqrt{5} = 2.24$

QUICK QUIZ 4.2

X	f	x′	fx′	x′²	fx′²
60–69	4	−3	−12	9	36
70–79	11	−2	−22	4	44
80–89	18	−1	−18	1	18
90–99	30	0	0	0	0
100–109	20	1	20	1	20
110–119	13	2	26	4	52
120–129	5	3	15	9	45
			9 = fx′		215 = fx′²

$$s^2 = \frac{[215 - (9)^2]/101}{100}(10^2) = \frac{215 - 0.8}{100}(100)$$

$$= \sqrt{214.2}$$

Since the standard deviation is computed as the square root of the variance, $s = \sqrt{214.2} = 14.6$.

QUICK QUIZ 4.3 (A) $z = \dfrac{23 - 20}{4} = \dfrac{3}{4} = 0.75$

(B) $z = \dfrac{415 - 500}{100} = \dfrac{-85}{100} = -0.85$

(C) $z = \dfrac{100 - 70}{12} = \dfrac{30}{12} = +2.50$

essential statistics for social research

QUICK QUIZ 4.4

$$Z_{89.5} = \frac{89.5 - 100}{15} = \frac{-10.5}{15} = -0.70 \text{ (Area = .2580)}$$

$$Z_{120.5} = \frac{120.5 - 100}{15} = \frac{20.5}{15} = +1.37 \text{ (Area = .4147)}$$

The total area is .2580 + .4147 = .6727. Thus, 67 percent of all scores fall between 89.5 and 120.5.

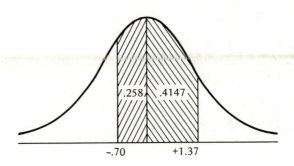

bases of statistical inference, I:
probability and the logic of hypothesis testing

In the first four chapters of this book we discussed simple descriptive statistics. In this chapter and subsequent chapters we shall deal with inferential statistics. Descriptive statistics provide us with a quantitative "picture" of some aspect of the world. Such statistics may be drawn from populations or samples and, strictly speaking, apply only to the population or sample from which the statistic was derived. For example, the decennial census of the United States gives us many descriptive measures of the American population. These census data apply only to the United States and cannot be used to describe any other population. Inferential statistics also give us a picture of some aspect of the world. But inferential statistics differ from descriptive statistics in that the former enable us to generalize beyond the data at hand. For example, public opinion polls, such as those of Gallup or Harris, measure the opinions of approximately 1,500 people, and from the descriptive measures derived from this sample *infer* a description of the opinions of the entire American population. What makes such inferences possible? How can we trust that the opinions of 1,500 people will accurately reflect the opinions of millions? The answers to such questions lie with the concepts of probability and sampling, the subjects of this and the next chapter.

probability: a way of viewing the world

5

1. The early morning weather forecast states that there is a 30 percent chance of rain today.

2. At the pregame coin toss, the football captain calls heads but knows that tails is equally likely to occur.

3. On a multiple-choice test with four options, a student who doesn't know the answer makes a pure guess, "c".

4. At the roulette table a chip is placed on number 13.

These are but a few of the many events in our day-to-day lives that are affected by the "laws" of probability. When probabilities are stated as above, they do not seem difficult to grasp. The statistician, however, uses the language of mathematics, and the above statements, as rendered by a statistician, might look like this:

(1) Pr(rain) = .30   [and, by implication, Pr(no-rain) = .70]
(2) Pr(heads) = .50   [and, by implication, Pr(tails) = .50]
(3) Pr(correct) = .25   [and Pr(incorrect) = .75]
(4) Pr(13) = .0263   [and Pr(not 13) = .9737]

Such probability statements are used for two purposes. First, they help us to make *inferences* about events that have not yet occurred; they do this, of course, by telling us how likely it is that the event in question will occur. Second, they help us to make certain kinds of *decisions* concerning those events. In example 1 above, we might make the following inference: in the past one hundred days when weather conditions were similar to those of today, it rained thirty of the days; therefore, it is reasonable to infer that the chances of rain today are $30/100 = 0.30 = 30$ percent. We can then use this inference to make a decision: shall we take an umbrella or not? The decision we actually make will be based on many factors beside the probability statement itself, such as whether we are wearing good or old clothes, whether the corn on our big toe is hurting, how much of a risk we are willing to take that we won't get wet, and the like. In example 2, the inference is simpler: when a fair coin is tossed, heads will come up as often as tails. The decision is equally simple: if the coin is fair, it really doesn't matter whether one calls heads or tails, and whichever choice is made will be perfectly idiosyncratic. In example 4 the inference might be: "I have one chance in thirty-eight of winning, so the odds against me are thirty-seven to one." The decision to bet or not to bet will again depend on many other factors. (But we might point out that since the house usually pays off at thirty-five to one when the true odds are thirty-seven to one, the only rational decision is: don't play roulette except for fun.)

How do we know that there is a 30 percent chance of rain today, or a 50 percent chance of observing a head when a coin is tossed? One way of knowing about the behavior of the coin toss is *empirical observation*, from which we obtain *empirical probability*. We could, for example, take a coin and toss it once, twice, a hundred times, and we could ask twenty friends to do the same. If we observe the result, or *outcome*, of each of these 2,000 tosses, or trials, we would undoubtedly see something like this:

Number of heads = 1,000 $Pr(heads) = \dfrac{1,000}{2,000} = .5$

Number of tails = 1,000 $Pr(tails) = \dfrac{1,000}{2,000} = .5$

Total   2,000   1.0

We might not get exactly 1,000 heads—there might be 1,013 heads and 987 tails—but the figure would be fairly close to 1,000. Because of this empirical observation that the number of heads is essentially equal to the number of tails, we could be quite confident that if we were to toss the coin another 2,000 times we would again get a result very close to a 50–50 split. In fact, this particular observation is so common in our experience that we rarely consider it.

Now suppose that at 6:00 A.M. every day we noted the temperature, wind velocity and direction, humidity, barometric pressure and activity and other meteorological data. We then note whether it rains that day. After many, many such days we might begin to detect certain weather patterns. Soon we would be able to make predictions about the day's weather. We do so, in part, on the basis of the empirical probabilities which were established by previous observation. In this sense we see that empirical probability enables us to make guesses or predictions about some unknown event on the basis of known past events.

Just as much of the physical world is "governed" by probability, so it is with the social world. If I buy a five-year term insurance policy, I am "betting" that I will die within five years. My insurance premium is the amount of my bet and the face value of the policy is the amount of the insurance company's wager. The ratio of the two bets gives the odds that I will die, and these odds are set by the company's actuarial tables which, from past experience, show that x-number of men in my age group die within five years.

In a similar fashion, a personnel manager wants to know whether the person to be hired will be a "success" or "failure" on the job. Therefore, she asks whether, in the past, people with certain background characteristics had better success records than persons with different background characteristics. In effect, she uses previous empirical observation to determine the probability of a future event. And on the basis of her inference, she decides to hire or not to hire the applicant.

A prison warden must decide whether or not to recommend parole for an inmate. Although there are many individual factors to consider, the final decision might be determined, in part, by the warden's formal or informal calculation of empirical probabilities for recidivism.

Just as coins, dice, human death and parole violations are to a certain degree *probable*, so are many other spheres of human activity. Indeed, the sociological concepts of norm and role might be thought of in probabalistic terms. A role can be defined as an expected pattern of behavior, and if we know that someone is playing a role, we can make certain predictions about that person's behavior. For example, if someone is occupying the role of teacher, it can be predicted that he will more often give than receive information in the classroom. Such predictions are not usually formalized into quantitative probability statements; they generally remain informal and subjective. But they do exist and we do use them to guide us in our everday behavior. We could even argue that the social order is nothing more than a set of informal probability statements.

Order implies *predictability* and *interdependence*. The opposite condition of chaos implies the lack of predictability, *independence*. If social interaction is not ordered, we often say it is random, or subject to laws of chance. But the real world in which we live is neither completely ordered nor completely random. No one can predict another's behavior with 100 percent accuracy, and no one could survive if the correct prediction rate was zero. The sociologist's real world lies somewhere between perfect order and complete chaos. It is a probabilistic world. It is so because our knowledge of the world is never complete, is always subject to uncertainty, randomness, fate, chance or probability.

Thus, any event (including a statistical event) is the result of two broad factors, those which are known and those which remain unknown. The former are called determining factors, the latter chance factors. For example, what "causes" delinquency? Some plausible causes are broken homes, association with delinquents, inadequate superego, failure in school, and so on. To a greater or lesser extent, delinquency is dependent on these factors, among others. But can we list *all* of the others? And do all children from broken homes become delinquents? Do all children from unbroken homes remain nondelinquent? Of course not. And this is where the unknown factors, or chance, come in. "Chance" is a residual category which includes all of the causes that we cannot specify. It is a measure of our ignorance. This ignorance need cause us no shame, since it is also important to know that-which-we-don't-know.

Having said all of this, let us now make what seems to be a totally contradictory statement: under certain conditions *chance itself behaves in regular patterns.* Such conditions resemble games of chance. This is so because "for statistical purposes chance factors are presumed to be (1) very numerous, (2) relatively minute, (3) independent of one another and (4) very largely unidentifiable and, therefore, not measurable; consequently, (5) they work collectively—as far as we know—to produce equally likely events" (Mueller, Schuessler and Costner, 1970: 210).

basic rules of probability

We have just seen that if it is possible to measure past outcomes, it is possible to calculate empirical probabilities. We do this by following several basic rules of probability.

Rule 1: The probability of any simple event (E) can be expressed as a ratio of the frequency (n) of any event to the total number (N) of trials in which the event might occur. This can be expressed as

$$Pr(E) = \frac{n}{N}$$ *(Formula 5.1)*

For example, suppose we record the sex of a random sample of 800 births in a given community. We note 412 girls and 388 boys. We can then make a prediction concerning the probability of a girl being born in that community. It is

$$Pr(girl) = \frac{412}{800} = .515$$

Often we are not interested in simple events, but in events that occur together, such as rolling two dice. We may want to know the probability of rolling "snake-eyes" (two one-spots). This leads us to

Rule 2: The probability of a *compound event* is equal to the product of probability of the individual events. This can be expressed as

$$Pr(E_1 \ and \ E_2) = Pr(E_1) \times Pr(E_2)$$ *(Formula 5.2)*

In our example, the probability of rolling a one-spot with the first die is $\frac{1}{6}$ and the probability of rolling a one-spot with the second die is also $\frac{1}{6}$. Therefore, the joint or compound probability is

$$\left(\frac{1}{6}\right)\left(\frac{1}{6}\right) = \frac{1}{36} = .028$$

Finally, we are sometimes interested in the probability of any one of several specified events. For example, there are six ways of rolling a 7 with a pair of dice: 1 + 6; 2 + 5; 3 + 4; 4 + 3; 5 + 2 and 6 + 1. If we are only interested in the event of a 7, regardless of how that 7 was achieved, we use the following rule for *alternative and mutually exclusive events.*

Rule 3: The probability of one of two or more mutually exclusive outcomes is equal to the sum of the probabilities of the individual outcomes. This can be expressed as

$$Pr(E_1 \ or \ E_2 \ or \ . \ . \ . \ E_n) = \Sigma \, Pr(E)$$ *(Formula 5.3)*

essential statistics for social research

Each of the six ways of rolling a 7 has an individual probability of $\frac{1}{36}$. Therefore, the probability of rolling a 7 is

$$\Pr(7) = \Pr(1,6) + \Pr(2,5) + \Pr(3,4) + \Pr(4,3) + \Pr(5,2) + \Pr(6,1)$$

$$= \frac{1}{36} + \frac{1}{36} + \frac{1}{36} + \frac{1}{36} + \frac{1}{36} + \frac{1}{36}$$

$$= \frac{6}{36} = \frac{1}{6} = .167$$

A slight modification of Rule 3 is necessary if we are working with alternative events which are not mutually exclusive. (Two events are mutually exclusive if the occurrence of one precludes the occurrence of the other. On a single roll of a die, each of the six outcomes is mutually exclusive of the others.) We can see an example of two outcomes which are not mutually exclusive in the following example. What is the probability of drawing a red card (heart or diamond) or a face card (J,Q,K) from a deck of fifty-two cards? Since there are twenty-six red cards, $\Pr(red) = 26/52 = 1/2 = .5$ and since there are twelve face cards, $\Pr(face) = 12/52 = .23$. But notice that six of the cards are *both* red and face. This means we have counted them twice (once as red, and once as face). To correct this obvious error, we must subtract the probability of this joint occurrence. Thus

$$\Pr(red \ or \ face) = \Pr(red) + \Pr(face) - \Pr(red \ and \ face)$$

$$= \frac{26}{52} + \frac{12}{52} - \left(\frac{26}{52}\right)\left(\frac{12}{52}\right)$$

$$= \frac{38}{52} - \frac{6}{52}$$

$$= \frac{32}{52}$$

$$= .62$$

By now you may be asking yourself what the relationship is between sociological research and dice and card games of chance. The following two simple problems may help you to answer such a question.

Problem A	*Problem B*
Suppose we toss twenty coins. What is the probability of observing ten heads?	Suppose a certain large city has an equal number of white and black workers. An employer is suspected of racial bias because of his

twenty employees, "only" seven are black. Is it reasonable to accuse the employer of bias?

At first glance it may seem that these two problems have nothing in common. One involves a trivial situation, while the other deals with a vital socioeconomic issue; one problem is a game of chance, the other is the game of life. While recognizing that Problem B is greatly over-simplified, let us examine how the use of probability statistics can help us solve both problems.'

One way of solving Problem A is by empirical observation. We could toss twenty coins many, many times, each time counting and tallying the number of heads. If we were to do this 1,000 times, we would observe results similar to those in Table 5.1. But we do not really want to take the time to toss 1,000 coins, and we already know that the "random" tosses of a coin are subject to very predictable behavior in the long run and on the average. This behavior is defined mathematically by the *binomial probability distribution*. A binomial situation is one in which each trial (1) is identical to every other trial; (2) is independent of (unaffected by) every other trial; (3) has two and only two possible outcomes, the probability of each being known. In coin tossing, each toss is considered to be identical; each toss is independent of the other tosses; each toss has only two possible outcomes (head or tail) and Pr(head) = Pr(tail) = .5. Schematically, the binomial distribution is defined by the following:

$$Pr(n) = \frac{N!(p^n)(q^{N-n})}{n!(N-n)!}$$ (*Formula 5.4*)

where n = the number of successes; N = the total number of trials; p = the probability of a success on a single trial; and q = (1 − p). (Note: N!, or N-factorial, is the product of N (N − 1) (N − 2) . . . (3) (2) (1). Zero factorial, 0!, is one.) A detailed discussion of Formula 5.4 is beyond the scope of this book. For further information, see Blalock (1972) or Mueller, Schuessler and Costner (1970).

When formula 5.4 is applied to Problem A,

$$N = 20 \qquad p = .5$$
$$n = 10 \qquad q = (1 - .5) = .5$$

and

$$Pr(10\ heads) = \frac{20!(.5^{10})(.5^{10})}{10!(20 - 10)!} = .176$$

table 5.1   a sampling distribution giving the probability of obtaining a given number of heads when twenty coins are tossed

NUMBER OF HEADS	BINOMIAL DISTRIBUTION	NORMAL APPROXIMATION
0	*	*
1	*	*
2	*	*
3	.002	.001
4	.005	.005
5	.015	.015
6	.037	.036
7	.074	.073
8	.120	.120
9	.160	.162
10	.176	.174
11	.160	.162
12	.120	.120
13	.074	.073
14	.037	.036
15	.015	.015
16	.005	.005
17	.002	.001
18	*	*
19	*	*
20	*	*
TOTAL	1.002†	0.998†

*Less than .001
†Does not equal 1.000 due to rounding error.

Thus the probability of observing exactly ten heads when twenty coins are tossed is about 18 percent.

Let us now turn to Problem B. Each time a person is hired could be considered as a trial, and each time a black person is hired could be termed a "success." (Of course, these terms are arbitrary; we could just as well define a success as the hiring of a white person.) Since the city's population contains an equal number of eligible blacks and whites, the theoretical probability of hiring a black, "all other things being equal," is $\frac{1}{2}$ or .5.. Therefore,

$$N = 20 \qquad p = .5$$

$$n = 7 \qquad q = .5$$

and

$$\Pr(7) = \frac{20!(.5^7)(.5^{13})}{20!(20-7)!} = .074$$

Thus, if *only chance* factors are operating, there is but a 7 percent probability of the employer hiring exactly seven blacks. Shall we conclude that hiring seven or fewer blacks is evidence of discrimination? Not yet—we must also consider the more extreme situations: six blacks hired, five blacks hired, and so on (including zero blacks hired). For if hiring only seven blacks constitutes discrimination, certainly hiring a smaller number than seven also constitutes discrimination. In other words, we are interested in the probability of an alternative, not mutually exclusive event. We are interested in Pr(7 or 6 or 5 or 4 or 3 or 2 or 1 or 0) which is

$$.074 + .036 + .015 + .005 + .002 + .0002 + .00002 + .000002 = .132.$$

What have we shown? If the situation described in Problem B is purely a matter of chance (that is, if it is independent of any external factors, such as discriminatory hiring practices), the outcome of hiring seven or fewer blacks would occur, on the average and in the long run, 13.2 percent of the time. If Pr(7 or fewer) = .132, is this evidence of discrimination? The answer to this question can*not* be derived from statistics, for we are now left with a question of judgment. Is something which can happen statistically only 13 percent of the time an unusual event, so unusual that we are ready to say that it could *not* have happened by chance? Again, we have a question of judgment, a question which our statistics cannot *prove*, but to which they can bring *evidence*. It is usually, but not always, the case in sociological work to consign an event to the realm of chance only if its probability is .05 or less (generally expressed as $p < .05$). If we apply this convention, we would conclude that there is not sufficient statistical evidence to reject the *chance model*.

Any binomial distribution which is based on a sufficiently large N (20 or more) bears a striking resemblence to a normal distribution. Even when N is as small as 10, the resemblance between the two distributions is quite close if both p and q are approximately .5. Furthermore, the mean and the standard deviation of a binomial distribution are easily computed from the following formulas:

THE BINOMIAL DISTRIBUTION AND THE NORMAL CURVE

$$\overline{X} = Np \qquad \text{(Formula 5.5)}$$

$$\sigma = \sqrt{Npq} \qquad \text{(Formula 5.6)}$$

Consider again our example of tossing twenty coins. We can perhaps intuitively "see" that the mean of the distribution is ten (Figure 5.1). But can we easily "see" the standard deviation? No. So let us use the formulas

essential statistics for social research

$$\overline{X} = 20(.5) = 10.0$$

$$\sigma = \sqrt{20(.5)(.5)} = \sqrt{5}$$

$$= 2.24$$

Since the data from Problem B are based on the same values of N and p, the mean of the distribution is also 10 and its standard deviation is 2.24.

Notice that we have now described our data as being approximately normal and that we know the mean and the standard deviation. We can, therefore, reconceptualize the entire problem as one involving z-scores.

However, we first must notice that the binomial distribution differs from the normal distribution in that the former is discrete; that is, it takes on only the whole numbers 1, 2, 3, . . . 19, 20. But the normal

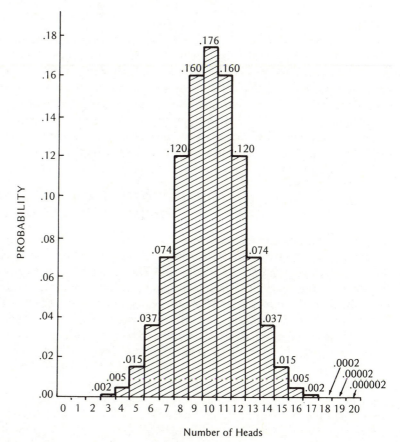

Figure 5.1   *The Probability of Observing a Given Number of Heads when Twenty Coins Are Tossed*

distribution is *continuous;* it can take on any value from 0.00 to 20.00, including 1, 2.24, 3.471, 18.9998 and $\sqrt{2}$. Because we are using a continuous curve (the normal distribution) to approximate a discrete distribution (the binomial), we must make a slight adjustment in our thinking: we must use the true upper and lower limits of any discrete number to define its location in the continuous distribution. Thus, the discrete number 7 is represented in its continuous form by all values between 6.5 and 7.5. (You might wish to review the discussion of true limits, pp. 15–16).

To solve Problem B, we must find the probability of observing 7.5 or fewer blacks in a group of twenty employees. Using z-scores (see Formula 4.15),

$$z = \frac{7.5 - 10.0}{2.24} = \frac{-2.5}{2.24}$$

$$= -1.12$$

Turning to Appendix Table B, we see that the area corresponding to a z-score of ± 1.12 is .3686 of the total area under the normal curve. Therefore, the area beyond $z = -1.12$ is $.5000 - .3686 = .1314$. Thus, we again see, using z-scores, that the probability of hiring seven or fewer blacks is about 13 percent. (The small discrepancy between 13.14 percent, the z-score probability, and 13.2 percent, the binomial probability, is due to the fact that the former figure is derived from a continuous distribution while the latter comes from a discrete distribution.)

probability and the logic of hypothesis testing

Let us now develop what we have learned thus far into some general principles for conducting statistical tests of hypotheses. Our first task will be to select an appropriate hypothesis. There can be a variety of hypotheses for any research problem. In tossing twenty coins we could hypothesize (1) the outcome will be ten heads, (2) the outcome will be eleven heads or (3) the outcome will be between eight and twelve heads, and so on. Any of these alternative hypotheses are plausible, but, statistically speaking, most are very difficult to test. (The reason for this difficulty is beyond the scope of this discussion.) There is, however, one general hypothesis that we can test. It is the hypothesis which says that the observed event occurs in conformity with a chance model. For example, Figure 5.1 describes a chance model of the possible outcomes when twenty coins are tossed. Of specific interest, this chance model tells us that the mean number of heads when twenty coins are tossed is ten. We can then formulate the following research question: is the

essential statistics for social research

number of heads actually observed *reasonably similar* to the number of heads that we should expect to observe? Stated more formally, since the true *population* mean is 10, we hypothesize that our *sample* mean will also be 10. This type of statement, which states that the sample value is no different from the population value, is called a *null hypothesis* (H_0), or the hypothesis of no difference. But the real meaning of the term null hypothesis lies in the fact that it is the hypothesis which we hope to nullify, that is, to disprove. Strictly speaking, the null hypothesis is the only hypothesis which can be statistically tested. For our example, the null hypothesis might be stated in any of the following ways:

1. H_0: The sample mean is no different from the population mean.
2. H_0: $\overline{X} = 10$
3. H_0: $\overline{X} - \mu = 0$*

In addition to the null hypothesis, researchers will also specify an alternative, or research, hypothesis. In our example, the research hypothesis (H_1) might be stated as (1) the sample mean is different from (or is greater than or less than) the population mean; (2) $\overline{X} \neq 10$; (3) $\overline{X} - \mu \neq 0$; (4) $\overline{X} - \mu < 0$; or (5) $\overline{X} - \mu > 0$ and so on. The null hypothesis is *always* a statement of no meaningful difference or of no meaningful relationship, while the alternative hypothesis is *always* a statement of some difference or of some relationship.

The null hypothesis is based on a known, or accurately estimated, characteristic of a population. We observe this characteristic in a sample. If the two observations yield contradictory values, we *reject* the null hypothesis. If the two observations do not show contradictory values, we *do not reject* the null hypothesis.

When does the sample observation contradict the null hypothesis? When it is highly improbable. *How improbable?* There is no statistical law which defines what is probable or improbable, but as stated earlier, statisticians generally consider that an event is statistically improbable only if it is among the extreme 5 percent of possible outcomes. This 5 percent value (or 1 percent or 10 percent as the case may be) is called *alpha* (α) and represents an important concept in statistical decision making: it is the level of risk which we are willing to assume that we will consider an outcome to be *improbable* when it is, in fact, *probable*. The technical name for such an error is a *Type I Error*. In a sampling distribution, alpha defines the *region of rejection*, or the proportion of the distribution which contains the specified highly improbable outcomes. In other words, alpha defines the probability of a Type I Error. In contrast, the *Type II Error* occurs when a null hypothesis which is actually false is not rejected.

*The symbol μ (Mu) is used to identify the population mean. It is to be distinguished from $\overline{X}$, the sample mean. The sample mean is used to estimate the population mean.

The problem of Type I and Type II Errors is analogous to the problem faced by a jury in a criminal case. The defendant is either guilty or not guilty. The jury may render a verdict of either guilty or not guilty. If the defendant is indeed guilty, and if that is also the jury's finding, there is no error. Similarly, if the defendant is truly not guilty and the jury so finds, there is no error. But if the defendant is guilty and the jury finds him not guilty, an error has been made, and if the defendant is truly not guilty and the jury finds him guilty, an error is made. Of the two errors, which is worse? In our system of justice, with its notion of "innocent until proven guilty" the latter error is usually deemed to be worse, so the legal system is designed to minimize that type of error. Consequently, our whole legal system is designed to protect the innocent, even if this means that an occasional guilty party will go unpunished.

The statistical analogues to the guilty-not-guilty problem are Type I and II Errors, which are described in Figure 5.2.

Returning to Problem A, if we toss a coin twenty times in order to determine whether it is fair (not subject to any controlling force except chance), we will regard any outcome in the vicinity of ten heads as probable and any outcome in the vicinity of zero heads or twenty heads as improbable. In statistical terms, such an hypothesis test is a *two-tail test*, a test in which either extreme outcome will lead us to reject the null hypothesis. In Problem B we are not interested in both extremes; we are only interested in one extreme, that in which blacks are underrepresented. A research hypothesis which tells us to look for one extreme outcome or the other, but not both, is a directional hypothesis, and the statistical tests used in such circumstances are called *one-tail tests*. Figure 5.3 illustrates directional or nondirectional hypotheses. In a one-tail test, alpha, the region of rejection, is located entirely at one end (or in one "tail") of the sampling distribution. In a two-tail test, alpha is divided in half, and there are, in essence, two regions of rejection, one in each tail, and each having a value of $\alpha/2$.

ONE-TAIL AND TWO-TAIL TESTS

To summarize: we have, in the last few pages, described the fundamentals necessary to conduct a statistical test. These are:

		The Null Hypothesis is	
		True	**False**
The Decision Concerning H_0 **is to**	**Reject**	Type I Error	Correct Decision
	Not Reject	Correct Decision	Type II Error

Figure 5.2   *Type I and Type II Errors*

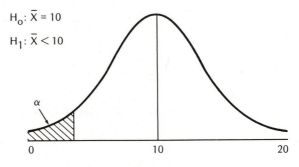

$H_0: \overline{X} = 10$

$H_1: \overline{X} < 10$

α

0   10   20

Number of Heads

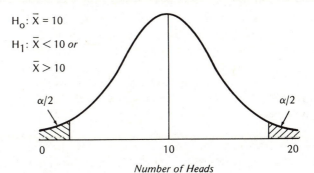

$H_0: \overline{X} = 10$

$H_1: \overline{X} < 10$ *or*

$\overline{X} > 10$

$\alpha/2$ $\alpha/2$

0   10   20

Number of Heads

Figure 5.3   (*Top*) *One-tail Test.* (*Bottom*) *Two-tail Test*

1. *A null hypothesis,* a statement which specifies some aspect of a population which is known or assumed to be true. It is this hypothesis which is actually subject to the statistical test.
2. *A research hypothesis,* a statement which contradicts the null hypothesis. This hypothesis is not directly tested, but we often accept its validity if the null hypothesis has been rejected.
3. *A region of rejection,* alpha, which specifies the risk that we will incorrectly reject the null hypothesis. Before testing, the researcher must decide whether alpha should be located in one or in both tails of a distribution; this decision depends on whether the research decision is directional or nondirectional.
4. *A test statistic* which is computed from data taken from a sample. The z-score is one example of a test statistic; many others will be described in Chapters 7–11.

Let us illustrate these elements of a statistical test with our problem concerning discriminatory hiring. Our null hypothesis is that there is no difference between the observed sample mean ($\overline{X} = 7$) and the theoretically expected population mean ($\mu = 10$). Stated formally,

$$H_0 : \overline{X} - \mu = 0$$

Our research hypothesis is that the difference between $\overline{X}$ and μ is not 0. More specifically, we might be willing to specify a directional hypothesis, since we suspect our sample data to reveal a bias against blacks. Stated formally,

$$H_1 : \overline{X} - \mu < 0$$

Thus, we will conduct a one-tail test. Our selection of alpha is arbitrary, but we shall follow a common convention and let $\alpha = .05$. As our test statistic, we have chosen to use the z-score. We are now ready to conduct our test of significance, and we shall evaluate the test in terms of the following *decision rules*.

Reject H_0 if the observed value of z is greater than the critical value obtained from Appendix Table B. (For our data, the critical value for a one-tail test when $\alpha = .05$ is 1.645.) *Do not reject* H_0 if the critical value is less than 1.645.

As we have already seen, the computed value of z is -1.12. The magnitude of z is thus less than that of the critical value. Following our decision rule, we do not reject the null hypothesis. Because the null hypothesis was not rejected, we conclude that an observed sample mean of 7 could have occurred "by chance" and that there is no statistical evidence of discrimination.

If our sample mean had been 5 rather than 7, then

$$z = \frac{5.5 - 10}{2.24} = \frac{-4.5}{2.24} = -2.01$$

In this instance, we would be led to reject the null hypothesis, since the observed value of z is greater than the critical value.

quick quiz
5.1

> From some population which consists of an equal number of males and females, a sample of $N = 36$ is drawn. (A) How many females would you expect to be included in the sample? (B) What is the probability that the sample will have 12 or fewer females?

essential statistics for social research

important terms to know

Probability
Empirical probability
Chance factors
Three rules of probability
Binomial distribution
Null hypothesis
Research hypothesis

Alpha (α)
Region of rejection
Type I Error
Type II Error
One-tail test
Two-tail test

suggested readings

Blalock (1972: 119–173); Loether and McTavish (1974b: 3–39); Mendenhall, Ott and Larson (1974: 151–185); Mueller, Schuessler and Costner (1970: 207–237).

answer section

QUICK QUIZ 5.1   (A) $\overline{X} = np = 36(.5) = 18$

(B) $s = \sqrt{npq} = \sqrt{9} = 3$

$$Z = \frac{12.5 - 18}{3}$$

$$= \frac{-5.5}{3}$$

$$= -1.83$$

$$p = .0336$$

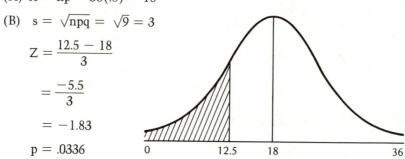

bases of statistical inference, II:

sampling and estimation

In Chapter 5 we learned how to use the laws of probability to assist us in making decisions about observed events. The examples used in Chapter 5 provided all of the information needed to reach those particular conclusions. In sociological research, however, we frequently do not have access to all of the necessary information. For example, we might want to know what the American people think about nuclear disarmament. Depending on how we define "American people," this population could have as many as 200,000,000 + people. It would require extraordinary resources to gather so much information, and such tasks are attempted only once every ten years. Given that no one but the Bureau of the Census has the capacity to study the entire 200,000,000 + "American people," does this mean that our original question cannot be answered, cannot even be asked? It does not, for we can, with a very high degree of confidence and with only a small amount of error, obtain the answer to our question by using data from a sample of the larger population. From the sample data, we can make inferences about the population. And the inferences which we make will not be at all haphazard.

It is not unusual for us to understand our world by making inferences, or generalizations: having touched one hot stove, we are unlikely to touch another; finding several rotten apples, we may reject the entire barrel; noticing that some Europeans eat with their forks in their left hands, we conclude that all Europeans do the same. Such inferences are reasonable. They help us to make sense out of what would otherwise be a chaotic universe. They guide our behavior.

6

But obviously, such generalizations are not always valid. A sensible person will reshape generalizations in the light of new information. On the other hand, a prejudiced person will use generalizations to reshape information. If a person is refused employment because of ethnic differences between employer and employee, shall we conclude that all or even most members of the employer's ethnic group are prejudiced? If my wallet is taken by a bearded youth, shall I infer that most bearded youths are thieves?

One of the functions of statistical sampling is to help us distinguish between valid and invalid generalizations; indeed, this is probably its most important function. But two other important functions should be mentioned. As indicated above, sampling permits us to save our resources of time, energy, money and personnel. Except for census purposes, there is no need to survey 200,000,000 people when we can get the same information from 1,500 people. Finally, sampling is at times necessary if the very process of measurement alters or even destroys what is being measured. For example, politicians are often the subject of "voter recognition" studies. In such studies, potential voters are asked, "Do you recognize the name of John Doe? Who is he?" But people who do not recognize Mr. Doe may be moved by the question and by their ignorance to seek information about Doe. In this example, simply asking the question alters, or may alter, a portion of the respondents.

populations and samples

The *population*, or universe, is the category about which an inference is made. The sample is a category within the population from which measurements are obtained. It is imperative that a population be well-defined; that is, the elements which constitute a population must be clearly specified. A population may be of any size, and it is generally determined by the research problem at hand. For example, given a particular research problem, any of the following may be considered as a population: (1) all American citizens age eighteen or older; (2) all registered voters in Tennessee; (3) all Democrats who voted in the last presidential election; (4) all undergraduate students now registered at this school; (5) all sophomore females at this school; and so on.

Some authors distinguish between the target, or theoretical population and the sampled population. The target universe is the universe we are seeking to know, such as "all registered voters in Chicago." While this universe is reasonably well-defined, it probably is difficult to obtain an accurate list of this population, since within any given time span a certain number of people die, or move out of or into the city, or for some other reason do not appear or mistakenly appear on the official voter list. But it is this list which defines the sampled universe and distinguishes it from the target universe.

A *sample* is a specified portion of the universe. Samples are of many kinds, but can generally be classified as *random* (or scientific or probability) or *nonrandom*. A random sample *is not* an accidental sample, that is, one that "just happens." Rather, it is random in the sense that every element in the population has a known, and often equal, chance of being included in the sample which is eventually drawn from the population. Let us illustrate this important point by means of an example. Suppose you wanted to draw a sample of five-hundred voters from your congressional district. You might simply go to the largest city and stop the first five hundred people you meet on the street. Or you might knock on five hundred doors in a nearby neighborhood. From a naive point of view, one might argue that it is a matter of chance which five-hundred people you happen to meet, *but* it is also true that these five-hundred are likely to be *unrepresentative* because they are found in a city, not in a rural area; the people who do not come to the city, or even to that part of the city, have no chance of being included in the sample; and so on. These five hundred people are unrepresentative of their district because not everyone in the district had an equal chance of being included in the sample. This bias may not have been intended; nonetheless it is real and present. A truly random sample minimizes the danger of such biased selection by using the laws of probability as the basis of sample selection. Thus, a sample is random if, and only if, it is selected by a process which is *statistically random.*

The most obvious type of random sample is the *simple random sample.* For instance, if we wanted to draw a sample of five students from a class of twenty-five, we could write each of the twenty-five names on a slip of paper, place the slips in a hat, thoroughly mix and blindly select five names.* Note that this procedure guarantees that each person has an equal and known probability of being included in the sample: Pr(inclusion) = 5/25 = .20. As a further technical point we might note that every possible sample of n = 5 has an equally likely chance of being selected.

A variation of the simple random sample is the *interval*, or systematic sample. If the sampling units are arranged in some kind of unbiased order, such as an alphabetical list of all students in a university, we can draw a reasonably representative sample simply by selecting every n-th name from the list, after a random starting point. (Some people argue, however, that an alphabetical list is confounded by ethnicity and may, therefore, be biased.)

Most social research problems involve populations much too large to permit us to draw names from a hat, but the principles of more advanced sampling techniques have the same end.

---

*To be technically correct, after we select each slip of paper we should return it to the hat before drawing the next slip because we must theoretically assume that the relevant population is infinitely large.

In research situations in which a crucial variable can be specified in advance, a *stratified random sample* will frequently be used. If we are sampling political attitudes in a town where voters are 50 percent Republican, 35 percent Democrat and 15 percent other, we might wish to first divide the total population into three groups, or strata, and then sample from each group. This procedure has two strong points in its favor. (1) It insures that our final sample will accurately reflect the population in terms of the political party variable; and (2) it enables us to achieve this with a smaller total sample size than would be required by simple random sampling. Figure 6.1 is a schematic representation of a stratified sample.

When the geographic area which includes the population is very large, researchers will often use an *area probability sample*. National polls, for example, would be too expensive to conduct if the researchers had to rely on samples drawn from all fifty states. Therefore, the country is divided into areas, and a sample of the area is drawn; then the areas are divided into smaller units, such as counties, and another sample is drawn. After several such steps, the final sampling units are drawn. In this type of sample, the first stage of sampling involves large geopolitical units, and it is only at the final stage that selection of individuals is made.

To the sociologist, sampling is especially important in the construction of research designs. To the statistician, sampling is important as a basis for inference. We sociologists who use statistics must appreciate both of these points. Most important, we must understand that a sample statistic can be seen as a sample value which, because it is only one value of many possible values (that is, the sample is but one of many possible samples), may or may not be truly representative of the corresponding population value. It is our task to develop means to de-

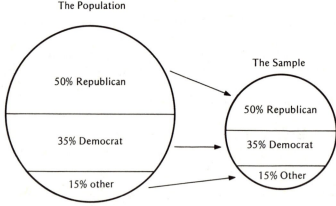

Figure 6.1   *A Stratified Sample*

essential statistics for social research

termine how representative our statistics really are. To do so, we must first understand the concept of a sampling distribution.

For the sake of familiarity, let us return to our example of tossing twenty coins (see page 63ff). Table 5.1 presented the probabilities of obtaining each of the twenty-one possible outcomes (from zero heads to twenty heads). The sum of these probabilities must equal 1.00. Using table 5.1, we can directly tell the probability of observing a given number of heads when twenty coins are tossed. Thus, $Pr(8) = .120$ and $Pr(15) = .015$. With a little manipulation, we can also quickly determine the probability of observing any set of heads; thus, the probability of five or fewer heads is

$$Pr(5 \text{ or } 4 \text{ or } 3 \text{ or } 2 \text{ or } 1 \text{ or } 0) = .015 + .005 + .002 \, (*) = .022$$

and the probability of observing between eight and twelve heads is

$$Pr(8 \text{ or } 9 \text{ or } 10 \text{ or } 11 \text{ or } 12) = .120 + .160 + .174 + .160 + .120$$
$$= .734$$

quick quiz
6.1

> What is the probability of observing (A) at least fourteen heads; (B) between nine and eleven heads, inclusive, when twenty coins are tossed?

A listing of all possible outcomes of any event is known as a *sampling distribution*. Thus, Table 5.1 gives the sampling distribution of the number of heads when twenty coins are tossed. Sampling distributions are calculated on the basis of a very large number, theoretically infinite, of the events in question. The importance of a sampling distribution is that it lists all possible outcomes and their probabilities and thus enables us to determine which of the outcomes are likely to occur and which are not. Since any and every sample statistic belongs to some sampling distribution, it is possible to determine how representative any sample statistic is as long as we know its sampling distribution. For instance, suppose we sample 1,500 families from a population of all American families and from each of these families we obtain a measure of family income. Can we be sure that our sample statistic is a reasonably accurate representation of the true population value? Figure 6.2 pictures the true (population) median income in the population, and in each of three

*The probability of two, one or zero heads is so small as to be negligible.

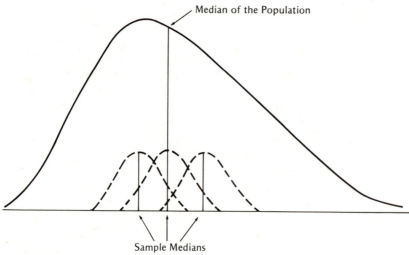

Figure 6.2 *A Population Value and Three Possible Sample Values*

samples. But suppose there were more than three samples in Figure 6.2; suppose there were hundreds and hundreds; try to imagine *all possible samples* and all possible sample medians. If we could develop a list of all possible sample medians, what would we have? The sampling distribution of the median family income for a sample size n = 1,500. If we could have such a sample distribution, we could easily tell whether any given sample was indeed representative, just as we could with our twenty coins. But in doing research we usually do not have a list of all possible samples, for, in fact, we usually draw only *one* sample. However, if we can locate that one sample relative to a *theoretical* list of all possible samples, we could determine the statistical probability that our observed sample reflects the true population value. Exactly how this is done is described below.

estimation

Up to this point we have discussed only a few of the obvious advantages of using a sample as the basis for statistical study. However, one noticeable disadvantage of sampling is that it inevitably involves a loss of information; consequently, measurements based on sample data contain some error. Since a sample is only an approximation of a population, one of the fundamental questions raised by sampling is: how much error is contained in sample statistics?

Let us suppose that we have a population which consists of the homicide rates of 145 SMSAs (see Table 2.1, p. 13). From this population we draw a random sample of size n = 30 (Table 6.1). We compute

table 6.1 **random sample of thirty homicide rates**

5	2	10	12	13
10	15	8	5	3
12	5	2	3	4
11	14	18	4	7
10	15	5	5	7
7	19	10	5	5

$$\overline{X} = 8.37$$

$$s = 4.75$$

a mean from this sample and find $\overline{X} = 8.37$. How certain can we be that this sample mean is a reasonably accurate estimation of the true population mean? How much confidence can we have in our sample statistic? Is it possible, because of an unknown bias or bad luck, that we have drawn a sample which does not represent the population? To answer such questions, we must reflect on both the sampling distribution of our sample statistic, in this case the sampling distribution of the mean, *and* on a new concept, the *standard error* of the sample statistic.

Let us put aside for a moment the problem described above. Instead, let us imagine a very different and very large population, such as all children currently enrolled in the seventh grade in a large school system. From this population we draw a sample of one hundred cases and obtain measures of some variable, such as IQ. We observe that this sample has a mean of 98.7 and a standard deviation of 17.8. Now we draw a second sample, also of n = 100. For this second sample we find a mean of 102.6 and a standard deviation of 14.2. We continue to draw new samples, each with n = 100, and obtain the same descriptive statistics for each sample. We repeat the process until we have collected one hundred (or even 1,000) samples, with one hundred sample means and one hundred sample standard deviations (Table 6.2). If we consider these one hundred means as a sample (that is, a sample of sample means), we can compute the mean of the sample means. Let us assume that this "grand mean" has a value of 100.0. This value is now our best estimate of the true

table 6.2 **partial list of one hundred sample values**

SAMPLE NO.	$\overline{X}$	s	x
1	98.7	17.8	−1.3
2	102.6	14.2	+2.6
3	105.5	15.9	+5.5
.	.	.	.
.	.	.	.
.	.	.	.
99	91.3	18.2	−8.7
100	109.4	15.3	+9.4

population mean. (The true population mean cannot be known, of course, as long as we rely on sample data.) Next, we can see that each of the one hundred sample means deviates from the grand mean by a certain amount—some are above 100.0, some are below. Since we can compute deviations of sample means from the grand mean, we can also compute a standard deviation of all the sample means about the grand mean. This type of standard deviation has a special name—*standard error*. (In our example, we are concerned with the standard error of the mean, but note that many other statistics have standard errors. We could, for instance, compute one hundred medians and then determine the standard error of the median.) Let us assume that this special standard deviation, the standard error of the mean, has a value of 2.5.

Figure 6.3 illustrates this point. The larger curve represents the population. (Its mean is actually unknown, but for the sake of clarifying what follows, let us suppose that we know that the true population mean is 98.5) The smaller curve represents the distribution of one hundred sample means; its mean, as we have seen, is 100.0. There is about this estimated mean of 100.0 a standard error of 2.5. Since this standard error is a standard deviation, it can be interpreted in relation to the normal curve, just as any other standard deviation. To be more precise, the distance from the estimated mean to ± one standard error will include the true population mean 68 percent of the time. In other words, 68 percent of all sample means lie within one standard error of the true population mean; conversely, since the grand mean of all sample means is the best estimate of the population mean, we can also say that the true population mean will fall within the range, $\overline{X} \pm s_{\overline{X}}$, 68 percent of the time. Further utilizing our knowledge of the normal distribution, we can also be certain that the distance, $\overline{X} \pm 2s_{\overline{X}}$, will include the true population mean 95 percent of the time, and $\overline{X} \pm 3s_{\overline{X}}$ will include the true population mean 99 percent of the time.*

If the sample mean is seen as a *point estimate* of the true population mean, the standard error provides us with information about the accuracy of that estimate. It does this by changing our estimated value of the population value from a single point (the sample mean) to a range of scores about which we can make a probability statement concerning the likelihood that the range includes the true population mean. This latter type of estimate is called an *interval estimate*.

In the example of one hundred sample means, we found a grand mean of 100.0 and a standard deviation of 2.5. We can, therefore, make the following interval estimates:

---

*To be precise, instead of $\overline{X} \pm 2s_{\overline{X}}$, use $\overline{X} \pm 1.96s_{\overline{X}}$; and instead of $\overline{X} \pm 3s_{\overline{X}}$, use $\overline{X} \pm 2.58s_{\overline{X}}$.

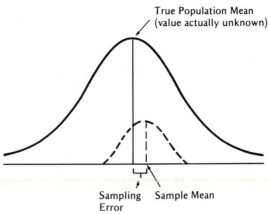

True Population Mean
(value actually unknown)

Sampling   Sample Mean
Error

Figure 6.3   *The Sample Mean and Error*

1. We can say that the true population mean will fall within the range, 100.0 ± 2.5, 68 percent of the time.
2. We can say that the true population mean will fall within the range, 100.0 ± (2.5)(1.96), 95 percent of the time.
3. We can say that the true population mean will fall within the range, 100.0 ± (2.5)(2.58), 99 percent of the time.

These interval estimates are often called *confidence intervals* (CI) because we frequently say that we are 95 percent confident that the true population mean lies within two standard errors of the sample mean. In our example, we are 95 percent confident that the true mean lies within the range 100.0 ± 4.9 or 95.1 to 104.9.

In the real-world situation, of course, we do not collect one hundred sample means in order to determine the standard error of the mean. We have only one sample, with one sample mean. How, then, do we obtain our best estimate of the true population mean, and how do we establish interval estimates (or confidence intervals)? Fortunately, this task is relatively simple, for the standard error is directly related to the sample size and standard deviation in the following way:

(Formula 6.1)
$$s_{\overline{x}} = \frac{s}{\sqrt{n}}$$

where s is the sample standard deviation, and n is the sample size. An alternative computing formula, perhaps simpler for computing the standard error is

(Formula 6.2)
$$s_{\overline{x}} = \sqrt{\frac{\Sigma x^2}{n(n-1)}}$$

where Σx^2 is the sum of squares, and n is the sample size. Given this information, we can compute a standard error on the basis of a single sample and from this we can readily set the 68 percent or 95 percent or 99 percent confidence intervals.

Let us now return to our example from page 81. Given that sample of n = 30, we can use as our point estimate of the mean the sample mean of 8.37. The sample of thirty homicide rates has a standard deviation of 4.75. Therefore, for these data, the standard error of the mean is

$$s_{\overline{X}} = \frac{4.75}{\sqrt{30}} = 0.87$$

To establish the 95 percent confidence interval around the sample mean, we simply do the following:

$$95\% \text{ CI} = \overline{X} \pm 1.96(s_{\overline{X}})$$
$$= 8.37 \pm 1.96(0.87)$$
$$= 8.37 \pm 1.71$$

Therefore, we are 95 percent certain that the true population mean lies within the range of 6.66 to 10.08.

quick quiz
6.2

(A) Compute the standard error of the mean for each of the following:
(1) n = 64; s = 16   (2) n = 640; s = 16
(3) n = 6,400; s = 16   (4) n = 400; s = 250

(B) For the data from the sample of thirty homicide rates, determine the 99 percent confidence interval.

There is yet another way of looking at confidence intervals. We can pose the following problem as our example: what is the probability that the true population mean lies within some specified range? If we let alpha be the probability that our observed sample mean will fall *outside* of some specified range, the problem can be represented graphically (Figure 6.4). The shaded areas represent the unlikely outcomes. In this case, what is unlikely is that the true population mean will fall in one of these areas. The unshaded areas represent the more probable outcomes; in this case, the probable outcome is that the true population mean will be here. The level of probability is set by alpha. In this sense, the establishment of a confidence interval is analogous to a hypothesis test.

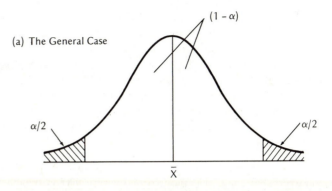

(a) The General Case

$\alpha/2$ $(1 - \alpha)$ $\alpha/2$

$\overline{X}$

(b) Specific Case when $\alpha = .05$ .95

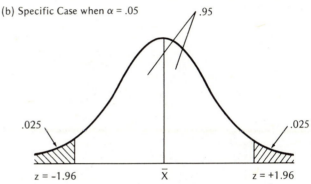

.025   .025

$z = -1.96$ $\overline{X}$ $z = +1.96$

Figure 6.4   *Probability and Confidence Intervals*

We have in this discussion dealt with only three confidence intervals (68 percent, 95 percent and 99 percent). We can, however, establish whatever confidence intervals we wish. The procedure involves the use of z-scores. You may have noticed that the values 68 percent, 95 percent and 99 percent correspond to the areas under the normal curve which are bounded by the z-scores of ± 1.00, ± 1.96, and ± 2.58, respectively. Therefore, it follows that if we wanted to construct another confidence interval, say 80 percent, the procedure would be to find the z-score whose positive and negative values correspond to 80 percent of the area under the curve. This value is $z = \pm 1.28$, and the 80 percent confidence interval is $\overline{X} \pm 1.28 s_{\overline{X}}$.

SAMPLE SIZE AND THE STANDARD ERROR
It should be obvious from Formula 6.1 that as the sample size gets larger, the standard error will get smaller. This is true regardless of how large the population may be. Mathematically, this is obvious, since increasing the size of n will result in a larger divisor in the formula and a correspondingly smaller quotient. In logical terms this means that *increasing the sample size is an excellent way to increase the reliability of a*

sample statistic. Increasing the size of n decreases the size of the standard error which in turn decreases the size of any given confidence interval; this means that we become increasingly certain about the accuracy of our sample statistics. Figure 6.5 may help to clarify this point. Figure 6.5(a) describes a population. In 6.5(b), each element in the sample corresponds to an element of the population, so the two distributions are identical and the standard error equals the standard deviation. In 6.5(c), the increased n results in a smaller standard error. Finally,

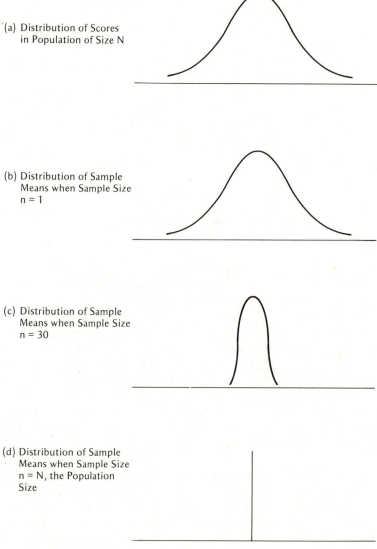

(a) Distribution of Scores in Population of Size N

(b) Distribution of Sample Means when Sample Size n = 1

(c) Distribution of Sample Means when Sample Size n = 30

(d) Distribution of Sample Means when Sample Size n = N, the Population Size

Figure 6.5   *Sample Size and Standard Error*

essential statistics for social research

in 6.5(d), there is no standard error at all; because the sample is identical to the population, there is no sampling error.

ESTIMATION FROM FINITE POPULATIONS   Although we have not emphasized the point, the above discussion of estimation assumes in theory that the population in question is infinitely large. But the sociologist rarely deals with an infinitely large population. So in practical terms, we must assume only a "very large" population. The definition of "very large" is arbitrary, and most populations with which we work are sufficiently large so that violation of the assumption does not damage our results. But *if we are dealing with relatively small populations*, such as the population of 145 homicide rates, and *especially if the ratio of sample size (n) to population size (N) is large*, that is, when n/N = .20 or greater, a certain adjustment should be made in the calculation of the standard error. In such circumstances,

(Formula 6.2)
$$s_{\overline{X}} = \frac{s}{\sqrt{n}} \sqrt{1 - \frac{n}{N}}$$

The reason for this adjustment is as follows. If the ratio of n/N is small, we would expect the standard error to be relatively large; if the ratio is large, we expect the standard error to be relatively small; and if the ratio n/N = 1, we would expect the standard error to be zero (since if the sample is 100 percent of the population there can be no sample error).

We can illustrate this by recomputing the standard error for the sample of thirty homicide rates.

$$s_{\overline{X}} = \frac{4.75}{\sqrt{30}} \sqrt{1 - \frac{30}{145}}$$
$$= (.87)(\sqrt{.7931}) = (.87)(.89)$$
$$= 0.77$$

Thus, we see that the adjusted standard error is smaller than the originally computed value (.77 < .87). This adjustment will, of course, also affect the size of our confidence intervals. For example, the 95 percent confidence interval, originally determined to be from 6.66 to 10.08, now becomes

$$95\% \text{ CI} = 8.37 \pm 1.96(.77)$$
$$= 8.37 \pm 1.51$$

or from 6.86 to 9.88.

important terms to know

Population	Sampling distribution
Sample	Standard error
Random sample	Point estimate
Stratified sample	Interval estimate
Area probability sample	Confidence interval

suggested readings

Blalock (1972: 201–215); Slonim (1960: 1–28; 43–53); Anderson and Zelditch (1975: 221–240); Loether and McTavish (1974b: 42–141); Mueller, Schuessler and Costner (1970: 343–392).

answer section

QUICK QUIZ 6.1   (A)   Pr = .06   (B)   Pr = .50

QUICK QUIZ 6.2   (A)   (1) 2.0   (2) 0.63   (3) 0.20   (4) 12.5
(B)   99% CI = $\overline{X} \pm 2.58(s_{\overline{X}})$

$$= 8.37 \pm (2.58)(0.87) = 8.37 \pm 2.24$$

testing for the difference between means

A common problem in sociological research involves the determination of whether two or more groups are meaningfully different on some variable. Are homicide rates higher in the North or South? Do minority group children learn more in integrated or segregated classrooms? Is family income higher among whites than among blacks? Are children reared in permissive environments more neurotic than children reared in strictly controlled environments? In this chapter we will discuss some statistical ways of answering such questions. (It should be clear by now that these questions are not to be answered in a simple "Yes-No" fashion, but rather in terms of probability statements.)

the t-test

If the populations in question are small enough, we can answer many such questions by simple enumeration. Thus, if we determine the homicide rate for *every* northern city and *every* southern city, we could simply compute the mean rate for each region and give a rather definite answer. But most social research involves collection of data from samples, not from populations, and in Chapter 6 we saw that any sample, no matter how carefully drawn, is subject to some error. Therefore, if we find that a sample of children from permissive home environments has a mean neuroticism score of 56.0, while a sample from rigid home environments has a mean score of 58.6, and if we realize that each sample mean is subject to some sampling error, can we safely conclude

7

that the two means are different, or is it possible that the observed difference is simply a function of sampling error?

In statistical terms, the problem is this: if we have two samples, each drawn from some population, can we determine whether the two population means are identical or different? Let us illustrate with a specific example. Table 7.1 presents data on the homicide rates for a random sample of thirty-six eastern and thirty western SMSAs. (Note that the following procedure requires a minimum sample size of thirty. If any sample is less than thirty, another technique, described below, must be used.) From the table we see that the sample of thirty-six eastern cities has a mean homicide rate (a point estimate) which is higher than the mean rate for the sample of thirty western cities. But we know that each of these means is subject to some sampling error, error which can be probabilistically measured by the standard error. Using data from Table 7.1 we can compute the standard error of each sample and establish the 95 percent confidence interval for each sample. An interval estimate of the true population mean of the eastern cities is

$$95\% \text{ CI} = \overline{X} \pm 1.96(s_{\overline{X}})$$

$$= 9.75 \pm 1.96\left(\frac{5.67}{\sqrt{36}}\right)$$

$$= 9.75 \pm 1.84$$

and an interval estimate of the true population mean of the western cities is

$$95\% \text{ CI} = 8.73 \pm 1.96\left(\frac{4.19}{\sqrt{30}}\right)$$

$$= 8.73 \pm 1.50$$

table 7.1 **homicide rates of thirty-six eastern and thirty western SMSAs**

		EASTERN				
3	13	15	12	6	17	$\overline{X} = 9.75$
12	21	2	3	14	7	$s = 5.67$
4	4	2	9	16	4	$s^2 = 32.14$
6	15	14	5	2	10	$s_{\overline{X}} = 0.94$
15	18	13	5	3	10	
5	16	16	14	16	4	95% CI is from 7.91 to 11.59
		WESTERN				
11	3	10	4	16	11	$X = 8.73$
8	4	9	5	5	13	$s = 4.19$
7	13	10	4	11	6	$s^2 = 17.58$
3	16	5	5	17	10	$s_{\overline{X}} = 0.77$
15	11	5	7	6	12	
						95% CI is from 7.23 to 10.23

testing for the difference between means

Notice that the point estimate of the eastern rate falls within the interval estimate of the western rate (and vice-versa). Figure 7.1 may help to clarify this observation. From this illustration we can see that it is reasonable to find a sample mean of 8.73 (the western mean) within the interval estimate of the eastern mean; it is also reasonable to find a sample mean of 9.75 (the eastern mean) within the interval estimate of the mean for western areas. This line of reasoning leads us to the inference that the two sample means may plausibly reflect two population means which, we may assume, are virtually identical.

If the interval estimate for eastern cities did *not* include the point estimate for the western cities (and if the interval for the western cities did not include the eastern sample mean), we could reasonably conclude that the two sample means represented two population means which were distinctly and truly different from one another. (Such a situation is described in Figure 7.2, page 94.

The "Student's t" statistic is a measure which, in similar logical fashion, tells us whether two sample means reflect two distinct population means. Stated differently, the t-test is a test for the significance of the difference between two sample means. It tells us whether an observed difference is a "true" difference, or is merely a difference which could have occurred "by chance."

(For the student who by now may be somewhat bored by statistics, we offer the following brief and irreverent digression. "Student" was the pen name of W. S. Gosset. Gosset was either a brewer who knew statistics, or a statistician who worked for a brewery. In planning to brew beer, he had to deal with the fact that the grains were often of different quality, that different water temperatures resulted in different brews and so on. However, the statistics of his day did not permit him to do the kind of scientific brewing that he wanted. Consequently, Gosset began to develop statistics that would do the trick; the t-test is the most famous

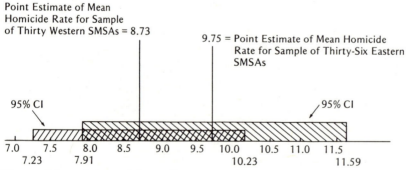

Point Estimate of Mean
Homicide Rate for Sample
of Thirty Western SMSAs = 8.73

9.75 = Point Estimate of Mean Homicide
Rate for Sample of Thirty-Six Eastern
SMSAs

95% CI   95% CI

7.0   7.5   8.0   8.5   9.0   9.5   10.0   10.5   11.0   11.5
    7.23   7.91   10.23   11.59

Figure 7.1   *Point and Interval Estimates from Table 7.1*

essential statistics for social research

of these. Gosset is long dead but that brewery still uses his method to prepare its beer, which is among the most famous in the world.)

Suppose we have two populations, one composed of children reared in a permissive environment, the other composed of children from a more rigid environment. We draw a sample from each population and record the *difference between the two sample means* $(\overline{X}_1 - \overline{X}_2)$. We then draw another pair of samples and record the difference between means. We do this again and again and again. If we do this often enough, we can build up a picture of the sampling distribution of the difference between means, $(\overline{X}_1 - \overline{X}_2)$. (A sampling distribution, as we learned in Chapter 6, is a list of all possible outcomes of a statistical event.) This list of all possible differences is normal in form and has its own mean $(\mu_1 - \mu_2)$ and its own standard error $(\sigma_{\overline{X}_1 - \overline{X}_2})$.

If we now think of the difference between the two observed sample means as a score, a score which may deviate from the true population mean, we can define the t-statistic as

(Formula 7.1)

$$t = \frac{\overline{X}_1 - \overline{X}_2}{\sqrt{\dfrac{s_1^2}{n_1} + \dfrac{s_2^2}{n_2}}} = \frac{\overline{X}_1 - \overline{X}_2}{s_{\overline{X}_1 - \overline{X}_2}}$$

Stated verbally, t is equal to the *difference between means* divided by the *standard error of the difference*. You may notice that the formula for t is analogous to the formula for z-scores (Formula 4.15, p. 53). As a matter of fact, when the sample sizes are sufficiently large (greater than 30) the sampling distribution of t is virtually identical to the sampling distribution of z.

Suppose our two samples of children had the following characteristics:

Permissive Environment	Rigid Environment
$n_1 = 100$	$n_2 = 95$
$\overline{X}_1 = 56.0$	$\overline{X}_2 = 58.6$
$s_1 = 6.2$	$s_2 = 8.3$

We can proceed to test the hypothesis that there is no difference between the two sample means; this hypothesis is our null hypothesis. Stated more formally, our test consists of the following elements:

1. H_0: $\mu_1 - \mu_2 = 0$
2. H_1: $\mu_1 - \mu_2 \neq 0$
3. Let $\alpha = .05$; two-tail test
4. Decision rules: Reject H_0 if the observed value of t is greater than ± 1.96; do not reject H_0 if the observed value is less than ± 1.96.

Inserting the sample data into Formula 7.1 we find

$$t = \frac{56.0 - 58.6}{\sqrt{\dfrac{6.2^2}{100} + \dfrac{8.3^2}{95}}} = \frac{-2.6}{\sqrt{.3844 + .7252}}$$

$$= \frac{-2.6}{\sqrt{1.1096}} = \frac{-2.6}{1.05}$$

$$= -2.47$$

Our observed value of t exceeds the critical value of ±1.96; we can, therefore, reject the null hypothesis, and by implication we can reasonably assume that there is evidence that the two samples were drawn from two populations whose means are truly different. Figure 7.2 illustrates this example. Notice that the 95 percent confidence interval surrounding $\overline{X}_1 = 56.0$ *does not* include $\overline{X}_2 = 58.6$, and the interval around 58.6 does not include 56.0. In other words, if one of the observed sample means reflects a true population value, the other sample mean could not have come from the same population.

quick quiz
7.1

Compute and interpret t for the data from Table 7.1. Let $\alpha = .05$, two-tail test.

small sample t-test

In the previous section we assumed that sample sizes were large (that is, $n_1 \geq 30$ and $n_2 \geq 30$). The reason for this is that the t distribution is

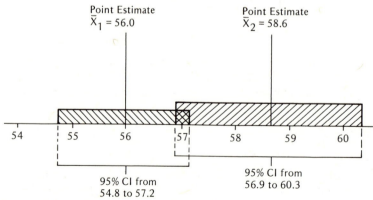

Figure 7.2   *Point and Interval Estimates*

virtually identical to the unit normal (or z) distribution when the samples are large. However, if the sample size is small, an adjustment must be made in the calculation of t. For small samples the formula is

(Formula 7.2)

$$t = \frac{\overline{X}_1 - \overline{X}_2}{\sqrt{\dfrac{n_1 s_1^2 + n_2 s_2^2}{n_1 + n_2 - 2}} \sqrt{\dfrac{n_1 + n_2}{n_1 n_2}}}$$

In the small sample case, the t distribution does not correspond to the z distribution. Furthermore, as the size of the samples changes, the shape of the t distribution also changes; thus, there is not one t distribution, but many. In statistical terminology, this happens because the *degrees of freedom* associated with t are a direct function of sample size.

DEGREES OF FREEDOM   We must again digress for a moment, this time to take up the concept of degrees of freedom, a concept which is related to many statistical problems. We have seen that we can use sample statistics to estimate true population values (commonly called *parameters*). In this chapter we are using a sample mean to estimate a population mean, and a sample standard deviation to estimate a population standard deviation. In computing a mean, there are no restrictions placed on the data; in other words, each of the several values which comprise the mean is "free to vary." For example, if N = 5, the five numbers may take on *any* values, and we can still compute the mean, no matter how great or small the five values are. However, when we compute a standard deviation, the data are not completely free. One restriction is imposed, namely that $\Sigma (X - \overline{X}) = 0$, the sum of the deviations about the mean must be zero. We then say that this restriction uses up one degree of freedom.

Let us use another example, from an artificial situation, to illustrate degrees of freedom. Suppose we have five numbers and for some strange reason we *require* that their mean be 10. How many of the five values are free to vary? To answer this, examine the four sets of data below. Each has a mean of 10.

	(a)	(b)	(c)	(d)
	7	6	25	6.8
	8	9	−14	13.7
	9	14	10	19.5
	10	3	−6	17.1
	?	?	?	?
$X =$	50	50	50	50
$\overline{X} =$	10	10	10	10

In each instance, the first four numbers are free—they may take on any value. But once these four numbers have assumed some value, the fifth term, the ? term, is not free; it is determined. In (a), the fifth number *must* be 16. If it is any other number, the requirement that $\overline{X} = 10$ cannot be met. In (b), the fifth value must be 18; in (c), 35; and in (d) it must be -7.1.

It is in this sense that the computation of a sample standard deviation uses up one degree of freedom.

In computing the t statistic we make use of not one, but two standard deviations, one from each sample. Therefore, the degrees of freedom for the t-test is

$$df\ (t) = (n_1 - 1) + (n_2 - 1) = n_1 + n_2 - 2 \qquad \text{(Formula 7.3)}$$

Because the small sample test involves degrees of freedom and different t distributions, we cannot use Appendix Table B to obtain critical values. Critical values for t are obtained from Appendix Table C.

Suppose an experiment yields the following data:

SMALL SAMPLE t: AN EXAMPLE

Experimental Group	Control Group
$n_1 = 16$	$n_2 = 25$
$\overline{X}_1 = 117$	$\overline{X}_2 = 112$
$s_1 = 14$	$s_2 = 12$

We wish to test the hypothesis that there is no difference between means. If we use a one-tail test with $\alpha = .05$,

$$t = \frac{117 - 112}{\sqrt{\dfrac{16(14^2) + 25(12^2)}{16 + 25 - 2}}\sqrt{\dfrac{16 + 25}{16(25)}}}$$

$$= \frac{5}{\sqrt{\dfrac{3{,}136 + 3{,}600}{39}}\sqrt{\dfrac{41}{400}}}$$

$$= \frac{5}{\sqrt{172.72}\sqrt{.1025}} = \frac{5}{13.14(.32)}$$

$$= 1.19$$

With $df = (16 + 25 - 2) = 39$, the critical value obtained from Appendix Table C is 1.68. (Actually, that is the value for $df = 40$, which is the closest value indicated in the table.) Our observed value is less than the critical value, so we do not reject the null hypothesis. In other words, we conclude that the two sample means are not different; given the size

essential statistics for social research

of the samples, a difference such as the one we observed could have occurred by chance.

quick quiz
7.2

Given the following data, compute and interpret t. Let $\alpha = .01$, one-tail test.

Anxiety Test Scores

Freshmen	Juniors
$\overline{X} = 49$	$\overline{X} = 43$
$s = 6$	$s = 5$
$n = 12$	$n = 16$

t-test for matched samples

In both the large sample and the small sample t-test, we assume that the two samples are *independent*; that is, we assume that whether a given unit is selected for inclusion in one sample has no bearing whatsoever on the selection of a given unit for the second sample. However, there are many instances in sociological research in which this assumption does not hold. In a study of husbands' and wives' attitudes, for example, the inclusion of one spouse in a sample implies the inclusion of the other spouse; or, in a study of homicide rates in large cities over a ten-year period, the inclusion of a city in the $Time_1$ sample implies that the same city will also be in the $Time_2$ sample. Such samples are said to be *matched*, or correlated. Matched samples are dealt with more efficiently by a special version of the t-test.

Table 7.2 lists the violent crime rate (murder, rape, robbery and assault) for fifteen large cities over a five-year period, 1968–1973. The table lists the differences (D) between the rate for each city in 1968 and 1973, the standard deviation of D, the mean difference, $\overline{D}$, and the standard error of $\overline{D}$. The value of t is then defined as a ratio of the mean difference to the standard error of the difference:

(*Formula 7.4*)

$$t = \frac{\overline{D}}{s_{\overline{D}}}$$

The degrees of freedom for this variation of the t-test is $(n - 1)$, where n is the *number of pairs* from which differences are obtained. For the data from Table 7.2,

table 7.2   violent crime rate (rounded) for fifteen cities, 1968 and 1973

CITY	1968	1973	D = DIFFERENCE	D²
New York	1060	1480	420	176,400
Chicago	920	1170	250	62,500
Los Angeles	950	1060	110	121,000
Philadelphia	420	750	330	108,900
Detroit	1220	1680	460	211,600
Houston	610	690	80	6,400
Baltimore	2060	1770	−290	84,100
Dallas	470	1000	530	280,900
Washington	1510	1560	50	2,500
Cleveland	630	1010	380	144,400
Indianapolis	580	340	−240	57,600
Milwaukee	220	290	70	4,900
San Francisco	1300	1200	−100	10,000
San Diego	200	370	170	28,900
San Antonio	380	590	210	44,100
			2430	1,235,300

Mean Difference: $\overline{D} = \dfrac{2430}{15} = 162$

Standard deviation: $s_D = 245.2$

Standard error: $s_{\overline{D}} = 65.53$

Source: FBI Uniform Crime Reports, 1973.

$$t = \frac{162}{65.53} = 2.47$$

Our null hypothesis is that there is no difference between means. If we specify a one-tail test with $\alpha = .01$, and with df $= 15 - 1 = 14$, the critical value obtained from Appendix Table C is 2.62. Our observed value of t falls short of the critical value; therefore, we *do not reject* the null hypothesis. (Had we established a level of $\alpha = .05$, our decision would have been to *reject* H_0. Here we see the importance of specifying alpha in advance of the statistical test.)

Recently, a new statistic has begun to displace the t-test for correlated samples. The reason for this displacement lies in the utter simplicity of computing A. Since Sandler derived A directly from t, the two statistics have essentially the same interpretation. To compute A, we need determine only the value of D, the difference (as in Table 7.2), and D^2. Then,

SANDLER'S A-STATISTIC

$$A = \frac{\Sigma D^2}{(\Sigma D)^2}$$

(Formula 7.5)

For Table 7.2,

$$A = \frac{1235300}{2430^2} = .209$$

Appendix Table D gives the critical values for A. With df = 14, the critical value is .202. Since our observed value of A exceeds the critical value when $\alpha = .01$, we do not reject the null hypothesis. Note that this is the same conclusion we reached when using the t-test.

analysis of variance

In this chapter we have described a procedure, the t-test, for testing whether a difference between two means is significant. The next logical questions is: what do we do when we have three or more means? One apparent answer is to repeat the t-test, taking two means at a time, until all possible comparisons have been made. Thus, if we have five groups of subjects, we would conduct ten separate t-tests to find out which pairs of means are significantly different. Running that many tests can be tedious, but there are two other, more important, reasons why this procedure is generally not accepted by most statisticians. (1) If we run a large number of tests of significance, we can expect as a matter of chance that a certain proportion of these tests, a proportion defined by alpha, will be significant. For example, if we conduct one hundred t-tests, the laws of probability tell us that five of these tests will be statistically significant at the .05 level, and one will be significant at the .01 level. Multiple tests, therefore, increase the likelihood of making an incorrect decision concerning the null hypothesis. (2) In more sophisticated research designs, where there are two or more independent variables, we must acknowledge the fact that these variables can and do *interact* with one another. Since the t-test does not "partial out" these interaction effects, it will necessarily produce results which are not free from this bias.

The procedure known as analysis of variance (ANOV) is used when we wish to make comparisons among three or more means. In this text we will examine only the most elementary form of ANOV, simple, or one-way, analysis of variance. One-way ANOV is used when there is but one independent variable, but three or more categories of that variable. (If there are two independent variables, a technique called two-way ANOV is used; this and other techniques are described in advanced texts, such as Edwards [1960] or Winer [1962].)

The logic of ANOV can be seen by an example. Suppose we have four income groups (I, II, III and IV). A sample of n = 5 is taken from each group. These twenty subjects are then given an instrument which measures some attitude on an interval scale. Table 7.3 gives two possible

table 7.3   comparison of four samples

(a) SMALL VARIATION WITHIN GROUPS

Income Group	I	II	III	IV
	80	81	84	91
	81	82	86	87
	81	82	87	88
	79	85	87	89
	79	80	86	90
Group Mean	80	82	86	89

(b) LARGE VARIATION WITHIN GROUPS

Income Group	I	II	III	IV
	85	76	87	79
	80	92	95	98
	75	86	80	99
	73	82	92	77
	87	74	76	92
Group Mean	80	82	86	89

outcomes of such a study. In 7.3(a) we observe four means which correspond exactly to the four means of 7.3(b). But would you be more inclined to conclude that one set of means is truly different, while the other set is different only by chance? You might, if you looked at the pattern of variation. In 7.3(a) the scores which go into $\overline{X}_I$ have only a small amount of within-group variation; they tend to cluster together. The same is true of the scores which comprise the other three within-group means. This clustering of scores is statistically measured by the variance, s^2. This clustering phenomenon is shown graphically in

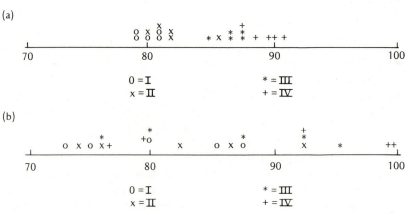

Figure 7.3   *Schematic Representation of Table 7.3*

Figure 7.3(a). Here the circles tend to cluster around 80, the stars around 86 and so on. Because the pattern of dispersion as measured by the variance is small, we have greater confidence in the accuracy and reliability of the sample mean. (Recall the discussion of sampling error in Chapter 6.)

Now focus attention on part (b) of Table 7.3. Again we have the same means. But notice the patterns of dispersion. The scores do not cluster closely about the mean; rather, they range widely. In Figure 7.3.(b) we see that there is great overlap among the constituent elements of the four categories. A statistical measure of the variance within each of the four income groups would be quite large, relative to the groups in (a). Consequently, we would have less confidence in the sample means of (b) as reliable indicators of true population means. We would be more likely to attribute differences among means to sampling error than to true differences.

Carefully examine Table 7.3 and Figure 7.3. Together they should help you to understand the concept of analysis of variance. Even if you do not grasp all of the mathematics of ANOV, you should be able to develop a "mental picture" of ANOV. It is a technique which provides a statistical answer to the question: does a pattern of dispersion, as measured by the variance, indicate that sample means are truly different, or does it indicate that the difference is due to chance or to sampling error?

We can think of our problem in yet another way. Let us focus attention less on the sample means and more on the sample variances. We can first speak of the total variance, s_T^2. In our example, we could compute the total variance by using Formula 4.7 (see p. 48):

(Formula 7.6)

$$s_T^2 = \frac{\Sigma x^2}{n - 1}$$

To do so, we would first find the grand mean of all twenty scores, determine the deviation of each score from the grand mean, square these deviations, sum them, and divide by $(n - 1)$. This procedure yields the total variance.

The total variance can, in turn, be divided into two components. The first is the *within groups variance*, s_w^2. This value is obtained by computing the variance *within each* sample, then finding the mean variance for *all* samples. In terms of a simple computational procedure:

(Formula 7.7)

$$s_w^2 = \frac{\Sigma s^2}{k}$$

where s^2 is a sample variance and k is the number of samples.

The second component of the total variance is the *between groups variance*, s_b^2. The between groups variance is obtained by using the difference between each sample mean and the grand mean as a deviation score, x, which is squared, weighted for sample size (n), summed, and then divided by $(k - 1)$. Thus:

$$s_b^2 = \frac{\Sigma (x^2 n)}{k - 1}$$

(*Formula 7.8*)

where x is a difference between a sample mean and the grand mean; n is a sample size and k is the number of samples.

The actual analysis of variance is then computed by means of the *F-test*, which is simply a ratio of the between groups variance to the within groups variance.

$$F = \frac{s_b^2}{s_w^2}$$

(*Formula 7.9*)

For this F-test the null hypothesis states that the two variances, s_b^2 and s_w^2, are equal, and that both are equal to the true population variance. If the two sample variances are indeed equal, or close to equal, the ratio of one to the other will be approximately 1.00. But if s_b^2 is greater than s_w^2, the F-ratio will become considerably larger than 1.00; this indicates that the null hypothesis cannot be accepted.

Let us now illustrate the analysis of variance with a specific example. Suppose we draw a sample of n = 6 students from each of k = 4 schools. Each student is measured on some standard achievement test and results are obtained as in Table 7.4. First, we calculate the within groups variance:

$$s_w^2 = \frac{2.0 + 2.4 + 4.3 + 2.0}{4} = \frac{10.7}{4}$$

$$= 2.675$$

and then we calculate the between groups variance:

x = Sample $\overline{X}$ − Grand $\overline{X}$	x^2	n	$x^2 n$	
−1.625	2.64	6	15.84	
1.375	1.89	6	11.34	$s_b^2 = \dfrac{28.14}{4 - 1}$
−0.125	.02	6	.12	
0.375	.14	6	.84	$= 9.38$
			28.14	

Finally we compute the F-ratio:

$$F = \frac{s_b^2}{s_w^2} = \frac{9.38}{2.675} = 3.51$$

We see that the F-ratio is larger than 1.00, but before we can determine whether this F is statistically different from one that could have occurred by chance we need one further piece of information: the degrees of freedom associated with each variance. (The reason for this is that, like the t distribution, there is not one F distribution, but many; in fact, there is a different sampling distribution of F for every different combination of degrees of freedom.) The degrees of freedom associated with the between groups variance is

(Formula 7.10)
$$df_b = k - 1$$

and the degrees of freedom associated with the within groups variance is

(Formula 7.11)
$$df_w = N - k$$

where N is the total number of subjects. The total degrees of freedom for the analysis of variance is thus $N - 1$. For our data, $df_b = 4 - 1 = 3$ and $df_w = 24 - 4 = 20$. To interpret F, we use the table of critical values of F (Appendix Table E) for df = 3 and 20. The critical value read from the Table (with $\alpha = .05$) is 3.10. Since our observed value of F is larger than this critical value, we reject the null hypothesis and, by implication, we conclude that there is a true difference between the sample means. Had we set the level of alpha at .01, the critical value from the Table E would be 4.94; we would not have rejected the null hypothesis and it would have been reasonable to assume that the observed differences between sample means could have occurred by chance.

table 7.4   *data for analysis of variance*

	SCHOOL 1	SCHOOL 2	SCHOOL 3	SCHOOL 4
	15	17	17	15
	14	17	15	17
	15	19	13	19
	16	19	18	18
	17	20	18	16
	13	16	18	17
X:	90	108	99	102
$\overline{X}$:	15.00	18.00	16.50	17.00
s^2:	2.00	2.40	4.30	2.00

Grand Mean = $\overline{X}_T$ = 16.625

This introductory discussion of ANOV has been kept deliberately simple and we have stressed the logical understanding of ANOV rather than the mathematical procedures in the hope that you will grasp the underlying meaning of this type of analysis. However, for purposes of computation we suggest a procedure which works directly from the raw data and does not require the computation of variances. This procedure makes extensive use of the quantity Σx^2, also known as the *sum of squares*, or SS. Again, there are three values: the total sum of squares, SS_T, the "between" sum of squares, SS_b, and the "within" sum of squares, SS_w.

The total sum of squares is found by computing the grand mean, $\overline{X}_T$, then measuring the deviation of each score from $\overline{X}_T$ as $(X - \overline{X}_T)$, squaring these deviations, and summing. (This procedure was described earlier in Formula 4.10, p. 49.) Expressed as a computing formula:

$$\Sigma x_T^2 = SS_T = \Sigma X^2 - \frac{(\Sigma X)^2}{n} \qquad \text{(Formula 7.12)}$$

For the data from Table 7.4:

$$SS_T = (15^2 + 14^2 + 15^2 + \ldots + 16^2 + 17^2) - \frac{399^2}{24}$$

$$= 6715 - 6633.375$$

$$= 81.625$$

The *between sum of squares* is found by squaring the difference between the mean of each group and the grand mean, multiplying this by the sample size of the group, and summing across all groups. (This procedure is contained in the numerator of Formula 7.8).

$$SS_b = \Sigma (\overline{X} - \overline{X}_T)^2 n = \Sigma (x^2 n) \qquad \text{(Formula 7.13)}$$

For our data:

$$SS_b = (15 - 16.625)^2 6 + (18 - 16.625)^2 6$$

$$+ (16.5 - 16.625)^2 6 + (17 - 16.625)^2 6$$

$$= 15.844 + 11.344 + 0.094 + 0.844$$

$$= 28.126$$

An alternative direct computing formula for SS_b is:

$$SS_b = \frac{(\Sigma X)^2}{n} - \frac{(\Sigma X_T)^2}{N} \qquad \text{(Formula 7.14)}$$

essential statistics for social research

where n = sample size; N = total of all samples; ΣX = sum of raw scores in a sample and X_T = sum of *all* raw scores. For our data:

$$SS_b = \left(\frac{90^2}{6} + \frac{108^2}{6} + \frac{99^2}{6} + \frac{102^2}{6}\right) - \frac{399^2}{24}$$

$$= 1350 + 1944 + 1633.5 + 1734 - 6633.375$$

$$= 28.125$$

Notice that the two procedures for computing SS_b yield identical values (within rounding error).

The *within sum of squares* might simply be obtained by subtracting SS_b from SS_T, since

$$SS_T = SS_b + SS_w$$

This would give us a value for SS_w of

$$SS_w = 81.625 - 28.125$$

$$= 53.5$$

However, as a useful check on the accuracy of your work, it is wise to independently compute SS_w. This can be done by the following formula:

(Formula 7.15)

$$SS_w = \Sigma \left[X^2 - \frac{(\Sigma X)^2}{n}\right]$$

(In Formula 7.15, the quantity within the brackets is computed for each group.) Thus for our data:

$$SS_w = \left(1360 - \frac{90^2}{6}\right) + \left(1956 - \frac{108^2}{6}\right) + \left(1655 - \frac{99^2}{6}\right)$$

$$+ \left(1744 - \frac{102^2}{6}\right)$$

$$= 10 + 12 + 21.5 + 10$$

$$= 53.5$$

With these independently computed values of the various sums of squares we can verify that $SS_b + SS_w = SS_T$, since

$$28.125 + 53.5 = 81.625$$

Finally, the *degrees of freedom* for SS_t is $(N - 1)$, since in computing the grand mean we use up one degree of freedom. The degree of

table 7.5   analysis of variance for table 7.4

SOURCE	df	SS	MS
Between Groups	3	28.125	9.375
Within Groups	20	53.5	2.675
Total	23	81.625	

F = 3.50
p < .05

freedom for SS_w is $(n - 1)$, since we use up one degree of freedom in computing the mean of each group. And the degree of freedom for SS_b is the number of groups less one, or $(k - 1)$.

It is a common practice in research writing to summarize all of this information in an ANOV table, such as Table 7.5. The ANOV table lists the various sources of variation (within and between), the respective df values, the SS values, and finally a value called the *mean square*, which is simply SS/df, and which is the variance.

important terms to know

The t-test (for large samples, small samples, and correlated data)	**Sandler's A-statistic**
	Analysis of variance
Standard error of the difference	**Total variance**
	Within groups variance
Degrees of freedom	**Between groups variance**
	F-ratio

suggested readings

Blalock (1972: 317–328); Freeman (1965: 199–209); Loether and McTavish 1974b: 161–176); Mueller, Schuessler and Costner, (1970: 404–419); Runyon and Haber (1976: 227–278).

answer section

QUICK QUIZ 7.1 $t = \dfrac{9.75 - 8.73}{\sqrt{\dfrac{5.67^2}{36} + \dfrac{4.19^2}{30}}} = \dfrac{1.02}{\sqrt{.8930 + .5852}}$

$\qquad\qquad = \dfrac{1.02}{\sqrt{1.4782}} = \dfrac{1.02}{1.2158} = 0.84$

Since the observed value of t does not exceed the critical value of $\pm\,1.96$, we *do not reject* the null hypothesis; we conclude that the two sample means reflect two population means which are not different. The observed difference between the sample means could have occurred "by chance"; the difference is not statistically significant.

QUICK QUIZ 7.2 $t = \dfrac{49 - 43}{\sqrt{\dfrac{12(6^2) + 16(5^2)}{12 + 16 - 2}}\sqrt{\dfrac{12 + 16}{12(16)}}}$

$\qquad = 2.70$

The observed value of t exceeds the critical value (which is 2.48), so we can *reject* the null hypothesis and conclude that the two means are truly different; the observed difference is not a function of sampling error; it could not have occurred by chance.

measuring the association between two nominal level variables

the concept of statistical association

In the first few chapters of this book, we studied various statistics which describe a set of data. Those measures of centrality and dispersion were applied to a single-variable, or univariate, data set. We saw, for example, ways of computing mean family income or modal religious preference. As important as such univariate descriptive measures are, their utility is clearly limited, since so many sociological problems usually call for a type of analysis far more complex than that which can be provided by the simple description of a single variable. Such analyses must also tell us how two or more variables are related to each other. In this chapter and Chapters 9–10, we will examine some of the many measures that sociologists use to assess the relationships between two variables. Such measures are called measures of relationship, association or correlation. In general, we shall say that *"two qualities are associated when the distribution of values of the one differs for different values of the other"* (Weiss, 1968: 158). In statistical language, the opposite of association is *independence*. We can illustrate these concepts of association and independence by using the data from Tables 8.1 and 8.2. In Table 8.1, the variables of sex and preference for Brand X are independent, or not associated: proportionately as many males as females prefer Brand X. However, in Table 8.2 the variables are associated: as we go from the category male to the category female, the proportion of people preferring

8

table 8.1

table 8.1   *sex and preference for brand x (percentage distribution)*

		SEX	
		Male	Female
Prefer Brand X	Yes	40	40
	No	60	60
	Totals	100	100

table 8.2   *sex and preference for brand y (percentage distribution)*

		SEX	
		Male	Female
Prefer Brand Y	Yes	40	10
	No	60	90
	Totals	100	100

Brand Y *changes* from 40 percent to 10 percent. This example illustrates another way by which we define association and independence. *If subgroup proportions of variable A differ within a given subgroup of variable B, we have association. If such subgroup proportions do not differ, we have independence.*

There are a great many things in the world that seem to be related to or associated with each other. As we noted earlier, height and weight are generally related so that in any population the tall people tend to weigh more than the short people. (The word "tend" is used to emphasize the point that the relationship is not perfect—some tall person may indeed weigh less than some short person.) Intelligence and academic success also are related to one another, as are religious preference and suicide rates, and a host of other variables.

To say that two variables are related is not necessarily to say that the two are causally related. That is, if we find that two variables, A and B, are related, it does not mean that A causes B, or that B causes A or that they are both caused by a third variable C. In fact, no *causal* inference can be drawn from a statistical measure of relationship. Causality is fundamentally a logical rather than a statistical problem; however, we can and do use the statistical method to help us develop our logical arguments, and there are certain advanced statistical techniques which we can use to detect causality.

To illustrate this distinction between association and causation, let us suppose that we found a statistically significant relationship between the number of storks in given geographic areas and the birth rates of those areas: the more storks in an area, the higher the birth rate. Such an association, however statistically accurate, does not mean that babies "cause" storks, or that storks "cause" babies (although a popular myth does support the latter explanation). To explain this relationship, we would have to look beyond the statistical measure. We might better explain the relationship by noting that storks are more frequently found in rural, as opposed to urban, areas and that rural populations typically have higher birth rates than do urban populations.

Users of the statistical method of analysis are not content with merely assuming the existence of a relationship; they want to know, in quantifiable terms, precise information about the relationship between phenomena. Most measures of relationship give us two such pieces of information. First, they tell us the *direction* of the relationship, that is, whether the phenomena in question vary directly (positively) or inversely (negatively) with one another. An example of a direct or positive relationship is the one usually found between income and education. Typically, as one of these variables increases, the other also increases; as measured income level increases, so too, generally, will measured education level. An example of an inverse, or negative, relationship might be found between social class position and rate of juvenile arrests: the higher one's social class, the lower one's rate of arrests. Inverse relationships are those in which one variable increases in magnitude while the other variable decreases. Statistical measures that tell us the direction of a relationship conventionally do so by the simple procedure of using a plus ($+$) or minus ($-$) sign before the statistic. The second piece of information we get from most statistical measures of relationship is an indication of the *strength* of the relationship. The indication of strength comes from the size of the computed statistic. Most measures of relationship vary between zero and one: a score of zero reflects the absence of a relationship, or no association, while a score of one (either $+1.00$, for a direction relationship, or -1.00 if the relationship is inverse) reflects a complete or perfect relationship.

There are many ways that we can use statistics to determine whether two variables are related to each other in any meaningful fashion. Weiss (1968: 161) has suggested five general procedures that can be used to identify relationships between variables.

1. *Departure from independence between two factors.* We imagine what the data would be like if there were no association. Then we say that there is association to the extent that the observed data depart from this. . . .
2. *Magnitude of subgroup differences.* Assuming that there is association, its degree may be measured by direct comparison of subgroup proportions with each other. . . .
3. *Summary of pair-by-pair comparisons.* Another approach would be to think of forming all possible comparisons of one member of the

essential statistics for social research

population with another. In each of these comparisons, we should decide whether the two factors under study occurred together or did not. We should then summarize the results of all these pair-by-pair comparisons, and association would be measured by the preponderance of one type of pair. . . .

4. *Proportional reduction of probable error.* We might imagine that we are called on to predict whether factor *A* exists or not, first without information regarding *B*, and then with information regarding *B*. The more we are helped by information regarding *B*, the more association we are willing to admit. . . .

5. *Extent to which increments in one factor occur together with increments in the other factor.* We might take as our meaning of association the extent to which increase in the one factor is accompanied by increase in the other, or decrease in one by decrease in the other. . . .

Further discussion of these five procedures will be provided at appropriate points in the next few chapters. We begin with an illustration of procedure 2.

percentage difference

A discussion of percentage difference as a measure of association was implicit in our discussion of the concept of association. Percentage differences are quite easy to determine: *within* a category of the *dependent* variable, we compute the percentage difference (if any) between categories of the *independent* variable. If the difference is zero, we can conclude that the two variables are not associated, as in Table 8.1. If the difference is 100, the variables are perfectly associated. Differences between zero and 100 indicate intermediate degrees of association.

This conceptualization of percentage difference applies only to a 2 × 2 table (a table with two rows and two columns). For larger tables, modification of the above is necessary.

Because of its ease of computation and its simple, obvious interpretation, percentage difference has much to recommend it as a measure of association. Its major weakness is that it does not tell us how much of an observed difference constitutes a meaningful difference. To compute this, we must turn to other measures.

chi-square: a test of statistical independence

The Chi-square test is one of the most prominent and frequently used statistical tests in sociological literature. With care, it is relatively easy to compute; but, before we turn to the computation of Chi-square, let us first come to an understanding of the logic which provides the basis for this statistic. Suppose we have two coins, a nickel and a dime. If we toss each coin twenty times, and if the coins are unbiased (that is, if they are "fair" coins, not subject to any controlling force except chance, *independent*) we could theoretically expect each coin to show ten heads and ten tails. From our earlier discussion of probability (Chapter 5), we know that we will not necessarily get a 10–10 split. Many other outcomes are plausible. For example, we might obtain thirteen heads from the nickel and eight heads from the dime. This outcome is presented in Table 8.3. Clearly, the coins have not adhered perfectly to the theoretically expected 10–10 outcome. Or, in more technical terms, we can suggest that the coins have departed from the *model of statistical independence*. But is this departure sufficiently large to be meaningful? Can it occur by chance? Is this difference between what we observed and what we expected to observe really big enough "to make a difference?" Should we begin to wonder if one, or both, of the coins is not statistically independent, if one, or both, is biased? A return glance to Chapter 5, especially Figure 5-1, may help you to answer this question without using Chi-square. Indeed, we will not now provide the Chi-square solution to this problem, but will first look at another example which is more likely to confront a sociologist.

Suppose we are interested in the relationship (if any) between religious preference and political preference (both nominal level variables). We might suspect, for example, that members of certain religious groups are more likely to vote for candidates from a particular political party. To test this notion, we might draw a random sample of two hundred people, ask them the relevant questions, and obtain the results given in Table 8.4. If we convert the raw frequencies from Table 8.4 to percentages (this is the second procedure suggested by Weiss), we might begin to suspect that there is some departure from the model of statistical independence: it *seems* that Catholics prefer the Democratic party, and, to a lesser extent, that Protestants prefer the Republican party. But are we ready to make a judgment on the basis of what seems to be? Can we come to a more definitive solution? We can, and we do so by using Chi-square. But first we must face a relatively simple logical problem, a logical problem with a mathematical solution.

In the previous discussion on coin tossing, we saw an example of a situation in which we know something about the expected outcomes. On the basis of previous knowledge and experience we know that unbiased coins should yield, on the average and in the long run, an equal number of heads and tails. But in the present situation can we hold any expectations about religious and/or political preferences? Can we suggest any plausible strategies for determining the appropriate expected

THE LOGIC OF DETERMINING EXPECTED FREQUENCIES

table *8.3*   **hypothetical coin-tossing results**

		COIN		
		Nickel	Dime	Totals
Outcome	Heads	13	8	21
	Tails	7	12	19
	Totals	20	20	40

frequencies for Table 8.4? One suggestion is to assume that the two hundred subjects distribute themselves equally throughout the nine cells of the table. Thus, we would expect to find a value of 22.2 in each cell—a pure "chance" relationship. But this strategy cannot be applied, for it forces us to ignore reality, since, in this instance, we know certain facts which contradict the possibility of equal cell values. For example, we already know that there are eighty Democrats in our sample. The assumption of equal-expected cell frequencies, as described above, would wrongly lead us to conclude that there were not eighty, but 66.6 Democrats (22.2 + 22.2 + 22.2), equally divided among Protestants, Catholics and others. Since it is foolish to *assume* 66.6 Democrats when we *know* there are eighty, we must seek another strategy for determining expected cell frequencies.

A more appropriate strategy is one which makes full use of what we do know about our data. We know that there are two hundred subjects, of whom eighty are Democrats, seventy are Catholics and so on. Let us consider these *marginal values*. (Marginal values are the column and row subtotals in any tabular distribution.) If chance factors only are operating, we would expect to find no differences in political preference *within* any of the religious categories. (And, alternatively, we would expect to find no differences in religious preference within any of the political categories.) Now let us note that the *proportion* of Democrats in our total sample is 80/200 or 0.40. Similarly, the proportion of Republicans in our sample is 70/200 or 0.35 and the proportion of Independents is 50/200 or 0.25. Therefore, since we have 100 Protestants

table *8.4*   **religious and political preferences (hypothetical data)**

		RELIGIOUS PREFERENCE						
		Protestant		Catholic		Other		Totals
		N	(%)	N	(%)	N	(%)	
Party Preference	Democrat	30	(30)	40	(57)	10	(33)	80
	Republican	40	(40)	20	(29)	10	(33)	70
	Independent	30	(30)	10	(14)	10	(33)	50
	Totals	100	(100)	70	(100)	30	(99)	200

table 8.5   expected cell frequencies based on data from table 8.4

		RELIGIOUS PREFERENCE			
		Protestant	Catholic	Other	Totals
Political Preference	Democrat	40	28	12	80
	Republican	35	24.5*	10.5	70
	Independent	25	17.5	7.5†	50
	Totals	100	70	30	200

*24.5 = 70 × 0.35 = (70 × 70)/200
† 7.5 = 30 × 0.25 = (50 × 30)/200

in our sample, the number of persons who are both Protestant *and* Democrat is 100(.4) = 40. The number of Catholic-Democrats is 100(.35) = 35, and the number of other-Democrats is 100(.25) = 25. In similar fashion we can calculate the remaining expected cell frequencies. The results of these calculations are found in Table 8.5.

It should be noted that identical results could be obtained by reversing the variables, that is, by first determining the *proportions* of Protestants (0.50), Catholics (0.35) and others (0.15) and then multiplying by the numbers of Democrats, Republicans and Independents. As an exercise, you might verify this.

We shall now examine a way of computing expected cell frequencies which is, for most people, simpler than the procedure employed above. In many instances, though not in the present example, it is also more accurate because it minimizes rounding error. However, before proceeding, please review this section to make certain that you *understand* the logic of determining expected cell frequencies. The procedure described below is a rote procedure that you should not use unless you understand the reason for doing so.

A SIMPLE PROCEDURE FOR DETERMINING EXPECTED CELL FREQUENCIES

Suppose we have a very simple 2 × 2 table whose cell values, marginal totals and grand total are identified by the letters a, b, c, d, k, l, m, n and N (Table 8.6). *The expected values for any cell can be obtained by multiplying the marginal totals associated with that cell, and dividing that product by the grand total,* as shown in Table 8.7. This procedure applies not only to 2 × 2 tables, but to tables with any number of rows and columns. Verify this procedure for the data in Table 8.4; your results should be identical to those in Table 8.5.

COMPUTING CHI-SQUARE

We now have the basis for developing a measure of statistical independence. From our expected frequencies we know how the data should "behave" in a pure chance situation, that is, in a situation of statistical independence. Comparing these expected values with a set of actually observed values will tell us the extent to which our observed

table 8.6   schematic representation of a 2 × 2 table

a	b	m
c	d	n
k	l	N

table 8.7   expected frequencies for table 8.6

$\dfrac{km}{N}$	$\dfrac{lm}{N}$	m
$\dfrac{kn}{N}$	$\dfrac{ln}{N}$	n
k	l	N

data depart from the chance model. But how shall we construct an appropriate statistic? We can quickly see that it would not be sufficient simply to compute the deviation between observed frequencies (f_o) and expected frequencies (f_e), since some deviations will be positive and others negative, and these will cancel each other out. Therefore, we need to eliminate the *sign* of the deviation. One way to do this is to *square* each deviation. (If we square a negative number we get a positive number.)

There is one final factor to consider. In examing the table of expected frequencies, we note that each cell in the table can carry a different "weight." Therefore, we must adjust each squared deviation in an appropriate manner. We do this by dividing each squared deviation by the corresponding f_e. This step gives us, for each cell, the mean squared deviation of the observed from the expected frequencies. Repeating this procedure for each cell, we then sum across all cells. The result is a statistic which indicates the extent to which our observed frequencies fit a model of statistical independence. This statistic is Chi-square (χ^2), and it can be simply presented by the formula:

(Formula 8.1)

$$\chi^2 = \sum \frac{(f_o - f_e)^2}{f_e}$$

where Σ is the summation command, f_o is an observed frequency and f_e is an expected frequency.

Let us now proceed to a solution of the question we posed earlier: are religious and political preferences related? To do so, let us set up a simple work table (8.8) to give us the necessary figures. From this table we see that the computed value of Chi-square is 14.57. You might ask,

table 8.8   **work table for computing chi-square using data from table 8.4**

f_o	f_e	$(f_o - f_e)$	$(f_o - f_e)^2$	$(f_o - f_e)^2/f_e$
30	40	−10	100	2.50
40	28	12	144	5.14
10	12	−2	4	0.33
40	35	5	25	0.71
20	24.5	−4.5	20.25	0.83
10	10.5	−0.5	0.25	0.02
30	25	5	25	1.00
10	17.5	−7.5	56.25	3.21
10	7.5	2.5	6.25	0.83
				$14.57 = \chi^2$

14:57 what? There is no simple answer to such a question. The Chi-square statistic has no clear conceptual meaning except to say that as χ^2 gets larger, there is greater departure from the chance model. Remember that Chi-square is defined as the *sum of the mean square deviations of observed from expected frequencies.* So the computed value of Chi-square is but an indication of the magnitude of these mean square deviations. The greater the magnitude, the greater the departure from a chance model. But again, how much of a difference is a meaningful difference? How large must a difference be before we reject the model of statistical independence? To answer these questions and to interpret Chi-square, we still need several pieces of information. Specifically, we must have information about the *sampling distribution* of the Chi-square statistic. (For a review of sampling distribution, see Chapter 6, page 79.) The relevant information about the sampling distribution of Chi-square is presented in Appendix Table F. A small portion of that table is reproduced here as Table 8.9.

A quick glance at Table 8.9 tells us that we need one final piece of information: the degrees of freedom associated with the computed statistic. As you will recall from Chapter 6, it is necessary to consider the degrees of freedom for any sampling distribution which changes its

DEGREES OF FREEDOM FOR CHI-SQUARE

table 8.9   **critical values of chi-square for various levels of alpha (α) and for varying degrees of freedom**

df	$\alpha = .10$	.05	.02	.01
1	2.71	3.84	5.41	6.64
2	4.61	5.99	7.82	9.21
3	6.25	7.81	9.84	11.34
4	7.78	9.49	11.67	13.28
5	9.24	11.07	13.39	15.09

    essential statistics for social research

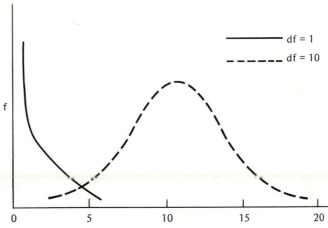

Figure 8.1 *Approximate Shape of the Chi-square Distribution when df = 1 and when df = 10*

shape as the degrees of freedom change. Chi-square is one such distribution. To illustrate this, the approximate shapes of the sampling distributions of Chi-square when df = 1 and when df = 10 are presented in Figure 8.1. You may notice that as df gets larger, the shape of the Chi-square distribution begins to approximate a normal curve.

For the Chi-square statistic, degrees of freedom are determined by the formula

(*Formula 8.2*)
$$df = (r - 1)(c - 1)$$

where r = the number of rows and c = the number of columns in the contingency table. Why is the degrees of freedom for Chi-square defined as $(r - 1)(c - 1)$? An illustration may help. Recall our coin-tossing example from the beginning of this section. We may set up this problem as in Table 8.10. If we accept certain "givens," namely, that the marginal totals are 20, 20, 21 and 19, we may ask: How many of the cells within the table are "free to vary?" If we look at a table whose marginals are fixed, but whose cell values are left open (Table 8.11),

table 8.10   coin-toss example

		COIN		
		Nickel	Dime	
Outcome	Head	13	8	21
	Tail	7	12	19
	Totals	20	20	40

we can see that it is possible to enter into any *one* of the cells any value between zero and the corresponding minimal value. However, once we enter a value, for example, as in Table 8.12, *every other value is fixed* as well. If 13 is entered in the upper-left cell, as in Table 8.12, or in any other cell, and if the corresponding row marginal is 21, the upper-right cell must have the value of 8. The other two cells are similarly fixed. In this sense, only one of the four cells is "free to vary"; the other three cells are fixed. (Convince yourself that this procedure for determining degrees of freedom holds true for any table of r rows and c columns.) Therefore, the degrees of freedom for our coin-tossing example is

$$df = (2 - 1)(2 - 1) = (1)(1) = 1$$

and for the example of religious/political preferences (Table 8.4)

$$df = (3 - 1)(3 - 1) = (2)(2) = 4$$

In the special case where $r = 1$ or $c = 1$ (for example, if we repeatedly roll a single die and observe the outcomes we would have a 6×1 table), df is defined simply as $(c - 1)$ or $(r - 1)$.

We are now ready to make a decision concerning the relationship between religious and political preferences. To do so, we first state our null hypothesis and our decision rules.

Null Hypothesis: Religious preference and political preference are statistically independent.

Decision Rule: Do not reject H_o if the computed value of Chi-square does not equal or exceed that table value of Chi-square when df = 4 and $\alpha = .05$.

Reject H_o if the computed value equals or exceeds the table value.

quick quiz
8.1   (A)   For the adjacent table, what is the value of df and what values must fill the empty cells?

		20	55
10			45
30	35	35	100

(B)   For tables of the following dimensions, what is the appropriate df?
(1) 2×3 (2) 4×5 (3) 6×1 (4) 1×4 (5) 4×4

essential statistics for social research

table 8.11   *illustration*

		21
		19
20	20	40

table 8.12   *illustration*

13		21
		19
20	20	40

From Table 8.9 or Appendix Table E, we see that the critical value when df = 4 and α = .05 is 9.49. Since our computed value, 14.57, clearly exceeds the critical value of 9.49, we reject the null hypothesis. We do so because we know that a computed value of 14.57 will occur by chance fewer than five times in one hundred (in fact, less than once in one hundred trials), and we consider such an improbable outcome to be due to a factor or factors other than chance. We conclude that the two variables are *not* statistically independent; they do *not* conform to a chance model of the universe. Very frequently we will go one step further and *infer* that the variables are somehow related. It should be noted, however, that on the basis of our statistical test alone, *we cannot specify that relationship:* we do not know if religious preference "causes" political preference, or the reverse, or if both are "caused" by a third factor, of if there is another explanation for the relationship. Such specification would require further logical and/or statistical analysis, and, ultimately, must be integrated into a relevant sociological theory.

ADDITIONAL NOTES ON CHI-SQUARE   *yates' correction.*   In the special case of the 2×2 table (or when df = 1), the computation of Chi-square presents a particular problem because of the fact that while the theoretical distribution of Chi-square is continuous, that is, it is able to take on any value within limits, the actual values of the Chi-square statistic are discontinuous, or discrete.

quick quiz 8.2

Given the following computed values for Chi-square, levels of α, and degrees of freedom, would you accept or reject the null hypothesis (the hypothesis of statistical independence)?

	χ^2	α	df
(A)	5.00	.05	1
(B)	5.00	.01	1
(C)	8.14	.05	3
(D)	2.96	.05	2
(E)	13.08	.01	4
(F)	13.08	.05	6

This problem can be quite crucial when df $= 1$, as well as and especially when any value of f_e is relatively small (less than 10). A full discussion of this problem can be found in other texts (for example, Blalock, 1972; Siegel, 1956); it will not be discussed here. For our purposes, we will simply note the problem and offer the appropriate computational formulas.

The following is a general formula which incorporates Yates' correction

$$\chi_y^2 = \sum \frac{(|f_o - f_e| - .5)^2}{f_e} \qquad \text{(Formula 8.3)}$$

where $|f_o - f_e|$ is the absolute value (that is the difference without regard to a positive or negative sign) of the deviation between observed and expected frequencies. In the special case of 2×2 table, such as Table 8.6, the appropriate formula is

$$\chi_y^2 = \frac{N\left(|ad - bc| - \dfrac{N}{2}\right)^2}{k \cdot l \cdot m \cdot n}$$

quick quiz 8.3

Compute χ_y^2 for Table 8.10. If $\alpha = .05$, what is your decision concerning H_o?

fisher's exact test. In cases where f_e is very small (less than 5), even Yates' correction can produce a misleading decision. Therefore, when $f_e < 5$ we must use a technique known as Fisher's exact test. We will not compute Fisher's test here, but you should note it as a special case which you might confront in some sociological literature. See Blalock (1972) or Siegel (1956) for a detailed discussion of this procedure.

cell collapsing. There is one further problem concerning the use of χ^2 that should be mentioned. In some cases, even if N and df are relatively large, we may encounter a situation in which several cells have a small value of f_e. Instead of applying Yates' correction, an alternative strategy is to collapse, or combine, cells. This can be done *as long as the collapsing procedure makes sense.* To illustrate, suppose that our original table of religious and political preferences was as given in Table 8.13. Clearly, the four right-hand columns (Jewish, Muslim,

table 8.13 **religious and political preferences (hypothetical data)**

		RELIGIOUS PREFERENCE						
		Prot.	Cath.	Jewish	Muslim	Mormon	Other	Total
	Democrat	30	40	9	1	0	0	80
Political Preference	Republican	40	20	5	1	3	1	70
	Independent	30	10	4	4	1	1	50
	Totals	100	70	18	6	4	2	200

Mormon, other) would have many cells where f_e is very small (less than 5). In such cases, the standard computation of Chi-square would be inappropriate. We have several ways of handling this difficulty. For example, we could increase our sample size, especially in the groups with small numbers. If we do not have the resources (of time, money, personnel, and so on), we can consider combining cells. This has the double effects of decreasing the degrees of freedom and building up the value of f_e in the resulting cells.

However, we must be extremely careful that the way the cells are combined makes sense in terms of the research problem. For example, in a study of political preference, it may be statistically helpful to combine Democrats and Republicans (assuming their expected frequencies were small), but to do so would be absolute nonsense in terms of studying a real-world political issue. In such cases the logic of the real world should govern the logic of the statistical world.

In the case of Table 8.13, and assuming that we must collapse cells, it probably makes logical sense to keep the two larger groups distinct and to combine the smaller groups into one category.

measures of association based on chi-square

THE PHI COEFFICIENT   One difficulty with the Chi-square statistic is that it does not lend itself to comparison with other statistics, and unless the values of N are equal, even two Chi-square values cannot meaningfully be compared with each other. In part, this happens because the value of χ^2 is a function of N. To illustrate, recall that for Table 8.10 we obtained a corrected Chi-square of 1.60. Now let us triple the size of our sample, so that N = 120 and let us keep the other cell and marginal values in similar proportion (see Table 8.14). The computed value of χ_y^2 is 6.55. With df = 1 and $\alpha = .05$, this value is statistically significant; it leads us to *reject* the null hypothesis. Note that the *proportion* of heads and tails

table 8.14   coin toss (N = 120)

		COIN		
		Nickel	Dime	Total
Outcome	Heads	39	24	63
	Tails	21	36	57
	Totals	60	60	120

has not changed from Table 8.10. All that has changed is the size of our sample. But notice the effect of this change. In Table 8.10 we conclude that the relationship is due merely to chance, but in Table 8.14 we reject the chance model! From this example, the importance of sample size should be evident.

Because of this difficulty in comparing various Chi-squares, other statistics which are related to χ^2 have been developed. We shall mention only three such statistics here; discussion of others can be found in other texts (for example, Weiss, 1968).

In the special case of a 2×2 table, as in Table 8.6, we can define the statistic Phi (ϕ) as

$$\phi = \frac{(ad - bc)}{\sqrt{klmn}}$$

(Formula 8.4)

It can be shown algebraically that ϕ is related to χ^2 as follows:

$$\phi = \sqrt{\frac{\chi^2}{N}} \quad \text{or} \quad \chi^2 = N\phi^2 \quad \text{or} \quad \phi^2 = \frac{\chi^2}{N}$$

(Note that in the equations given just above, Yates' correction has *not* been applied to Chi-square.) It is in the comparison of Phi for Tables 8.10 and 8.14 that we can see the utility of this statistic. Unlike Chi-square, the computed values of Phi for these two tables are identical. In both cases, $\phi = 0.25$. The reason for this is that, unlike Chi-square, Phi is unaffected by sample size. (Note that ϕ^2 is χ^2 divided by sample size, N.) Phi also has the feature of taking on values only between zero and ± 1.00. (But with nominal level data, the sign is meaningless.) Consequently, values of Phi may be readily compared. There are other uses of Phi which will be touched on in later chapters. The major disadvantage of Phi in dealing with nominal level data is that it cannot be applied to tables with dimensions greater than 2×2.

Some authors prefer to use the Phi-square statistic, rather than Phi. The advantage of Phi-square is that it is more directly related to Chi-square than is Phi. Furthermore, in a 2×2 table, Phi-square is equal to

Goodman and Kruskal's Tau, a statistic which has a PRE interpretation. (See below.)

quick quiz
8.4

(A) Compute φ for Table 8.10.
(B) Compute φ for Table 8.14.
(C) From the answers to A and B, what can you say about the effect of sample size on Phi?

THE CONTINGENCY COEFFICIENT (C)

For tables larger than 2 × 2, for which Phi is not appropriate, we may use the contingency coefficient (C) whose formula is

(Formula 8.5)

$$C = \sqrt{\frac{\chi^2}{N + \chi^2}} = \sqrt{\frac{\phi^2}{1 + \phi^2}}$$

One difficulty with the contingency coefficient is that while its lower limit is zero, its upper limit is always less than 1.00. In a 2 × 2 table, for example, the upper limit of C is 0.707. As the dimensions of the table increase, the upper limit of C also increases, but it never reaches unity. Therefore, two values of C cannot be meaningfully compared unless they are based on two tables possessing identical degrees of freedom. Mendenhall, Ott and Larson (1974: 351) have described a procedure for computing an adjusted value of C which minimizes the upper limit problem in those cases where the table is "square," that is, where the number of rows equals the number of columns. This adjusted C does have 1.00 as its upper limit.

CRAMER'S V

For tables which are larger than 2 × 2 and which are not square, we can use as a measure of association Cramer's V:

(Formula 8.6)

$$V = \sqrt{\chi^2/N \left(\min \begin{matrix} (r - 1) \\ (c - 1) \end{matrix} \right)}$$

where $\left(\min \begin{matrix} (r - 1) \\ (c - 1) \end{matrix} \right)$ is the smaller of $(r - 1)$ or $(c - 1)$.

quick quiz
8.5

Compute C for Table 8.4.

lambda: a "proportional reduction in error" measure of association for nominal level data

In this section we shall discuss a statistic, lambda (λ), which measures association between two nominal level variables, and which is interpreted according to a proportional reduction of error (PRE) model. The meaning of this phrase will be illustrated shortly. The PRE model which is a basis for many statistics other than lambda, is quite different from the model of statistical independence which we used in describing Chi-square.

Suppose we have a group of fifty adolescent boys and we know that thirty of them have no record of delinquency while twenty do have a delinquent record. Knowing nothing else, we are asked to predict for each individual whether his record is delinquent or nondelinquent. Since our information is minimal, our best strategy would be to determine the mode for this group of fifty, and in each individual case, use the mode as our best prediction. Here, the mode is nondelinquent and by guessing that each of the fifty boys is nondelinquent we will be correct thirty times (the modal frequency) and we will be wrong twenty times. Our *prediction rule* ("Guess the mode") has resulted in twenty *errors in prediction*, or an error rate of 20/50 = 40 percent. Given the very limited information we have, we cannot do much better than this. But suppose we add a second variable, and, hence, a second piece of information: twenty-six of the boys have a background of Kids Club membership and twenty-four do not. We can arrange this information in a 2×2 cross-classification table (Table 8.15). Again, let us predict delinquency, but this time we shall do so while knowing the club background of each boy. Again our prediction rule will make use of the mode, *but not the overall mode;* rather, we shall predict *within-category modes*. Thus, for the twenty-six boys who do have a club background, the within-category mode is nondelinquent and using this as our predictor results in four errors, or an error rate of 4/26 = 15 percent. Similarly, for the twenty-four boys who do not have a club background, we predict delinquent (since within the category of nonmember the mode is delinquent) and make eight errors in prediction for an error rate of 8/24 = 33 percent. In total we have made 4 + 8 = 12 errors, and our error rate is (4 + 8)/(26 + 24) = 12/50 = 24 percent. We can now easily see the utility of having the additional piece of information (club background): it enables us to reduce our error rate from 40 percent to 24 percent. Stated differently, we have reduced the number of prediction errors from twenty to twelve, a reduction of eight errors.

table 8.15   **club membership and delinquency (hypothetical)**

| | | CLUB BACKGROUND | | |
		Member	Nonmember	Totals
Record	Delinquent	4	16	20
	Nondelinquent	22	8	30
	Totals	26	24	50

We can now define the statistic lambda as the amount by which we reduce errors in prediction when we move from one prediction scheme (the overall mode) to another (within-category modes), divided by the amount of original error. In general, we can compute a value of lambda by using the formula

(*Formula 8.7*)

$$\lambda = \frac{(\Sigma \max f_i) - \max F_d}{N - \max F_d}$$

where $\max f_i$ = the *maximum* frequency *within* a *subclass* of the *independent* variable, and $\max F_d$ = the modal frequency of the *dependent* variable. For Table 8.15, N is 50; $\max F_d$ is 30; we have two categories of the independent variable (the independent variable is club background) and the maximum frequencies within these categories are 22 and 16. Using Formula 8.7, λ_r is computed as follows:

$$\lambda_r = \frac{(22 + 16) - 30}{50 - 30} = \frac{8}{20} = 0.40$$

The subscript r indicates that we have designated the *row* variable as *dependent*. We do this because we are predicting delinquency (the row variable) from our knowledge of club background (the column variable). We could similarly compute a value of λ_c by predicting club membership from our information about delinquency. As an exercise, verify that for Table 8.15 the value of $\lambda_c = 0.50$.

INTERPRETATION   PRE measures of association generally tell us the proportional (or relative) reduction in error that is achieved when we shift from one prediction rule to another. In the case of lambda, the first prediction rule is

Prediction Rule 1 (λ): To predict the dependent variable, use its own mode.

and the second prediction rule is

Prediction Rule 2 (λ): Within categories of the independent variable, predict the dependent variable by using the within-category modes.

Lambda may vary from 0.0 to 1.0. It cannot be negative. A value of $\lambda = 1.0$ means that knowledge of the independent variable enables us to perfectly predict the dependent variable; a value of $\lambda = 0.0$ means that knowledge of the independent variable is of no help in predicting the dependent variable. Intermediate values indicate the proportional reduction in error. A value of $\lambda = 0.40$ means that, in shifting from Prediction Rule 1 to Prediction Rule 2, we reduce the amount of prediction error by 40 percent.

It should be noted that a value of $\lambda = 0.0$ does not *necessarily* mean that there is no association between variables. It means that the shift in prediction rules is of no help. To illustrate this point, let us consider Table 8.16. Even a casual examination of this table should convince us that there is a relationship between these variables, since *none* of the boys with a club background are delinquent, while $11/24 = 46$ percent of the boys without club backgrounds are delinquent. Yet the computed value of lambda is zero!

$$\lambda_r = \frac{(26 + 13) - 39}{50 - 39} = \frac{39 - 39}{11} = \frac{0}{11} = 0.0$$

It is zero, *not* because there is no association, but because *the within-category modes are identical to each other and to the overall mode; hence, there is no difference in prediction, no difference in error,* and lambda is zero. In such situations, lambda is said to be *insensitive*, and is clearly an inadequate measure of association. In these specific instances, we must use another measure of association (such as Goodman and Kruskal's Tau, described on pp. 131–134).

Thus far in our discussions we have presented lambda as an *asymmetric* measure of association. A measure of association is said to be asymmetric if, for a given contingency table, *two* values of that measure can be computed: one value computed with the row variable conceived of as the independent variable and a second value computed with the column variable conceived of as independent. (We saw an example of lambda as an asymmetric measure when we computed λ_r and λ_c for Table 8.16 and obtained two distinct results.) On the other hand, a *symmetric* measure yields only a single computed value.

Asymmetric measure always describe *one-way,* as opposed to *mutual,* association. It should be noted that whether a measure is asymmetric or symmetric is a question of statistical formulation, while the question of one-way versus mutual association is a logical question. To paraphrase

ASYMETRIC, SYMMETRIC, ONE-WAY AND MUTUAL ASSOCIATION

essential statistics for social research

table 8.16   club membership and delinquency (hypothetical)

		CLUB BACKGROUND		
		Member	Nonmember	Totals
Record	Delinquent	0	11	11
	Nondelinquent	26	13	39
	Totals	26	24	50

Weiss (1968. 180), If we want our measure of association to tell us the extent to which all club members are delinquent, but we are not interested in the extent to which all delinquents are club members, we want a measure of one-way association. But if we want to measure the extent to which both phenomena go together, we need a measure of mutual association. In choosing an appropriate measure, we thus face both a statistical and a logical choice; the question of logic should always be answered before the statistical question. If we wish to measure one-way association, we select, whenever possible, an asymmetric measure. (We say, *whenever possible,* because we will occasionally encounter situations which are logically one-way but for which we have available only a symmetric measure. An example is the Pearson r discussed in Chapter 10.) If we wish to measure mutual association, we *always* select a symmetric measure.

To illustrate the difference between these several types of relationships let us consider Tables 8.17 and 8.18. Table 8.17 presents hypothetical data on fathers' and sons' religious preferences. Here, logic (or common sense) tells us that the pattern of influence (or cause) should be such that the fathers' preferences are independent and the sons' preferences are dependent on the fathers'. Thus, we have a logical one-way relationship and we measure it by using an asymmetric measure of association. Table 8.18 presents hypothetical data on husbands' and wives' religious preferences. But, is the relationship between husbands' and wives' preferences one-way or mutual? We might logically argue

table 8.17   fathers' and sons' religious preferences (hypothetical)

		FATHER'S RELIGION			
		Protestant	Catholic	Other	Totals
Son's Religion	Protestant	10	1	1	12
	Catholic	2	8	1	11
	Other	3	6	13	22
	Totals	15	15	15	45

table 8.18   **husbands' and wives' religious preferences (hypothetical)**

		HUSBAND'S RELIGION			
		Protestant	Catholic	Other	Totals
Wife's Religion	Protestant	10	1	1	12
	Catholic	2	8	1	11
	Other	3	6	13	22
	Totals	15	15	15	45

that men traditionally dominate husband-wife relationships, and, therefore, the relationship is one-way, with the wife's religion being dependent. Conversely, we might argue that in religious matters the wife is more influential and, therefore, the wife's religion is the independent variable. Finally, we might suggest that each partner equally influences the other, and that the relationship is not one-way but mutual. Which interpretation is correct? To answer this question, the good sociologist would look to the body of relevant theory and previous research and take into account whether the sample has any important characteristics. (For example, one might opt for the first interpretation if the subjects were blue-collar, and for the third if the subjects were white-collar.) We will not answer this question here, but for purposes of illustration, let us assume that the relationship is indeed mutual. In that case, we would prefer to have a symmetric statistical measure.

symmetric lambda.   The symmetric lambda, λ_s can be computed by the formula

$$\lambda_s = \frac{(\Sigma \max f_r + \Sigma \max f_c) - (\max F_r + \max F_c)}{2N - (\max F_r + \max F_c)}$$ (Formula 8.8)

where r and c are row and column subscripts; max f is the maximum frequency *within* a row or column; and max F is the maximum *marginal* frequency of a row or column. Applying this formula to the data from Table 8.18

$$\lambda_s = \frac{(10 + 8 + 13) + (10 + 8 + 13) - (15 + 22)}{2(45) - (15 + 22)}$$

$$= \frac{(31 + 31) - (37)}{90 - 37}$$

$$= \frac{25}{53}$$

$$= 0.47$$

quick quiz
8.6

For Table 8.18, compute λ_r.

Symmetric lambda is a PRE measure, and can be interpreted as any other PRE measure: it measures the amount of error reduction achieved as we move from one prediction rule to a second prediction rule. Symmetric lambda differs from asymmetric lambda in that, with the former, each variable is used to predict the other *simultaneously*.

the general logic of PRE: prediction rules and error rules

Our discussion of lambda has provided an example of a measure of association based on the PRE model. Let us now examine this model in closer detail.

All PRE statistics depend on two sets of *predictions* that we make about the *dependent variable*. These predictions come from the application of certain well-specified *prediction rules*. However, the prediction rules are subject to error which can be measured.

Every PRE measure has two prediction rules, one that is based on a concept of no association and one that is based on a concept of complete association. If we have two variables, A and B, they are said to be perfectly associated if our knowledge of variable A enables us to perfectly predict variable B. Tables 8.19 and 8.20 illustrate two instances of perfect association. In Table 8.19, knowing the father's political preference enables us to perfectly predict the son's preference—it will be the

table 8.19   *father-son political preferences*

		FATHER	
		Democrat	Republican
Son	Democrat	10	0
	Republican	0	10

table 8.20   *father-son political preferences*

		FATHER	
		Democrat	Republican
Son	Democrat	0	10
	Republican	10	0

measuring the association between two nominal level variables   129

same as the father's. Table 8.20 also gives us a perfect, but exactly opposite prediction—the son's political preference will be different from the father's. In examining any square cross-classification table, it is easy to spot perfect association, for in any given row (or column) of the table, all entries will fall in only one cell; all other cells in that row (or column) will have frequencies of zero. In these cases of perfect association, knowledge of one variable enables us to predict the second variable without error.

In this text, the perfect association prediction rule of any PRE statistic will be known as *Rule 2*, and the errors that result from this rule will be identified as E_2. For lambda, Rule 2 is, in operational terms, "predict the dependent variable by using the within-category mode of the independent variable." *If* we have perfect association, we will have no errors, and lambda will be 1.0. To the extent that the association is less than perfect, as in Table 8.17, we will have some error in prediction, and lambda will be less than 1.0.

The concept of no association, and its corresponding rule, *Rule 1*, and the resultant error, E_1, suggests that knowledge of variable A is of no use whatsoever in predicting variable B. In fact, under Rule 1, *we do not use one variable to predict another*. Rather, we predict a variable *on the basis of its own marginal distribution*. Returning to Table 8.19 we can see that the marginal totals for the sons are identical: ten Democrats and ten Republicans. Hence, we could use as our prediction rule, "all sons are Democrats" or "All sons are Republicans." Since the marginals are identical, each of these rules would be as good as the other. (These are not the only prediction rules possible. Since we know that there is an equal number of Democrats and Republicans, we could base our rule on the toss of a coin—"If heads, Democrat; if tails, Republican." In the long run and on the average, this rule, too, would yield ten errors.) In this particular example, these three prediction rules are equally good; in general, however, this will not be the case, and one of our main tasks is to determine which prediction rules result in the fewest errors.

As we have already indicated, for lambda, Rule 1 is "Predict the dependent variable by using its own mode."

In general, any PRE statistic can be defined by

$$\text{PRE} = \frac{E_1 - E_2}{E_1}$$

(*Formula 8.9*)

Where E_1 and E_2 are the number of errors resulting from the application of Prediction Rule 1 and Prediction Rule 2.

We earlier presented a computational formula for lambda (Formula 8.7) which used a more direct computational procedure than that indicated in Formula 8.9. However, we can show that the two procedures produce identical results. In our discussion of Table 8.15 we noted that

Prediction Rule 1 resulted in twenty errors and the Prediction Rule 2 resulted in twelve errors. Thus, we can compute λ_r for Table 8.15 as follows:

$$\lambda_r = \frac{E_1 - E_2}{E_1} = \frac{20 - 12}{20} = \frac{8}{20} = 0.40$$

which is identical to the result obtained from Formula 8.7.

5	8	13
10	11	21
15	9	24
30	28	58

For the above table,
(A)   What is λ_r?
(B)   What is λ_c?
(C)   What is λ_s?

goodman and kruskal's tau

TAU   On page 126, we mentioned a situation in which lambda is not an appropriate statistic because it is insensitive. In this event, we may get a computed value of lambda = 0.0 even when association is truly present (see Table 8.16). Goodman and Kruskal's Tau (τ)* is a PRE measure of asymmetric association for nominal level data which can help us in such cases. It can do so because its prediction rules are different from those of lambda.

Whereas the prediction rules for lambda are based on modes, the prediction rules for Tau are based on the concept of random assignment of subjects within the table, given the set marginal values for the table. Review Table 8.16. Our first prediction rule for Tau, as with all such PRE prediction rules, uses only information about the distribution of the dependent variable. This rule is:

---

*Goodman and Kruskal's Tau is a measure of association for nominal level data. It should not be confused with Kendall's Tau which will be discussed in Chapter 9, and which is a measure of association for ordinal level data.

Prediction Rule 1 (τ): All N cases are to be *randomly* assigned to categories of the dependent variable.

If, in Table 8.16, we randomly assign eleven of the fifty cases to the delinquent category of the dependent variable, our error rate will be 78 percent (that is, 39/50). Since we are making eleven such assignments, we will make, in the long run and on the average, (11) (39/50) = 8.58 errors. Similarly, the random assignment of thirty-nine cases to the nondelinquent category will yield an error rate of 22 percent (11/50) and we will make (39)(11/50) = 8.58 errors. Therefore, E_1, the number of errors made from using Prediction Rule 1, is (8.58 + 8.58) = 17.16.

Our second prediction rule, as with all such PRE prediction rules, uses additional information: knowledge of the independent variable. For Goodman and Kruskal's Tau, this rule is:

Prediction Rule 2 (τ): *Within* each category of the *independent* variable, each case is to be *randomly assigned* to a category of the dependent variable.

In Table 8.16 we have twenty-six cases within the category of club member. If we randomly assign these twenty-six cases to the delinquent category we shall have an error rate of 100 percent (that is, 26/26) and we will make (0)(26/26) = 0 errors. If we assign the twenty-six cases to the nondelinquent category, we shall have an error rate of 0 percent (that is, 0/26) and will make (26)(0/26) = 0 errors in prediction. In the independent variable category, Non club member, we have twenty-four cases. If we randomly assign these twenty-four to the delinquent category of the dependent variable we shall have an error rate of 54 percent (13/24) and will make, in the long run and on the average, (11)(13/24) = 5.96 errors. If we assign the twenty-four cases to the Nondelinquent category, we shall have an error rate of 46 percent (that is, 11/24) and we will make (13)(11/24) = 5.96 errors. Therefore, E_2, the number of errors made from using Prediction Rule 2 is (0 + 0 + 5.96 + 5.96) = 11.92.

Using the general PRE formula (Formula 8.9), we can now determine the value of Tau for Table 8.16.

$$\tau_r = \frac{E_1 - E_2}{E_1} = \frac{17.16 - 11.92}{17.16} = \frac{5.24}{17.16} = 0.31 \qquad \textit{(Formula 8.10)}$$

If you understand the rationale behind Tau (that is, the use of prediction rules based on the concept of random assignment of cases to categories and cells), we can proceed to a simple formula for computing Tau. However, if you do not understand the underlying rationale for Tau, you should review the above material.

**COMPUTING
FORMULAS
FOR TAU**

Although it is very beneficial to "think through" the logic of random assignment to determine E_1 and E_2, most people will find the following formulas simpler and more direct for purposes of computation.

(Formula 8.11)

$$E_1 = \sum \left(\frac{N - F_d}{N}(F_d) \right) = \sum \left(F_d - \frac{F^2}{N} \right)$$

(Formula 8.12)

$$E_2 = \sum \frac{(F_i - f)f}{F_i} = \sum \left(f - \frac{f^2}{F_i} \right)$$

Where N is the total number of cases in a table; F is a marginal frequency; f is a cell frequency; i and d are subscripts indicating independent and dependent variables. The first version of Formula 8.11 is derived from the logic of Prediction Rule 1, while the second version is a more direct, but not as intuitively obvious, computing formula. The same is true with regard to Formula 8.12 and Prediction Rule 2.

With some algebraic manipulation we can combine the two formulas and develop a direct computing formula for Tau, a formula that allows us to bypass the computation of E_1 and E_2. Again, you should not use these formulas unless you fully understand the logic of the statistic in question. The direct computing formula for Goodman and Kruskal's Tau is:

(Formula 8.13)

$$\tau = \frac{N \sum \frac{f^2}{F_i} - \sum F_d^2}{N^2 - \sum F_d^2}$$

(Note that in Formula 8.13 the term f^2/F_i is to be interpreted as follows: square each cell frequency; divide the result by the independent variable marginal total associated with that cell.)

We can illustrate the application of these three formulas with the data from Table 8.16.

$$E_1 = \left(11 - \frac{11^2}{50} \right) + \left(39 - \frac{39^2}{50} \right) = 8.58 + 8.58$$

$$= 17.16$$

$$E^2 = \left(0 - \frac{0^2}{26} \right) + \left(26 - \frac{26^2}{26} \right) + \left(11 - \frac{11^2}{24} \right) + \left(13 - \frac{13^2}{24} \right)$$

$$= 0 + 0 + 5.96 + 5.96$$

$$= 11.92$$

These values for E_1 and E_2 are identical with those we computed earlier. Finally,

$$\tau_r = \frac{50\left(\dfrac{0^2}{26} + \dfrac{26^2}{26} + \dfrac{11^2}{24} + \dfrac{13^2}{24}\right) - (11^2 + 39^2)}{50^2 - (11^2 + 39^2)}$$

$$= \frac{50(38.08) - 1642}{2500 - 1642} = \frac{262}{858} = 0.31$$

A final word: since Tau is an asymmetric measure of association, we can also compute a value for τ_c. For τ_c, you should verify that $E_1 = 24.96$, $E_2 = 17.33$, and $\tau_c = 0.31$. You may notice that for Table 8.16 $\tau_r = \tau_c$. In a 2×2 table, τ_r will always equal τ_c. However, in tables larger than 2×2, generally τ_r and τ_c will not be the same.

Tau may range from 0.0 to 1.0. It cannot be negative. A value of Tau = 0.0 indicates that we have no reduction in error in shifting from Rule 1 to Rule 2, and a value of Tau = 1.0 indicates perfect prediction. Values of Tau between 0.0 and 1.0 indicate the degree to which prediction errors are reduced by substituting random assignment of cases to categories within the independent variable for random assignment of cases to categories of the dependent variable.

important terms to know

Association	Lambda (λ)
Statistical independence	Proportional reduction in
Chi-square (χ^2)	error (PRE)
Marginal value	Prediction rule
Expected cell frequency	Error in prediction
Degrees of freedom	Asymmetric measure
(for χ^2)	Symmetric measure
Yates' correction	One-way association
Fisher's exact test	Mutual association
Phi and Phi-square	Goodman and Kruskal's
(ϕ and ϕ^2)	Tau (τ)

suggested readings

Blalock (1972: 275–303); Siegel (1956: 42–47, 96–111, 175–179, 196–202); Weiss (1968: 158–196); Mueller, Schuessler and Costner (1970: 239–263); Mendenhall, Ott and Larson (1974: 316–372).

answer section

QUICK QUIZ 8.1 (A) $df = (2 - 1)(3 - 1) = 2$

20	15	20	55
10	20	15	45
30	35	35	100

(B) (1) 2
 (2) 12
 (3) 5
 (4) 3
 (5) 9

QUICK QUIZ 8.2 (A) Since $\chi^2 = 5.00$ exceeds the critical value of 3.84 *reject* H_o.
(B) Since $\chi^2 = 5.00$ does not exceed the critical value of 6.64, *accept* H_o.
(C) Since $\chi^2 = 8.14$ exceeds the critical value of 7.82, *reject* H_o.
(D) Since $\chi^2 = 2.96$ does not exceed the critical value of 5.99, *accept* H_o.
(E) Since $\chi^2 = 13.08$ does not exceed the critical value of 13.28, *accept* H_o.
(F) Since $\chi^2 = 13.08$ exceeds the critical value of 12.59, *reject* H_o.

QUICK QUIZ 8.3

$$\chi_y^2 = \frac{40\left((13)(12) - (7)(8) - \frac{40}{2}\right)^2}{(20)(20)(19)(21)}$$

$$= \frac{40(80)^2}{(20)(20)(19)(21)}$$

$$= 1.60$$

$$df = 1$$

Since this value does not exceed the table value of 3.84, we *accept* the null hypothesis. The "behavior" of the coins does not differ significantly from chance.

QUICK QUIZ 8.4 (A) $\phi = \frac{156 - 56}{\sqrt{(20)(20)(19)(21)}}$

$$= \frac{100}{399.5}$$

$$= 0.250$$

(B) $\phi = \dfrac{1404 - 504}{\sqrt{(60)(60)(63)(57)}}$

$= \dfrac{900}{3595.5}$

$= 0.250$

(C) The value of Phi is unaffected by sample size.

QUICK QUIZ 8.5 Since we know that $\chi^2 = 14.57$ (See Table 8.8),

$C = \sqrt{\dfrac{14.57}{200 + 14.57}} = 0.261$

QUICK QUIZ 8.6 $\lambda_r = \dfrac{(10 + 8 + 13) - 22}{45 - 22} = \dfrac{31 - 22}{23} = \dfrac{9}{23} = 0.39$

QUICK QUIZ 8.7 (A) $\lambda_r = \dfrac{15 + 11 - 24}{58 - 24} = \dfrac{2}{34} = .06$

(B) $\lambda_c = \dfrac{8 + 11 + 15 - 30}{58 - 30} = \dfrac{4}{28} = .14$

(C) $\lambda_s = \dfrac{(8 + 11 + 15 + 15 + 11) - (24 + 30)}{2(58) - (24 + 30)}$

$= \dfrac{60 - 54}{116 - 54} = \dfrac{6}{62} = .10$

essential statistics for social research

measuring association between two ordinal level variables

In Chapter 8 we examined several ways of measuring the relationship between two nominal level variables. In this chapter we shall look at measures of association for ordinal level variables. Remember that the distinction between nominal and ordinal measurement is that the former is purely qualitative and involves the assignment of data to classes or categories, while ordinal measurement introduces the dimension of ranks. When two categories of a variable are nominally different, the only thing that we can say about them is that they are not the same, but when two categories of a variable are ordinally different we can also specify which of the two is larger (or greater, stronger, and so on). This ability to specify differences in rank order gives an added dimension to our measurement capacities.

In this chapter we shall examine four major measures of ordinal association. The computing formulas for these statistics are, for the most part, rather simple. What may not be so simple is the logic which underlies the statistics. In studying this material, pay special attention to the discussions which deal with the *why* of a statistic. Computing a statistic is easy; understanding why you are doing so may take effort.

gamma: a symmetric measure of one-way association

Gamma is a measure of association developed by Goodman and Kruskal (1954: 1959). It measures one-way association; that is, it uses information

9

about one variable to tell us something about a second variable. Gamma is a symmetric measure because any contingency table yields only one value of gamma, regardless of whether the row variable or column variable is logically dependent or independent. Gamma has a PRE interpretation, but its fundamental meaning is based on the notion of pair-by-pair comparisons.

THE LOGIC OF PAIR-BY-PAIR COMPARISON

In the previous chapter we introduced five strategies for measuring association (p. 110) and discussed three of these (percentage differences, departure from independence and proportional reduction in error), in detail. We now introduce the logic of *pair-by-pair comparison* as the basis for understanding certain of the ordinal measures of association.

If we assign a subject to some rank on each of two ordinal variables, we can think of that subject as being "paired" with any and every other subject in a sample. We can then compare the members of each *pair* to determine whether the relative rankings of the two members on *both* variables are similar or dissimilar. If we summarize all of these paired comparisons and determine whether there is a preponderance of similar or dissimilar pairs, we can derive a measure of association. For example, suppose we have three subjects (A, B and C) which are ranked on each of two variables (Table 9.1). We can think of these three subjects forming themselves into all possible pairs. In our example, it is easy to see that the possible pairs are AB, AC and BC. However, if the number of subjects is large, it will not be so easy to list all possible pairs. Fortunately, the statistics we shall be dealing with do not require such a list, but they do require that we know *how many* pairs can be formed. The number of pairs that can be formed for a given value of N is

$$\text{No. of possible pairs} = \frac{N(N-1)}{2} \qquad \textit{(Formula 9.1)}$$

We can verify for Table 9.1 that the number of pairs is $3(3-1)/2 = 3$.

Let us focus our attention on pair AB in Table 9.1. We see that on variable X, A is ranked above B and on variable Y, A is also ranked above B. Therefore, on both variables the rank ordering of the pair members is said to be similar (or the same). It is similar in the sense that one

table 9.1   *example of three subjects ranked on two variables*

SUBJECT	RANK ON VARIABLE X	RANK ON VARIABLE Y
A	1	1
B	2	3
C	3	2

member of the pair is ranked above the other member on *both* variables. Pair AC also shows a *similar* pattern of ranking because subject A is ranked above subject C on *both* variables. If we look at pair BC we see that B is ranked higher than C on variable X but lower than C on variable Y. This pattern of ranked pairs is said to be *dissimilar* (or reversed).

The measures of association discussed below and in the next two sections are based on the logic of pair-by-pair comparison. These measures involve a determination of the number of similar and dissimilar pairs (symbolized as n_s and n_d), an expression of the differences between such pairs (symbolized as S and equal to $n_s - n_d$), and a ratio of S to some defined quantity.

GAMMA:
AN EXAMPLE
Suppose we ask two sociology students to rank five occupations. Three possible sets of rankings are given in Table 9.2. We can easily see that in (a) there is perfect positive agreement between the two students. Student X places an architect first; so does Student Y. Both students rank the bank manager second. Their rankings are completely consistent. We should expect any measure of the relationship between the two sets of ranks to have a value of $+1.00$. In 9.2(b) it is equally easy to see that the agreement is also perfect, but negative. The occupation which is ranked first by Student X is ranked last by Student Y. Each student's rank ordering is the perfect opposite of the other student's ranking. However, the situation in 9.2(c) is not so clear, for there is both agreement and disagreement in the two sets of ranks. For example,

table 9.2   ***ranking of five occupations by two students***
(three hypothetical examples)

	OCCUPATION	STUDENT X	STUDENT Y
	Architect	1	1
	Bank Manager	2	2
(a)	Clergyman	3	3
	Dentist	4	4
	Engineer	5	5
	OCCUPATION		
	Architect	1	5
	Bank Manager	2	4
(b)	Clergyman	3	3
	Dentist	4	2
	Engineer	5	1
	OCCUPATION		
	Architect	1	1
	Bank Manager	2	2
(c)	Clergyman	3	4
	Dentist	4	5
	Engineer	5	3

measuring association between two ordinal level variables   139 both students agree that the dentist ranks below the architect. But X and Y disagree about the ranking of the dentist and clergyman—student X places the dentist above the clergyman, while Y places the clergyman above the dentist. In the terms of pair-by-pair comparison, the architect-dentist pair is said to be *similar* and the clergyman-dentist pair is said to be *dissimilar*. In like fashion, every possible pair can be similar or dissimilar.

After counting the number of similar and dissimilar pairs, how shall we determine the level of association between the two sets of ranks? Perhaps the most straightforward procedure is to simply count the number of similar pairs and the number of dissimilar pairs and then find some value which expresses the preponderance of one type of pair over the other. There are

$$\frac{N(N-1)}{2} = \frac{5(4)}{2} = 10$$

possible pairs. We list these pairs in Table 9.3 and also record, for each of the three hypothetical examples, whether a given pair is similar (s) or dissimilar (d). Of the ten possible pairs in (a), all ten are similar. Of the ten pairs in (b), all ten are dissimilar. And of the ten pairs in (c), eight are similar and two are dissimilar. Let us examine some of the pairs in (c). For pair AB, A is ranked above B by both Student X and Student Y; therefore, this pair is similar (s). For pair CE, Student X ranks C above E but Student Y ranks C below E; this pair is dissimilar (d). Pair DE is also dissimilar.

table 9.3   list of pairs from table 9.2

PAIR	9.2 (a)	9.2 (b)	9.2 (c)
AB	S*	D†	S
AC	S	D	S
AD	S	D	S
AE	S	D	S
BC	S	D	S
BD	S	D	S
BE	S	D	S
CD	S	D	S
CE	S	D	D
DE	S	D	D

For (a): $n_s = 10$, $n_d = 0$
For (b): $n_s = 0$, $n_d = 10$
For (c): $n_s = 8$, $n_d = 2$

*S = similar
†D = dissimilar

If we let n_s indicate the number of similar pairs and n_d the number of dissimilar pairs, we can express the difference as $(n_s - n_d)$; we shall indicate this difference by the symbol S. We can also define the total number of similar and dissimilar pairs as $(n_s + n_d)$. Finally, we can define a ratio which expresses the preponderance of similar or dissimilar pairs to the total number of similar and dissimilar pairs; this value is Gamma (G or γ). The simple computing formula for Gamma is

(Formula 9.2)
$$G = \frac{(n_s - n_d)}{(n_s + n_d)} = \frac{S}{(n_s + n_d)}$$

We can now compute a measure of association for the data in Table 9.3.

$$\text{From (a), } G = \frac{10 - 0}{10 + 0} = \frac{10}{10} = +1.00.$$

$$\text{From (b), } G = \frac{0 - 10}{0 + 10} = \frac{-10}{10} = -1.00.$$

$$\text{And from (c), } G = \frac{8 - 2}{8 + 2} = \frac{6}{10} = +0.60.$$

In (a), the value of $G = +1.00$ indicates that the two variables are perfectly and positively ordered in terms of pair-by-pair comparison. In (b), the value of $G = -1.00$ indicates that the two variables are perfectly and inversely ordered in terms of pair-by-pair comparison. In (c), the value of $G = +0.60$ indicates the extent to which similar pairs are preponderant over dissimilar pairs, relative to the total number of pairs which are similar or dissimilar. In addition to this explanation of the meaning of G, we shall see below that we can obtain a more precise interpretation of G by using the PRE model.

Before concluding this introductory discussion of Gamma, we must say a word about tied ranks. In the examples cited thus far, we have purposely avoided this problem. But now that you have a basic grasp of Gamma, you should note that it is possible for a judge to be unable to decide how certain ranks should be filled. To illustrate, suppose Student X was able to assign ranks 1, 2 and 3 to the architect, bank manager and clergyman, but felt that it was really impossible to discriminate between the dentist and engineer; in other words, the dentist and engineer were tied for fourth place. As we shall soon see, different statistics treat tied ranks in different ways. With Gamma, the procedure is to *ignore tied pairs*. Any pair in which a tie exists on either ranking, or both, is excluded from the computation of n_s and n_d. Table 9.4 shows how tied ranks affect the computation of Gamma. It is clear that, because of the tied rank on X, we cannot consider the pair DE as either similar or dissimilar.

table 9.4   computation of G with tied ranks, ungrouped data

OCCUPATION	STUDENT X	STUDENT Y
A	1	1
B	2	2
C	3	4
D	4⎤	5
E	4⎦ tie	3

PAIR	S, D OR T (ie)	
AB	S	
AC	S	
AD	S	
AE	S	$n_s = 8$
BC	S	$n_d = 1$
BD	S	
BE	S	$G = \dfrac{8-1}{8+1} = \dfrac{7}{9} = +0.78$
CD	S	
CE	D	
DE	T	

Clearly, as the number of cases under analysis becomes large, the number of ranks and the number of possible pairs also become large, and attempts to list all similar and dissimilar pairs become quite cumbersome. Also, there are many research situations in which the number of cases is quite large, but the number of ranks in a variable is quite small. In such circumstances, it is usual to group the data into categories. Table 9.5 illustrates such a situation. With N = 40, there are 780 possible pairs to consider in the computation of Gamma; to attempt to list these would be terribly tedious and time-consuming. However, there is an easier and more direct way to determine n_s and n_d, and, thereby, to compute Gamma. Consider the six subjects who occupy the upper-left cell of Table 9.5. Each subject, when paired with anyone else in the same *cell*, is a member of a pair which is tied on both variables. When paired with anyone else in the same *row*, each is tied on the ranking of the income variable. And when paired with anyone else in the same *column*, each is tied in rank on the education variable. Remembering

COMPUTING GAMMA FOR GROUPED DATA

table 9.5   income and education (hypothetical data)

		LEVEL OF EDUCATION (X)				
		I (= Low)	II	III	IV	Total
	Low	6	3	3	2	14
LEVEL OF INCOME (Y)	Med	3	3	7	3	16
	High	1	3	2	4	10
	Totals	10	9	12	9	40

that in the computation of Gamma ties are not counted, we eliminate these pairs from further consideration. We now can see in Figure 9.1(a) that each of the six members of the upper-left cell, when paired with each member of the remaining cells, results in a *similar* pair. Each member of the upper-left cell is ranked "less than" each member of the remaining cells on *both variables*. There are 132 such similar pairs: (6) (3) + (6) (7) + (6) (3) + (6) (3) + (6) (2) + (6) (4). Now consider the cell in the first row, second column. After eliminating its tied pairs, we find that there are forty-eight similar pairs (see Figure 9.1[b]). For the cell in the second row, third column, there are twenty-eight similar pairs (Figure 9.1[c]). In general, *we obtain* n_s *by multiplying each cell frequency by the sum of the cells below and to the right, and summing all such products.* For Table 9.5

$$n_s = 6(3 + 7 + 3 + 3 + 2 + 4) + 3(7 + 3 + 2 + 4) + 3(3 + 4)$$
$$+ 3(3 + 2 + 4) + 3(2 + 4) + 7(4)$$
$$= 132 + 48 + 21 + 27 + 18 + 28$$
$$= 274$$

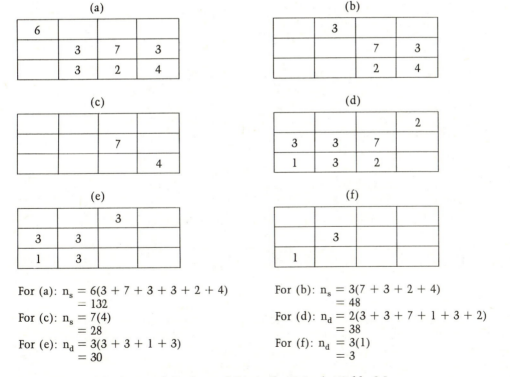

For (a): $n_s = 6(3 + 7 + 3 + 3 + 2 + 4)$
$\qquad = 132$

For (c): $n_s = 7(4)$
$\qquad = 28$

For (e): $n_d = 3(3 + 3 + 1 + 3)$
$\qquad = 30$

For (b): $n_s = 3(7 + 3 + 2 + 4)$
$\qquad = 48$

For (d): $n_d = 2(3 + 3 + 7 + 1 + 3 + 2)$
$\qquad = 38$

For (f): $n_d = 3(1)$
$\qquad = 3$

Figure 9.1 *Calculation of Similar and Dissimilar Pairs for Table 9.5*

To find n_d, we must find all pairs in which one member is ranked higher than the other on one variable, but lower on the second variable. Consider the cell in the first row, fourth column (Figure 9.1[d]). We first eliminate tied pairs, that is, those formed within the same row and same column. Now each member of the upper-right cell forms a *dissimilar* pair with each member of the six remaining cells; there are thirty-eight such dissimilar pairs. The cell in the first row, third column yields thirty dissimilar pairs (Figure 9.1[e]) and the cell in the second row, second column yields three dissimilar pairs (Figure 9.1[f]). In general, *we obtain n_d by multiplying each cell frequency by the sum of the cells below and to the left, and summing all such products.* For Table 9.5

$$n_d = 2(3 + 3 + 7 + 1 + 3 + 2) + 3(3 + 3 + 1 + 3) + 3(3 + 1)$$
$$+ 3(1 + 3 + 2) + 7(1 + 3) + 3(1)$$
$$= 38 + 30 + 12 + 18 + 28 + 3$$
$$= 129$$

We can now compute Gamma.

$$G = \frac{n_s - n_d}{n_s + n_d} = \frac{274 - 129}{274 + 129} = \frac{145}{403} = +0.36$$

This value can be interpreted as follows. If there were perfect association, the preponderance of similar (or dissimilar) pairs would equal the number of possible pairs (excluding ties) and the ratio of the former to the latter would be ± 1.00. If there were no association, the number of similar pairs would equal the number of dissimilar pairs, there would be a preponderance of neither and the ratio would be 0.00. Values between zero and one indicate the extent to which one type of pair is predominant over the other type, divided by the number of possible pairs (ties excluded).

In the above example, the positive sign tells us that the similar pairs are preponderant, and that the pattern of association is, therefore, direct, or positive. If the sign were negative, the dissimilar pairs would be preponderant, and the pattern of association would be inverse, or negative.

In addition to the above interpretation, Gamma can be viewed as a PRE measure. (For a review of the proportional reduction in error concept, see pp. 129–131.) To compute a PRE measure we need two Prediction Rules, one which predicts the dependent variable from knowledge of its own distribution, and one which predicts the de-

GAMMA AS A PRE MEASURE

For the data below, compute Gamma.

Rank on X

		1	2	3
Rank on Y	1	10	10	20
	2	10	20	10
	3	20	10	10

pendent variable from knowledge of the independent variable. Each prediction rule results in some error, E_1 and E_2, and the PRE measure is defined as $(E_1 - E_2)/E_1$.

For Gamma, we want to predict whether a *pair* is similar or dissimilar in its rankings on *both* variables. From knowledge of the dependent variable only, we have no reason to predict whether pairs will be similar or dissimilar. The best we can do is to assume that n_s will equal n_d. In simpler terms, we trust to chance, to a flip of a coin, to predict similarity or dissimilarity. To predict rank order on the dependent variable for a pair member, we are just as likely to be correct if we predict the rank to be higher than the rank of the independent variable, of if we predict it to be lower than the rank of the independent variable. This logic can be generalized as

Prediction Rule 1 (G): Predict all pairs to be the same, either similar or dissimilar.

Fundamentally, this is a "guessing" rule, and results in a theoretically expected error rate of 50 percent. In the long run and on the average, the number of errors, E_1, will be

(Formula 9.3)
$$E_1 = \tfrac{1}{2}(n_s + n_d).$$

Prediction Rule 2 utilizes knowledge of order on the independent variable to predict order on the dependent variable. If we know that there are more similar-order pairs than dissimilar-order pairs, it makes sense to predict "similar" for all pairs. And if the dissimilar-order pairs outnumber the similar-order pairs, we should predict "dissimilar" for all pairs.

Prediction Rule 2 (G): (a) If $n_s > n_d$, predict all pairs to be similar. (b) If $n_s < n_d$, predict all pairs to be dissimilar.

In essence, this rule says "go with the majority." (If there is no majority, that is, if $n_s = n_d$, $G = 0$). In situation (a), the number of errors, E_2, will equal n_d, and in (b), the number of errors will equal n_s. In general,

$$E_2 = min\ (n_s,\ n_d) \qquad (Formula\ 9.4)$$

Where $min\ (n_s,\ n_d)$ is the smaller of n_s and n_d. Let us use the above rules to compute Gamma for Table 9.5.

$$E_1 = \tfrac{1}{2}(n_s + n_d) = \tfrac{1}{2}(274 + 129)$$

$$= \tfrac{1}{2}(403)$$

$$= 201.5$$

$$E_2 = min\ (n_s,\ n_d) = min\ (274, 129) = 129$$

$$G = \frac{E_1 - E_2}{E_1} = \frac{201.5 - 129}{201.5}$$

$$= +0.36$$

This value is identical with that computed from Formula 9.2. It can be interpreted as the amount by which we reduce errors in prediction of similar or dissimilar pairs when we shift from a rule based on "chance" prediction to a rule based on "majority" prediction. When Gamma = ± 1.00, the reduction in error is total and we have perfect or complete association. When Gamma = 0.00, we have no error reduction and zero association. Intermediate values of Gamma indicate the relative amount of error reduction.

YULE'S Q AS A SPECIAL CASE OF GAMMA

Years before Gamma was developed and became quite prominent in sociological literature, a statistic called Yule's Q was frequently used as a measure of association for a 2 × 2 table. If the four cells of a 2 × 2 table are identified as in Figure 9.2, then

a	b
c	d

$$Q = \frac{ad - bc}{ad + bc} \qquad (Formula\ 9.5)$$

Figure 9.2

It is directly evident that $ad = n_s$ and $bc = n_d$; Yule's Q is, therefore, a special case of Gamma.

This point is mentioned here for purposes of information. In reading some of the older research literature you may come across the Q statistic. Since it is now understood to be a special case of Gamma, you should recognize it for what it is, and interpret Q not simply as a measure of association with no inherent meaning, but as a PRE measure of ordinal association.

kendall's tau: a symmetric measure of mutual association

Kendall (1962) has described a series of three symmetric measures of mutual association for ordinal data. All three, like Gamma, are based on the logic of pair-by-pair comparison. Our discussion of these measures will be brief; for a more complete discussion, see Kendall (1962), Blalock (1972), or Weiss (1968).

Let us first compare the three Tau measures and Gamma. All four measures involve the computation of n_s and n_d. All involve the quantity $(n_s - n_d) = S$ in the numerator of the computational formula. However, the four differ in the determination of the maximum possible number of pairs which are to be considered in the computation of the statistic.

(1) For Gamma, the maximum number of pairs is $(n_s + n_d)$, that is, the total number of pairs that are either similar or dissimilar; *ties are excluded.*

(2) Tau-a (τ_a) takes as its maximum number of pairs the total number of pairs, including ties, that can be formed. This value was defined in Formula 9.1 and is equivalent to $\frac{1}{2}N(N - 1)$. The computing formula for Tau-a is

(Formula 9.6)

$$\tau_a = \frac{S}{\frac{1}{2}N(N - 1)}$$

(3) Tau-b (τ_b) takes as its maximum value the number of pairs, *excluding ties*, that could be formed *if* there were complete mutual association between both variables. Figure 9.3 illustrates two cases of complete mutual association. Complete mutual association exists when both variables have the same number of ranks and all nondiagonal cell values are zero. If we have complete mutual association, knowledge of a subject's rank in either variable enables us to perfectly predict that subject's rank on the other variable. For Figure 9.3(a), the maximum number of pairs is not $\frac{1}{2}N(N - 1) = 105$ (as it would be for Tau-a) because in the upper-left cell there are $\frac{1}{2}(4)(3) = 6$ pairs which are tied on both variables; these pairs must be excluded; in the middle cell there are $\frac{1}{2}(6)(5) = 15$ tied pairs which must be excluded; and in the lower-right cell there are $\frac{1}{2}(5)(4) = 10$ ties which must be excluded. In this case of complete mutual association, the maximum number of untied pairs is, therefore, $105 - (6 + 5 + 10) = 74$.

quick quiz **9.2**	What is the number of untied pairs in Figure 9.3(b)?

(a)			
4	0	0	4
0	6	0	6
0	0	5	5
4	6	5	15

(b)			
0	0	65	65
0	70	0	70
48	0	0	48
48	70	65	183

Figure 9.3 *Illustration of Complete Mutual Association*

In the computing formula for Tau-b we use S in the numerator; in the denominator we use an estimate of the maximum number of untied pairs, assuming complete mutual association (Weiss, 1968).

$$\tau_b = \frac{S}{(\tfrac{1}{2})\sqrt{(N^2 - \Sigma F_r^2)(N^2 - \Sigma F_c^2)}} \qquad (Formula\ 9.7)$$

where F_r and F_c are, respectively, the *row totals* and *column totals*.

(4) A limitation of Tau-b is that it is applicable only to tables in which the number of rows is the same as the number of columns. Tau-c (τ_c) incorporates a correction which enables us to compute a measure of association for any rxc table. The computing formula for Tau-c is

$$\tau_c = \frac{S}{\tfrac{1}{2}N^2[(m-1)/m]} \qquad (Formula\ 9.8)$$

where m is the *smaller* of the number of rows or number of columns.

For Table 9.5 we computed a value of Gamma $= +0.36$. For that same table, let us now compute and compare values of Tau-a, Tau-b, and Tau-c.

$$\tau_a = \frac{S}{\tfrac{1}{2}N(N-1)} = \frac{145}{\tfrac{1}{2}(40)(39)} = \frac{145}{780}$$

$$= +0.19.$$

$$\tau_b = \frac{S}{\tfrac{1}{2}\sqrt{(N^2 - \Sigma F_r^2)(N^2 - \Sigma F_c^2)}}$$

$$= \frac{145}{\tfrac{1}{2}\sqrt{[40^2 - (14^2 - 16^2 + 10^2)][40^2 - (10^2 + 9^2 + 12^2 + 9^2)]}}$$

$$= \frac{145}{\tfrac{1}{2}\sqrt{(1600 - 552)(1600 - 406)}} = \frac{145}{\tfrac{1}{2}\sqrt{(1048)(1194)}}$$

$$= \frac{145}{\tfrac{1}{2}\sqrt{1251312}} = \frac{145}{\tfrac{1}{2}(1118.62)} = \frac{145}{559.31}$$

$$= +0.26$$

$$\tau_c = \frac{S}{\frac{1}{2}N^2\left(\frac{m-1}{m}\right)} = \frac{145}{\frac{1}{2}(40)^2\left(\frac{3-1}{3}\right)} = \frac{145}{\frac{1}{2}(1600)(\frac{2}{3})}$$

$$= \frac{145}{533.33}$$

$$= +0.27$$

(Note that, although the values of Tau-b and Tau-c are very close to each other in this example, values for the various Tau measures will not necessarily be the same.)

WHICH MEASURE TO USE? All four measures described so far in this chapter are *symmetric* measures of association. Gamma differs from the Tau measures in that Gamma measures *one-way* association while Tau measures *mutual* association. Tau-a has fairly limited application in sociological research. It is preferred to Tau-b or Tau-c "only when the investigator has some reason to believe that ties are relevant cases against the interpretation of association" (Weiss, 1968, 204). In other words, we use Tau-a only in those circumstances where ties do not, or in theory should not, exist. As for Tau-b and Tau-c, there is little to choose between them except that Tau-b applies to those tables where the number of rows equals the number of columns, while Tau-c applies to cases where r ≠ c. Tau-c is easier to compute, but its interpretation is not as clear as that of Tau-b. Finally, note that Kendall's Tau measures do not have a PRE interpretation, except for a very special case of Tau-b (Wilson, 1969).

somers' d: an asymmetric measure of association

Somers (1962) has introduced an asymmetric measure of association for ordinal data which is becoming increasingly popular in the sociological literature. Like Gamma and Kendall's Tau, Somers' d is based on the logic of pair-by-pair comparison. Unlike Gamma and Tau, d is an asymmetric measure. This means that, like asymmetric lambda (pp. 126–128), there are *two* values for d that can be computed for any contingency table. We shall follow common usage and refer to these two values as d_{yx} and d_{xy}. (That is, if we have two variables, X and Y, and we wish to predict Y from our knowledge of X, the resulting statistic is d_{yx}. Similarly, d_{xy} measures the extent to which the X variable can be predicted from the Y variable.)

Somers' d is logically very similar to Gamma, with one notable exception: *the denominator includes those pairs which are tied on the dependent variable only* but excludes those which are tied on the independent variable only and those tied on both variables. The numerator

STATISTIC	COMPUTING FORMULA	TYPE OF ASSOCIATION	PRE INTERPRETATION?	OTHER INTERPRETATION	MAJOR ADVANTAGE	MAJOR DISADVANTAGE(S)
G	$\dfrac{S}{n_s + n_d}$	One-way and symmetric	Yes	Excess of similar (or dissimilar) pairs relative to the total number of similar and dissimilar parts. Ties are excluded.	Can be interpreted as a PRE measure	Insensitive to asymmetry
τ_a	$\dfrac{S}{\frac{1}{2}N(N-1)}$	Mutual and symmetric	No	Excess of similar (or dissimilar) pairs relative to number of all possible pairs. Ties are included.	Useful when presence of ties is an argument against association	Lacks PRE interpretation
τ_b	$\dfrac{S}{\frac{1}{2}\sqrt{(N^2 - \Sigma F_x{}^2)(N^2 - \Sigma F_y{}^2)}}$	Mutual and symmetric	In limited circumstances	Excess of similar (or dissimilar) pairs relative to all possible pairs, assuming complete mutual association. Ties are excluded.	Best measure of mutual association	Limited PRE interpretation
τ_c	$\dfrac{S}{\left(\frac{1}{2}N^2\,\dfrac{m-1}{m}\right)}$	Mutual and symmetric	No	As τ_b but modified for tables of any dimensions.	As τ_b	As τ_b
d_{yx}	$\dfrac{S}{\frac{1}{2}(N^2 - \Sigma F_x{}^2)}$	One-way and asymmetric	No	As G, except pairs tied on the independent variable are excluded. Also analogous to the percentage difference	Statistically distinguishes between independent and dependent variables	Lacks PRE interpretation
d_{xy}	$\dfrac{S}{\frac{1}{2}(N^2 - \Sigma F_y{}^2)}$	One-way and asymmetric	No	As d_{yx}	As d_{yx}	As d_{yx}

Figure 9.4 Summary of Characteristics of Measures of Ordinal Association

of d is the now familiar quantity S. The computing formulas for d_{yx} and d_{xy} are

(Formula 9.9)
$$d_{yx} = \frac{S}{\frac{1}{2}(N^2 - \Sigma F_x^2)}$$

(Formula 9.10)
$$d_{xy} = \frac{S}{\frac{1}{2}(N^2 - F_y^2)}$$

where F_x and F_y are the marginal (that is, column or row) totals of the X and Y variables. Let us compute d_{yx} and d_{xy} for the data from Table 9.5.

$$d_{xy} = \frac{274 - 129}{\frac{1}{2}[40^2 - (10^2 + 9^2 + 12^2 + 9^2)]}$$

$$= \frac{145}{\frac{1}{2}(1600 - 406)} = \frac{145}{597}$$

$$= +0.24$$

$$d_{xy} = \frac{274 - 129}{\frac{1}{2}[40^2 - (14^2 + 16^2 + 10^2)]}$$

$$= \frac{145}{\frac{1}{2}(1600 - 552)} = \frac{145}{524}$$

$$= +0.28$$

Somers' d does not have a distinct PRE interpretation. Otherwise, the interpretation of d is analogous to that of Gamma. Indeed, the interpretations of all six measures discussed thus far (G, τ_a, τ_b, τ_c, d_{yx} and d_{xy}) are similar in that all are based on the logic of pair-by-pair comparison. The six measures differ in the manner in which tied pairs are treated. *Gamma completely eliminates all tied pairs*, whether tied on the independent variable, the dependent variable or both. *Tau-a includes all tied pairs. Tau-b* (and, by modification, *Tau-c*) treats all pairs as if there were complete mutual association, and *excludes all tied pairs.* Somers' d treats all pairs as does Gamma, but *excludes all pairs which are tied on the independent variable.* A summary of these six measures is presented in Figure 9.4.

The decision as to which measure should be used is not an easy one to make. Costner (1965) has argued that, because of its clear PRE interpretation, Gamma is always the preferred measure. But Gamma does not measure mutual association, nor does it statistically distinguish between the independent and dependent variables. If we wish to measure mutual association, we may prefer one of the Tau measures, but the interpretation of Tau (except in limited circumstances) is not as clear as that of Gamma. Somers' *d* does give us an asymmetric measure, but one which lacks a clear conceptual interpretation (except in a 2 × 2 table, where *d* is analogous to the percentage difference. See Somers, 1962).

testing for significance of gamma, tau and d

All of the measures described above are subject to tests of statistical significance. More properly, it is not the measures themselves which are subject to test, but the value of S. Whether we are ultimately interested in Gamma, Tau or *d*, it is essential that we first compute the value of S, and since every cross classification table has only one value of S, we need concern ourselves with only a single test of significance. A test for the significance of S is, indirectly, a test for the significance of Gamma, Tau and *d*.

The logic of this test involves the determination of the sampling distribution of S. From this, we compute the probability that we will observe any given value of S. If the number of cases involved is small (if $N \leq 10$), the procedure is very simple. When N is above 10, the procedure becomes a bit complicated.

Kendall (1962) has prepared a table which enables us to directly determine the probability of observing a given value of S when $N \leq 10$. This table is reproduced in Appendix Table G. To use this table, simply compute $S = (n_s - n_d)$ and enter the table for the given values of S and N. The table value is the exact probability of obtaining the observed value (or a greater value) of S under a one-tail test. (For a two-tail test, proceed as above, but *double* the probability values in the table.) For example, in Table 9.1(c), we computed a value of S = 6. With N = 5, the one-tailed probability of observing a value of $S \geq 6$ is 0.117. If we had specified a level of $\alpha = .05$, the result of this test would lead us to accept (or more accurately, we would fail to reject) the null hypothesis. We would conclude that the pattern of association observed in Table 9.1(c) is a pattern which could occur "by chance." (For a two-tail test, the probability of observing a value of $S \geq 6$ is 0.234.)

DETERMINING THE SIGNIFICANCE OF S WHEN $N \leq 10$

quick quiz
9.3

With N = 8, what is the probability (one-tail test) of observing a value of S = 8? What is the probability for a two-tail test?

Kendall (1962) has shown that when N $\geq$ 10 the sampling distribution of S is approximately normal with a mean S = 0 and a standard deviation of $\sigma_s = \sqrt{(\frac{1}{18})N(N-1)(2N+5)}$. (This last value, whose derivation need not concern us, is technically correct only when no ties exist. Because such a situation rarely occurs, a necessary correction, described below, must be made for σ_s whenever the number of ties is not negligible.) Because we have a close approximation to the normal curve, we can test for the significance of S by using z-scores.

$$z = \frac{S - \bar{S}}{\sigma_\text{B}} = \frac{S - 0}{\sigma_\text{B}} = \frac{S}{\sigma_\text{B}}$$

The above statistic tests the null hypothesis that S = 0; in other words, we are testing a hypothesis of no association.

Because the distribution of S is finite and discrete, while the normal distribution is infinite and continuous, it is necessary to correct S and σ_s. (This is analogous to Yates' correction for Chi-square.) Freeman (1965) has provided us with the following procedures for estimating the corrected values of S (called $\hat{S}$) and σ_s (called $\sigma_{\hat{s}}$). These are

(Formula 9.11)

$$\hat{S} = |S| - \frac{N}{2(r-1)(c-1)}$$

where |S| is the absolute value of S; N is the number of cases; and r and c are the number of rows and columns.

(Formula 9.12)

$$\sigma_{\hat{s}} = \sqrt{\frac{R_2 C_2}{N-1} - \frac{R_2 C_3 + R_3 C_2}{N(N-1)} + \frac{R_3 C_3}{N(N-1)(N-2)}}$$

Where R_2 (and C_2) is the *sum* of the products of the row (column) totals taken two at a time; and R_3 (and C_3) is the *sum* of the products of the row (column) totals taken three at a time. To test the significance of S, we compute a z-score using the corrected values $\hat{S}$ and $\sigma_{\hat{s}}$.

(Formula 9.13)

$$z = \frac{\hat{S}}{\sigma_{\hat{s}}}$$

As an example, let us return to the data from Table 9.5.

1. Null Hypothesis (H$_o$): S — 0. Or, there is no association between the two variables.
2. Let α = .05, one-tail test.
3. Decision Rule: Reject H$_o$ if z $\leq$ 1.64; do not reject H$_o$ if z > 1.64.

The computation of $\hat{S}$ and $\sigma_{\hat{s}}$ is as follows. (See Table 9.6 for figures.)

$$\hat{S} = 145 - \frac{40}{2(2)(3)} = 145 - \frac{40}{12} = 145 - 3.33$$

$$= 141.67$$

$$\sigma_{\hat{s}} = \sqrt{\frac{(524)(597)}{39} - \frac{(524)(3942) + (597)(2240)}{40(39)} + \frac{(2240)(3942)}{40(39)(38)}}$$

$$= \sqrt{8021.23 - 2181.34 + 148.96}$$

$$= \sqrt{5988.85}$$

$$= 77.39$$

and

$$z = \frac{141.67}{77.39} = 1.83$$

Because our computed value of z exceeds the critical value from the table ($1.83 > 1.64$), we reject the null hypothesis (which states that there is no association). By extension, we can conclude that the two variables are related.

spearman's rank-order correlation coefficient, rho

In the final section of this chapter, we focus on the oldest of the frequently used measures of ordinal association, Spearman's rank-order correlation coefficient, Rho (ρ), and its associated value, Rho-square (ρ^2). Rho is a measure of the extent to which two sets of ranks are in agreement or disagreement with each other. Rho may take on values between 0.00 (indicating no rank-order correlation) and ± 1.00 (indicating perfect association of ranks).

The underlying logic of Rho centers on the differences between ranks. Suppose we have the rankings as described in Table 9.2 (p. 139). Clearly, for (a), we want a measure which yields a coefficient of $+1.00$; for (b) we want a measure which yields a coefficient of -1.00; and for (c), we want a measure which yields an intermediate value, one which expresses the amount of agreement or disagreement between the two sets of ranks. Spearman's Rho gives us such a value. For computation purposes, Rho is defined as

$$\rho = 1 - \left(\frac{6 \Sigma D^2}{N(N^2 - 1)} \right)$$

(Formula 9.14)

6	3	3	2	14
3	3	7	3	16
1	3	2	4	10
10	9	12	9	40

$S = n_s - n_d = 274 - 129 = 145$
$N = 40$
$r = 3$
$c = 4$

$R_2 = 14(16) + 14(10) + 16(10)$
$\quad = 224 + 140 + 160$
$\quad = 524$

$R_3 = 14(16)(10)$
$\quad = 2240$

$C_2 = 10(9) + 10(12) + 10(9)\ 9(12) + 9(9) + 12(9)$
$\quad = 90 + 120 + 90 + 180 + 81 + 108$
$\quad = 597$

$C_3 = 10(9)(12) + 10(9)(9) + 10(12)(9) + 9(12)(9)$
$\quad = 1080 + 810 + 1080 + 972$
$\quad = 3942$

where D is the difference between ranks assigned to an object. For the first two examples given in Table 9.2:

(a)

X Rank	Y Rank	D	D^2
1	1	0	0
2	2	0	0
3	3	0	0
4	4	0	0
5	5	0	0
			$\Sigma D^2 = 0$

$\rho = 1 - \dfrac{6(0)}{5(24)}$
$\quad = 1 - 0$
$\quad = +1.00$

(b)

X Rank	Y Rank	D	D^2
1	5	-4	16
2	4	-2	4
3	3	0	0
4	2	2	4
5	1	4	16
			$\Sigma D^2 = 40$

$\rho = 1 - \dfrac{6(24)}{5(24)}$
$\quad = 1 - \dfrac{240}{120} = 1 - 2$
$\quad = -1.00$

quick quiz
9.4

For Table 9.2(c), what is the value of Rho?
(c) X Rank: 1 2 3 4 5
     Y Rank: 1 2 4 5 3

TIED RANKS   It occasionally happens that a judge cannot distinguish between two objects, and declares that the objects are tied at some rank. In such cases, the common procedure is to assign to each object the mean value of the tied ranks. Suppose eight objects are ranked by two judges. Judge A cannot decide which two objects belong in the sixth and seventh places; Judge B cannot decide which three belong in the second, third and fourth places. Table 9.7 shows these rankings. For Judge X, objects VI and VII are assigned the mean of ranks 6 and 7; for Judge Y, objects II, V, and VII are assigned the mean of ranks 2, 3, and 4, $(2 + 3 + 4)/3 = 3$. Rho is then computed in the usual fashion, and yields a value of $+0.64$.

Note that when the number of ties is relatively large, the value of Rho becomes inflated. Kendall (1962:32) has described a procedure to correct this.

Rho is like Chi-square in that it has no inherently logical meaning, except to say that as the value of Rho moves from zero to unity, there is evidence of increasing association. However, if we square the value of Rho and obtain Rho-square, we have a measure which has a PRE interpretation.

Rho-square is a symmetric measure of one-way association for ranked data. Because it can fit the general formula,

$$\text{PRE} = \frac{E_1 - E_2}{E_1},$$

it is a proportional reduction in error measure. We have already seen that every PRE measure is derived from the errors associated with two prediction rules. For Rho-square, the first prediction rule, which yields E_1, uses only knowledge of the dependent variable.

Prediction Rule 1 (ρ^2): To predict the Y-rank for a given object, use the mean of all ranks on Y. In symbols, predict $R_y = \overline{R}_y$.

If N items are being ranked, the mean rank, $\overline{R}_y$, is defined as the sum of all ranks divided by N, and can be easily computed as

table 9.7   *computing ρ with tied ranks*

OBJECT	JUDGE X	JUDGE Y	D	D²	
I	1	1	0	0	
II	2	3	−1	1	$\rho = 1 - \dfrac{6(30.5)}{8(8^2 - 1)}$
III	3	5	−2	4	
IV	4	7	−3	9	
V	5	3	2	4	$= 1 - \dfrac{183}{504}$
VI	6.5	6	0.5	0.25	
VII	6.5	3	3.5	12.25	$= 1 - .36$
VIII	8	8	0	0	$= +0.64$
			0	$30.50 = \Sigma D^2$	

$$\overline{R}_y = \frac{N + 1}{2}$$

If we apply Rule 1 to Table 9.8 we shall predict a value of $\overline{R}_y = (5 + 1)/2$ = 3 for each object being ranked on Y.

The second prediction rule, which yields E_2, uses knowledge of the X ranks (R_x) to predict the Y ranks. We obtain the predicted value of rank $Y(R_y)$ from a formula which incorporates the computed value of Rho.

Prediction Rule 2 (ρ^2): Predict a value for Y, $\hat{R}_y$, such that

$$\hat{R}_y = (R_x)(\rho) + \frac{N + 1}{2}(1 - \rho)$$

For Rho-square, the definition of error is slightly different from other error definitions we have already seen. *Error is defined in terms of square deviations:* $E_1 = (R_y - \overline{R}_y)^2$ and $E_2 = (R_y - \hat{R}_y)^2$. The computing formulas for E_1 and E_2 are

(Formula 9.16)

$$E_1 = \frac{N(N^2 - 1)}{12}$$

(Formula 9.17)

$$E_2 = \frac{N(N^2 - 1)}{12}(1 - \rho^2)$$

Why do we use the squared deviations? One reason is that the sum of the deviations, $(R_y - \overline{R}_y)$ and $(R_y - \hat{R}_y)$ will always be zero, since some deviations are positive and others are negative, and the two cancel each other. To eliminate this difficulty, we square each error value before summing. (This procedure is analogous to that used in computing the

table 9.8   computation of E_1 and E_2 for ρ^2

RANK OF X = (R_x)	RANK OF Y = (R_y)	$\overline{R}_y$*	$(R_y - \overline{R}_y)$	$(R_y - \overline{R}_y)^2$	$\hat{R}_y$†	$(R_y - \hat{R}_y)$	$(R_y - \hat{R}_y)^2$
1	1	3	−2	4	1.6	−0.6	0.36
2	2	3	−1	1	2.3	−0.3	0.09
3	4	3	1	1	3.0	1.0	1.00
4	5	3	2	4	3.7	1.3	1.69
5	3	3	0	0	4.4	−1.4	1.96
			0	$E_1 = 10$		0.0	$E_2 = 5.10$

$$\rho^2 = \frac{E_1 - E_2}{E_1} = \frac{10 - 5.10}{10} = \frac{4.90}{10} = 0.49$$

*$\overline{R}_y = (N + 1)/2 = 6/2 = 3$
†$\hat{R}_y = (R_x)(\rho) + (N + 1)/2(1 - \rho) = (R_x)(0.7) + (3)(0.3) = .7R_x + 0.9$

standard deviation, in which deviations from the mean were squared, then summed. See Chapter 4.)

The computing formulas for E_1 and E_2 should be used in preference to the "logical" formulas for two reasons: (1) the computing formulas are far easier to use, and (2) the logical formulas do not adequately handle tied ranks.

While Rho-square has a PRE interpretation, it is not an adequate measure of the *direction* of association; that is, it does not tell us whether a pattern of association is direct (or positive) or inverse (or negative). However, we can get such information from Rho, which can be positive, zero, or negative.

Finally we note that it is possible to determine Rho-square not through the PRE procedures just described, but by simply computing the value of Rho and squaring. There is no reason why you should not use the simpler computing procedure as long as you understand that Rho and Rho-square are two different statistics with two different interpretations.

Appendix Table H contains critical values for testing the significance of Rho. As an example of its use, let us use the data from Table 9.8. We first state our null hypothesis and decision rules. (For Rho, df (N − 2), where N is the number of pairs.)

TESTING FOR THE SIGNIFICANCE OF RHO

1. *Null Hypothesis* (H_o): $\rho = 0$. Or, there is no association between the two sets of ranks.
2. Let $\alpha = .05$, one-tail test.
3. *Decision Rule:* If the observed value of Rho equals or exceeds the table value (.900), reject H_o; if the observed value is less than the table value, do not reject H_o.

Our computed value of Rho is 0.70, which is less than the critical value from the table. Therefore, we do not reject H_o. A reasonable conclusion is that this pattern of association could occur "by chance" (where the level of "chance" is defined by $\alpha = .05$).

quick quiz
9.5

> For Table 9.7, test for the significance of Rho. Let $\alpha = .01$, one-tail test.

essential statistics for social research

important terms to know

Pair-by-pair comparison	Tau-a (τ_a)
Similar pair	Tau-b (τ_b)
Dissimilar pair	Tau-c (τ_c)
Tied pair	d_{yx} and d_{xy}
Yule's Q	Spearman's Rho (ρ)
	Rho-square (ρ^2)

suggested readings

Blalock (1972: 415–426); Costner (1965); Siegel (1956: 202–223); Freeman (1965: 79–88, 162–175); Goodman and Kruskal (1954; 1959; 1963); Kendall (1962); Mueller, Schuessler and Costner (1970: 267–292); Mendenhall, Ott and Larson (1974: 262–276); Somers (1962).

answer section

QUICK QUIZ 9.1

$n_s = 1100$
$n_d = 2200$

$$G = \frac{S}{n_s + n_d} = \frac{-1100}{1100 + 2200}$$

$S = n_s - n_d$
$\quad = 1100 - 2200$
$\quad = -1100$

$$= \frac{-1100}{3300}$$

$$= -.33$$

QUICK QUIZ 9.2 We first determine the total number of possible pairs as $\frac{1}{2}N(N - 1) = \frac{1}{2}(183)(182) = 16653$, and then eliminate the tied pairs. The number of tied pairs is $\frac{1}{2}(48)(47) + \frac{1}{2}(70)(69) + \frac{1}{2}(65)(64) = 1128 + 2415 + 2080 = 5623$. Our solution, therefore, is $16653 - 5623 = 11030$.

QUICK QUIZ 9.3 For a one-tail test, p = 0.199; for a two-tail test, p = 0.398

QUICK QUIZ 9.4 $\Sigma D^2 = 6; \rho = 1 - \dfrac{6(6)}{5(24)} = +0.70$

QUICK QUIZ 9.5 With $\alpha = .01$, one-tail test and N = 8, the critical value of Rho is .833. Since our observed value is less than the critical value, we do not reject H_o.

measuring association between two interval level variables

In this chapter we will devote our attention almost exclusively to two statistical measures of association, the Pearson product-moment correlation coefficient, r, and its associated value, r^2, the coefficient of determination. In Chapters 8 and 9 we encountered several statistics, each of which is, in the proper circumstances, an appropriate measure of association for nominal or ordinal level data. However, this diversity of available measures means that one of our data analysis problems will be to select the "best" statistic to use. When working with interval (or ratio) level data, our problem is greatly minimized by the fact that the Pearson r, or r^2, is the almost universal choice as *the* measure of association. (An exception to this statement will be made at the end of this chapter.) The Pearson r is also of great importance because it is the basis of many advanced statistical techniques which are used in sociological analysis. We will not discuss these techniques, such as path analysis, in this book, but an understanding of r will at least enable you to read more advanced research literature with increased comprehension.

One of the important distinctions between interval level measurement and measurement at lower levels (nominal and ordinal) concerns the nature of prediction errors. With the lower levels of measurement, an error is simply an error: we cannot determine the magnitude of error. If we recall the hypothetical example used in describing lambda (p. 124), our prediction of delinquency based on club background resulted in either a correct prediction or an incorrect prediction (error); for any given case, we were either right or wrong. We could not measure the

10

magnitude of error because of the nature of nominal level measurement. Similarly, with ordinal measures, such as Gamma, we predicted pairs of data to be either similar or dissimilar; again, such predictions were either right or wrong, with no information as to *how* wrong an error might be. We could not determine the magnitude of error because of the nature of ordinal measurement. But because of the properties of interval level measurement, the Pearson r *can* be used to tell *how much* change in one variable can be expected, given a set amount of change in the other variable. It is in this sense that r provides us with an example of the fifth way of viewing association, as described in Chapter 8 (p. 111). The Pearson r describes the extent to which an increase or decrease in one variable is accompanied by an increase or decrease in the other. In the history of statistics, this notion is usually referred to not as association, but as *correlation* or as *linear regression*.

The Pearson r and r^2 are two very useful and versatile statistics. Each has several important interpretations, and each interpretation focuses on a different aspect of the data. We shall begin our discussion with a PRE interpretation of r^2.

the pearson r^2 as a pre measure

Following the general logic of PRE measures of association, we wish to develop two measures of error, one based on a prediction rule which uses only information about the dependent variable, and one based on a prediction rule which uses information about the independent variable.

We shall use an overly simplified example to illustrate the PRE interpretation of r^2. Suppose five students are to take a quiz in their statistics course. Each spends the amount of time studying, and receives the quiz grade indicated in Table 10.1.

Since both variables are interval or ratio measures, the Pearson r, or r^2, is an appropriate measure of association. Upon simple inspection of the data we can see that as study time increases, the quiz grade also tends to increase. We also note that this tendency is not perfect: student D, who studied three hours, received a lower grade than student C, who studied only two hours.

It is reasonably clear that the dependent variable is the Y-variable, quiz grade. If we know nothing about these data except the distribution of grades, what would be our best guess of the grade received by any individual? It should be clear by now that with interval data, the best guess for any individual score in a distribution is the mean of the distribution. The mean is the best guess in the sense that it is the mean which minimizes the sum of squared deviations. (See Chapter 4 for a review of this concept.) This line of thought leads us to our first PRE prediction rule for r^2.

table 10.1 **hours studied and quiz scores**

STUDENT	HOURS STUDIED (X)	QUIZ SCORE (Y)
A	0	4
B	1	6
C	2	8
D	3	7
E	4	10

Prediction Rule 1 (r^2): To predict a value of the dependent variable, use its mean.

With our data we are interested in predicting the quiz scores. The quiz score variable has been designated as the Y-variable, so we must find the value of $\overline{Y}$, the mean of Y. In Table 10.1, we see that $\overline{Y} = 7$.

We measure E_1, the error resulting from the application of Prediction Rule 1, by finding the deviation of observed Y-scores; this value is the deviation score, y, or $Y - \overline{Y}$. But since the sum of deviation scores about a mean will always equal zero, we must *square* the deviation scores, and sum these squared deviations, thus obtaining $y^2 = (Y - \overline{Y})^2$.

(Formula 10.1)
$$E_1 = \Sigma (Y - \overline{Y})^2 = \Sigma y^2$$

From Table 10.2 we see that $E_1 = 20$.

Prediction Rule 2 and computation of E_2 are more complex. Let us approach it slowly, visually. In Figure 10.1, we have plotted the X and Y scores as a coordinate system. If we look at this graph we can see that there is a crude pattern of positive association. We can also "see" how E_1 was determined, for we can see that there is a certain amount of distance, or deviation, which is equal to $(Y - \overline{Y}) = y$, between any Y value and $\overline{Y}$. The mean of Y is indicated by the dashed line, and the deviations are indicated by brackets. When these distances (that is, deviations from the mean) are squared and summed, we have E_1. We might now ask: is there some line other than $\overline{Y}$ which would result in even *less* error than that which we have in Figure 10.1?

table 10.2 **calculation of E_1**

Y	$\overline{Y}$	$y = Y - \overline{Y}$	y^2
4	7	-3	9
6	7	-1	1
8	7	1	1
7	7	0	0
10	7	3	9
35	35	0	$20 = E_1$

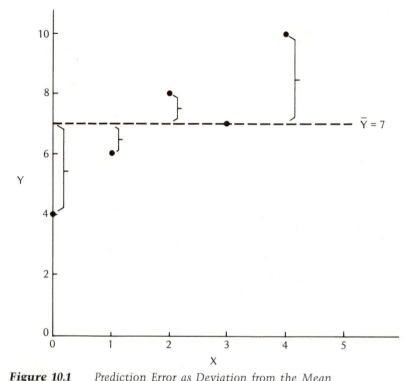

Figure 10.1   *Prediction Error as Deviation from the Mean*
• *indicates an observed value*
— — — *indicates the mean of Y, a predicted value*
} *indicates the difference between the observed and predicted values* $(Y - \overline{Y})$.
The sum of these distances squared, $\Sigma (Y - \overline{Y})^2$, *is* E_1.

If we can now introduce information about the independent (X) variable, we will be able to define a "best fitting" straight line (*regression* line), a line which minimizes the sum of squared deviations. Figure 10.2 anticipates part of the discussion yet to come, and illustrates the best-fitting straight line for our data. Where does this line come from?

Any straight line can be defined by the equation

$$\hat{Y} = a_{yx} + b_{yx}X$$ (*Formula 10.2*)

where $\hat{Y}$ is the predicted value of Y; a_{yx} is the *Y-intercept*, or point where the line crosses the Y-axis; and b_{yx} is the *slope* of the line. It is the slope of the line which tells us how much of a change in Y will occur as a result of change in X. To be more specific, for every unit of change in X, there will be bX change in Y. Formula 10.3 defines the slope of the regression line. (The derivation of this formula is beyond the scope of the present discussion.)

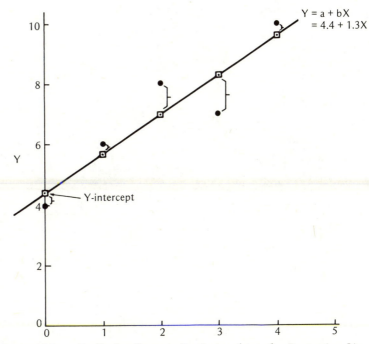

Figure 10.2 *Prediction Error as Deviation from the Regression Line*
● *indicates an observed value*
◧ *indicates a predicted value derived from the "best-fitting straight line"*
} *indicates the difference between observed and predicted values* $(Y - \hat{Y})$.
The sum of these distances squared, $\Sigma(Y - \hat{Y})^2$, *is* E_1.

(*Formula 10.3*)
$$b_{yx} = \frac{\Sigma(X - \overline{X})(Y - \overline{Y})}{(X - \overline{X})^2} = \frac{N(\Sigma XY) - (\Sigma X)(\Sigma Y)}{N(\Sigma X^2) - (\Sigma X)^2}$$

From Table 10.3 (p. 166) we see that, for our data, $b_{yx} = 1.3$. We can now define the Y-intercept as

(*Formula 10.4*)
$$a_{yx} = \overline{Y} - b\overline{X}$$

For our data, $a_{yx} = 4.4$.

Now that we have the values of a and b we can solve the straight line equation for any value of X. We use the formula

$$\hat{Y} = 4.4 + 1.3X$$

to obtain the Y values found in Table 10.4 (p. 166), and by using these values, we plotted the straight line in Figure 10.2.

table 10.3   calculation of a_{yx} and b_{yx}

X	Y	X²	Y²	XY
0	4	0	16	0
1	6	1	36	6
2	8	4	64	16
3	7	9	49	21
4	10	16	100	40
10	35	30	265	83

$$\overline{X} = 2 \qquad \overline{Y} = 7$$

$$b_{yx} = \frac{5(83) - 10(35)}{5(30) - 10^2}$$

$$= \frac{415 - 350}{150 - 100} = \frac{65}{50}$$

$$= 1.3$$

$$a_{yx} = 7 - (1.3)(2)$$

$$= 7 - 2.6$$

$$= 4.4$$

Prediction Rule 2 (r^2): To predict any value of Y, use the straight-line equation, $\hat{Y} = a + bX$.

As with E_1, E_2 is defined in terms of squared deviations of the observed scores of Y from the predicted values of Y.

$$E_2 = (Y - \hat{Y})^2 \qquad \text{(Formula 10.5)}$$

From Table 10.4 we see that E_2 is 3.10. We can now compute r^2 as a PRE measure of association.

$$r^2 = \frac{E_1 - E_2}{E_1} = \frac{20 - 3.10}{20} = \frac{16.90}{20} = 0.84$$

table 10.4   calculation of $\hat{Y}$ and E_2

X	Y	$\hat{Y} = 4.4 + 1.3X$	$(Y - \hat{Y})$	$(Y - \hat{Y})^2$
0	4	4.4	−0.4	0.16
1	6	5.7	0.3	0.09
2	8	7.0	1.0	1.00
3	7	8.3	−1.3	1.69
4	10	9.6	0.4	0.16
10	35	35	0.0	3.10 = E_2

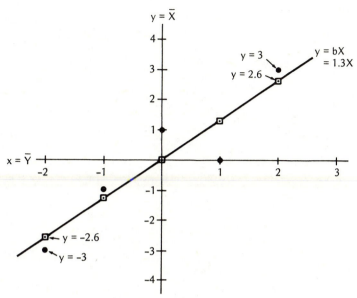

Figure 10.3   *Using Deviation Scores*

For computational purposes, it is usually more convenient to think of data not in terms of raw scores, but in terms of deviation scores. Figure 10.3 presents our data in deviation format. Note that the general configuration of Figure 10.3 is identical with that of Figure 10.2, except that the X axis has shifted to $\overline{X}$ and the Y axis is now $\overline{Y}$.

quick quiz
10.1

For the following data, determine the values of a_{yx} and b_{yx}.

X	Y
2	6
3	8
4	7

One notable consequence of expressing the data as deviation scores is that the y-intercept, or a_{yx}, becomes 0; as a result, the straight line equation for deviation scores is

(Formula 10.6) $\hat{y} = b_{yx}x$

table 10.5   deviation scores

X	Y	x	y	x^2	y^2	xy	$\hat{y} = bx$	$\hat{y}^2$
0	4	−2	−3	4	9	6	−2.6	6.76
1	6	−1	−1	1	1	1	−1.3	1.69
2	8	0	1	0	1	0	0.0	0.00
3	7	1	0	1	0	0	1.3	1.69
4	10	2	3	4	9	6	2.6	6.76
10	35	0	0	10	20	13	0.0	16.90

$$a_{yx} = 0$$

$$b_{xy} = \frac{13}{10} = 1.3$$

The computing formula for b_{yx} can be expressed as

$$b_{yx} = \frac{\Sigma xy}{\Sigma x^2} \qquad \text{(Formula 10.7)}$$

From Table 10.5 we see that $b_{yx} = 1.3$, which is, of course, identical to the value computed from raw scores (Table 10.3). With our scores now expressed in deviation form, we can calculate values for $\hat{y}$ and $\hat{y}^2$, and, thereby, utilize a more direct computing formula for r^2.

$$r_{yx}^{\,2} = \frac{\Sigma \hat{y}^2}{\Sigma y^2}$$

Again using Table 10.5, we first see that $\Sigma y^2 = 20$ and $\Sigma \hat{y}^2 = 16.90$. This value is identical with the value of r^2 computed earlier. It represents the proportional amount by which we reduce error when we shift from using the mean of Y to predict Y to using the best-fitting straight line as a predictor of Y, when error is defined in terms of squared deviations.

There is another way of viewing r^2 which we must mention. Consider $E_1 = \Sigma(Y - \overline{Y})^2 = \Sigma y^2$ to be the *total variation in Y;* that is, let E_1 represent the sum (or total) of the squared deviations (or variation) from the mean of Y. Then $E_2 = \Sigma(Y - Y)^2 = \Sigma \hat{y}^2$ is the amount of *unexplained variation* in Y; it is the amount that is *not* "explained" by our information concerning the independent variable, X. Viewed in this light

$$r^2 = \frac{\text{Total Variation} - \text{Unexplained Variation}}{\text{Total Variation}}$$

$$= \frac{\text{Explained Variation}}{\text{Total Variation}}$$

This conceptualization of r^2 as a *ratio of explained to total variation* is important for an understanding of many advanced statistical techniques which will not be examined in this book. However, make a mental note of this interpretation, for you will surely encounter it as you read through the sociological literature, and you will then have at least a simple intuitive idea of what is being discussed.

the pearson r

Despite the logical PRE interpretation and the logical "explained variation" interpretation of r^2, r is the more frequently used measure of association. One reason for this is the purely historical fact that early statisticians worked with r, not with r^2. Another reason is that r^2 varies between 0 and +1 and, therefore, does not indicate the *direction* of any relationship; from r^2 we cannot determine whether a relationship is positive or negative.

To understand the meaning of r, let us use the same set of data with which we have been working. But let us transform these data into *standard scores* (that is, z-scores, as described on pp. 52–55). To do this, we first express each raw score as a deviation score, then divide the deviation score by the standard deviation. For our data, these computations are presented in Table 10.6. Next we compute the cross-products of the z-scores and sum. If we divide this sum by N, the number of cases, we will have computed the *mean* of the z-score cross-products. *This value is the Pearson r; it is also the slope of the best-fitting straight line when data are recorded as standard scores.* The computing formula for this value is

(Formula 10.8)

$$r_{yx} = \frac{\Sigma (z_x z_y)}{N}$$

For our data, r = 4.62/5 = .92.

table 10.6   **standard scores as a basis of calculating the pearson r**

x	y	x^2	y^2	$z_z = x/\sigma_z$	$Zy = y/\sigma_y$	$Zx\ Zy$
−2	−3	4	9	−1.42	−1.50	2.13
−1	−1	1	1	−0.71	−0.50	0.36
0	1	0	1	0.00	0.50	0.00
1	0	1	0	0.71	0.00	0.00
2	3	4	9	1.42	1.50	2.13
0	0	10	20	0.00	0.00	4.62

$$\sigma_x = \sqrt{\Sigma x^2/N} \qquad \sigma_y = \sqrt{\Sigma y^2/N}$$
$$= \sqrt{10/5} \qquad\qquad = \sqrt{20/5}$$
$$= \sqrt{2} \qquad\qquad\quad = \sqrt{4}$$
$$= 1.41 \qquad\qquad\quad = 2.00$$

table 10.7   calculation of $\hat{Z}y$

z_z	$\hat{z}_y = rz_z$
-1.42	-1.31
-0.71	-0.65
0.00	0.00
0.71	0.65
1.42	1.31
---------	---------
1.00	0.92
-2.00	-1.84
2.50	2.30
-1.08	$-.99$

From the above discussion you can perhaps see why the full technical designation of r is "the Pearson product-moment correlation coefficient." (In mathematics, a *moment* can be a mean; the *product* refers to the multiplication of z-scores; and it was Karl Pearson who pioneered the development of this correlation coefficient.) With this understanding we can offer the following interpretation of r: *it is the mean change in Y for every unit of change in X, when data are expressed as standard scores.* Let us apply this interpretation to our data. The value of r = .92 means that, for every *standard unit* (z-score unit) of increase or decrease in Y, there is .92 standard units of increase or decrease in X. If X increases by $1\sigma_x$, Y increases by $.92\sigma_y$; if X decreases by $2\sigma_x$, y decreases by $2(.92)\sigma_y$. Consequently, if we can express any X score as a standard score or z-score, we should be able to predict a Y score expressed in its standard form. Just as we earlier were able to compute Y on the basis of our knowledge of X, we can now predict a value of $\hat{z}_y$, given knowledge of z_x. We do this by the formula

$$\hat{z}_y = r(z_x)$$

(Formula 10.9)

For our data, Table 10.7 provides the computational details, and the results are presented graphically in Figure 10.4.

computing formulas

We did not present the above discussion of r and r^2 for the purpose of computing these statistics. Rather we tried to logically demonstrate the meanings of r and r^2. Once these meanings are understood, we can move on to simpler and more direct procedures for computing this measure of

UNGROUPED DATA

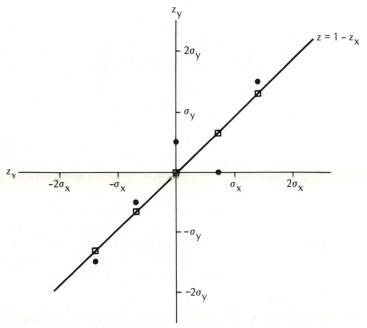

Figure 10.4   *Using z-scores*

association. Specifically, we offer the following formulas for computing r from ungrouped data.

(Formula 10.10)
$$r_{yx} = \frac{\Sigma\, xy}{\sqrt{\Sigma\, x^2\, \Sigma\, y^2}}$$

(Formula 10.11)
$$r_{yx} = \frac{N\Sigma\, XY - \Sigma\, X\, \Sigma\, Y}{\sqrt{[N\Sigma\, X^2 - (\Sigma\, X)^2][N\Sigma\, Y^2 - (\Sigma\, Y)^2]}}$$

Table 10.5 contains the necessary information to compute r using Formula 10.10.

$$r = \frac{13}{\sqrt{(20)(10)}} = \frac{13}{\sqrt{200}} = \frac{13}{14.14}$$
$$= .92$$

And Table 10.3 provides the necessary information to compute r using Formula 10.11.

$$r = \frac{5(83) - 10(35)}{\sqrt{[5(30) - 10^2][5(265) - 35^2]}}$$

$$r = \frac{415 - 350}{\sqrt{(150 - 100)(1325 - 1225)}}$$

$$= \frac{65}{\sqrt{50(100)}} = \frac{65}{70.71}$$

$$= .92$$

As is evident, both computing formulas yield a value of r which are identical to each other and to the value computed using z-score cross-products (p. 169).

It should be pointed out that although Formula 10.11 *looks* forbidding, it provides probably the easiest method of computing r for ungrouped data. All it requires is the computation of five sums: ΣX, ΣY, ΣX^2, ΣY^2 and ΣXY. In using this formula, do not worry about deviations, standard scores, cross-products, and the like; the raw data quickly and accurately yield the value of r.

We should also note that there is no similar simple, direct computing formula for r^2. We may, however, easily determine r^2 by computing r (using any of the above methods) and squaring. For our data $(.92)^2 = .8467 = r^2$. Within rounding error, this value is identical to the value of r^2 computed earlier (p. 166).

For the data below, compute r and r^2.

X	Y
2	5
3	2
4	3
7	-2

GROUPED DATA

(NOTE: This section can be considered optional. Only rarely will you need to compute r from grouped data. In general, if the number of cases is large enough to require grouping, a computer is used. However, the procedure for grouped data will be presented both to illustrate the method and to provide the computational tools for those instances in which a computer is not readily available.)

We saw in Chapter 3 that the procedure for computing the mean of a set of grouped data was essentially the same as the procedure for computing the mean of ungrouped data, with two exceptions: (1) the *frequency* of any score had to be accounted for, and (2) an assumption had to be made that all scores within a class interval were located at the midpoint of that interval. In computing r for grouped data, the procedure and exceptions will be analogous. Note that Formula 10.12, below, is essentially the same as Formula 10.11 except that (1) the frequency of scores is accounted for—thus each deviation score is multiplied by some frequency, f; and (2) the raw scores X and Y are replaced with the deviation scores x' and y' which represent midpoints of class intervals.

The computing formula for r, with grouped data, and using deviation scores is

(*Formula 10.12*)

$$r = \frac{N\,\Sigma(fx'y') - \Sigma(fx')\,\Sigma(fy')}{\sqrt{[N\,\Sigma(fx'^2) - (\Sigma\,fx')^2]\,[N\,\Sigma(fy'^2) - (\Sigma\,fy')^2]}}$$

Although this is indeed a complicated-looking formula, it, like Formula 10.11, demands only five sums: $\Sigma\,fx'$, $\Sigma\,fy'$, $\Sigma\,fx'^2$, $\Sigma\,fy'^2$ and $\Sigma\,fx'y'$. (Note that fx'^2 is *not* the same as $(fx')^2$; fx'^2 can be more clearly expressed as $(f)(x')(x')$, which is *not* the same as $(fx')(fx')$.) All else in the computation is simple arithmetic manipulation.

We shall illustrate the application of Formula 10.12 with a set of hypothetical data. Suppose we tabulate the homicide rates and suicide rates for thirty medium-sized cities. These data are presented in their ungrouped and grouped form in Table 10.8 (p. 174).

First let us visually inspect the data. We do this most efficiently by means of a *scatterplot* of the X and Y scores (Figure 10.5, p. 175). On a graph we find the (X,Y) coordinate points. That is, for each of the thirty cities, we plot the homicide rate and the suicide rate as a single point. Most researchers will agree that a scatterplot is a useful device to use when preparing to assess correlation. A glance at Figure 10.5 immediately tells us that (1) the relationship between homicide rate (X) and suicide rate (Y) is *linear* (or rectilinear); that is, there is a tendency for the scatter points to fall along a straight line, as opposed to a curved line (Figure 10.6 illustrates other linear and *curvilinear* plots); and (2) the relationship is positive; that is, as the homicide rate increases, the suicide rate also increases. The first piece of information, that the relationship is linear, is vital, for the Pearson r is applicable *only* to data which are linear or reasonably close to being linear. If the data markedly depart from linearity, as in Figure 10.6(c) and 10.6(d), the Pearson r is *not* an appropriate measure of association (p. 176). (Instead, eta-square is used. See pp. 180–182.)

There is one other assumption which must be met before r can be properly and fully utilized: if we were to compute the variance (the

table 10.8   homicide and suicide rates

(a) UNGROUPED DATA

HOMICIDE RATE	SUICIDE RATE	HOMICIDE RATE	SUICIDE RATE
3	6	4	8
0	5	9	15
6	12	14	20
3	7	10	18
8	16	10	23
5	19	5	9
1	4	13	22
4	12	4	10
9	20	11	16
6	11	1	2
1	1	6	13
2	3	7	13
8	23	7	17
7	18	5	11
12	24	8	14

(b) GROUPED DATA

HOMICIDE RATE	F	SUICIDE RATE	F
0–2	5	0–4	4
3–5	8	5–9	5
6–8	9	10–14	8
9–11	5	15–19	7
12–14	3	20–24	6
	30		30

(c) JOINT FREQUENCIES

	HOMICIDE RATE					
SUICIDE RATE	0–2	3–5	6–8	9–11	12–14	
0–4	4	0	0	0	0	4
5–9	1	4	0	0	0	5
10–14	0	3	5	0	0	8
15–19	0	1	3	3	0	7
22–29	0	0	1	2	3	6
	5	8	9	5	3	30

standard deviation squared) for each of the class intervals within each variable, the variances for each variable should be similar in value. This property of equal class variances bears the technical label of *homoscedasticity*. A scatterplot can be used to give us a rough visual estimate of whether our data are homoscedastic (Figure 10.7, p. 177). If data are homoscedastic, the points will fall within a cigar shape as in 10.7(a) and 10.7(b); marked deviations from such a shape indicate heteroscedasticity as in 10.7(c), (d), and (e).

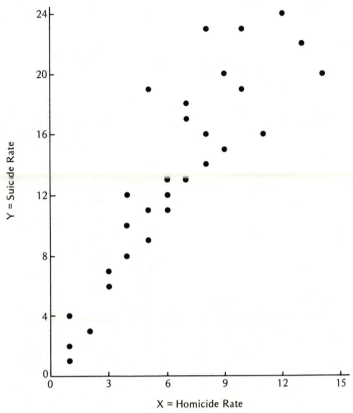

Figure 10.5   *Homicide and Suicide Rates*

(Note that we have now established *three critical assumptions* which must be met in order to properly use the Pearson r: (1) the data must be at the *interval level* of measurement; (2) the pattern of the relationship must be *linear*, that is, it must fall along a straight line; and (3) the data must be *homoscedastic*.)

To compute r for grouped data, we shall follow the procedure described by Mueller, Schuessler and Costner (1970) and use a correlation work table (Table 10.9, p. 178). (1) The central portion of this table contains as many rows and columns as there are class intervals of the X and Y variables. We arbitrarily divide our data into five intervals for the X variable (homicide rate) and five for the Y variable (suicide rate). We then clearly label each row and column. (2) We now enter the *joint frequencies* of X and Y into the appropriate cells. For example, we see in the upper-left cell that there are four cities which have a homicide rate between 0–2 and a suicide rate of 0–4; in the fourth row, third column, we find three cities which have a homicide rate between 6–8 and a

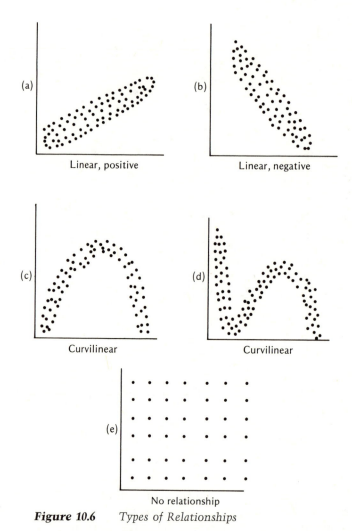

(a) Linear, positive

(b) Linear, negative

(c) Curvilinear

(d) Curvilinear

(e) No relationship

Figure 10.6   *Types of Relationships*

suicide rate between 15–19. (3) Next we sum the row and column frequencies, and enter these values as our first marginal frequencies. (4) We
record the adjusted deviation (from the mean) scores, x' and y'. Here
we follow the procedure described in Chapter 3 (p. 32). (5) We now
multiply frequency totals by adjusted deviation scores, obtaining fx'
and fy'. (6) We square x' and y', and multiply by the corresponding f to
obtain $f(x'^2)$ and $f(y'^2)$. (7) Now we must obtain the deviation cross-
products, x'y'. For each cell in the table, we find the corresponding values
of x' and y' and multiply them. We enter this value in the upper left
corner of each cell. For example, the cell in the second row, first column
has an x' value of -1 and a y' value of -2; the cross-product is, therefore, $(-2)(-1) = 2$. (8) Now we obtain fx'y' by multiplying each x'y'

essential statistics for social research

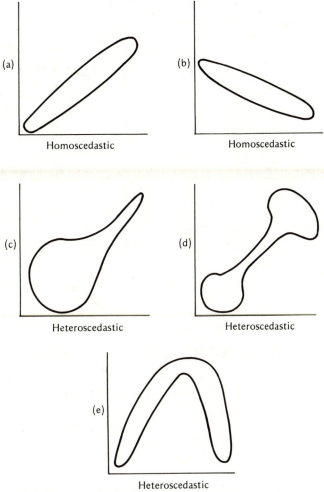

(a)

Homoscedastic

(b)

Homoscedastic

(c)

Heteroscedastic

(d)

Heteroscedastic

(e)

Heteroscedastic

Figure 10.7   *Homo- and Heteroscedasticity*

cross-product by its corresponding frequency. For each cell, we enter this value in the lower-right corner. (9) Finally we obtain Σ fx'y; by summing all fx'y' values across all *rows only*. We check the accuracy of our work by summing across all *columns only*. These two sums should be identical.

The above procedure yields all of the values necessary to compute r, which for these data has a value of .88. The work involved can be tedious, so it is advisable to proceed carefully.

We have not discussed any separate procedure for computing r^2 for grouped data. If r^2 is the value in which we are interested, we compute r, as above, and square it.

table 10.9   work sheet for grouped data

X = HOMICIDE RATE

Y = SUICIDE RATE	0–2	3–5	6–8	9–11	12–14	row f	x'	fx'	f(x'²)	fx'y'
0–4	^{4}4$_{16}$					−4	−2	−8	16	16
5–9	^{2}1$_2$	^{1}4$_4$				5	−1	−5	5	6
10–14		^{0}3$_0$	^{0}5$_0$			8	0	0	0	0
15–19		$^{-1}$1$_{-1}$	^{0}3$_0$	^{1}3$_3$		7	1	7	7	2
20–24			^{0}1$_0$	^{2}2$_4$	^{4}3$_{12}$	6	2	12	24	16
Col. f	5	8	9	5	3	30 = N	0	6	52	40
y'	−2	−1	0	1	2	0		= Σ fx'	= Σ fx²	= Σ fx'y'
fy'	−10	−8	0	5	6	−7	= Σ fy'			
f(y'²)	20	8	0	5	12	45	= Σ fy²			
fx'y'	18	3	0	7	12	40	= Σ fx'y'			

testing for the significance of r

The null hypothesis that r = 0 may be tested directly by using Appendix Table I. To use the table, first calculate the degrees of freedom associated with r. For r,

$$df = N - 2$$

(Formula 10.13)

If the observed value of r equals or exceeds the table value, reject H_0; if the observed value is less than the table value, do not reject H_0. As an example, we can test the hypothesis that r = 0 for the data found in Table 10.8(a).

1. *Null Hypothesis:* There is no correlation between the homicide rates and suicide rates in the thirty cities. Or, the correlation between homicide rates and suicide rates is zero.
2. *Decision Rules:* Let $\alpha = .01$; one-tail test; df = 28.
3. *Reject* H_0 if r ≥ .423. Do *not* reject if r < .423.

Since our observed value of r = .88 is larger than the critical value found in Table I, we can safely reject the hypothesis of no association. A reasonable further inference is that the homicide rates and suicide rates are associated.

summary

interpretation. Pearson's r^2 is a PRE measure of association for interval level data. It measures the relative reduction in error achieved when we shift from a prediction rule which states that any Y-value is equal to the mean of Y, to a prediction rule which uses the formula for a straight line, $Y = a + bX$. The Pearson r^2 may also be interpreted as a ratio of explained to total variation.

The product-moment correlation coefficient, r, is a measure of the extent to which a change in one variable is associated with a change in a second variable. Specifically, for every standard deviation unit of change in the independent variable, we predict that the dependent variable will change by $(r)(\sigma)$ units. The Pearson r may also be viewed as the slope of the regression line when data are presented as standard scores.

type of measure. Both r and r_2 are symmetric measures of one-way association. They differ, however, in that r indicates direction; r_2 does not.

mathematical relationship between r and r^2. It is too easy and possibly misleading, to simply say that $r = \sqrt{r^2}$, for while this is arithmetically correct, it has no logical meaning. The Pearson r is not "the square root of explained variation" and r^2 is not "the squared slope of the regression line." For computational purposes we can, of course, use one value to derive the other (except that when we extract the square root of r^2, we do not know which sign to use for r), but we should be careful not to confuse the meanings of the two. Furthermore, since r will always be larger than r^2 (except when both are zero or unity), we should be certain that the appropriate value, r or r^2, is chosen so that we deal properly with the aspect of the data being discussed.

reversibility. Because they are symmetric measures of association, $r_{yx} = r_{xy}$ and $r^2_{yx} = r^2_{xy}$. Given two variables, X and Y, the measure of association will have the same value whether X or Y is designated as the independent variable. However, this observation should not mask the fact that for any set of raw (or unstandardized) data there can be *two* regression lines: (1) $Y = a + bX$ (or $\hat{z}_y = rz_x$), *and* (2) $X = a + bY$ (or $\hat{z}_x = rz_y$). Figure 10.8 (p. 180) illustrates this for the data from Table 10.3. These two regression lines can be plotted for any set of data expressed as raw scores, deviation scores, or standard scores. However, note that if $r = 1.00$, the two lines will be identical, and if $r = 0$, there is no best-fitting line.

Finally, in computing r^2_{xy} rather than r^2_{yx}, care must be taken to adjust computing formulas. For example, Formula 10.3,

$$b_{yx} = \frac{N(\Sigma\, XY) - \Sigma\, X\, \Sigma\, Y}{N(X^2) - (X)^2} \quad \text{becomes} \quad b_{xy} = \frac{N(\Sigma\, XY) - \Sigma\, X\, \Sigma\, Y}{N(Y^2) - (Y)^2}$$

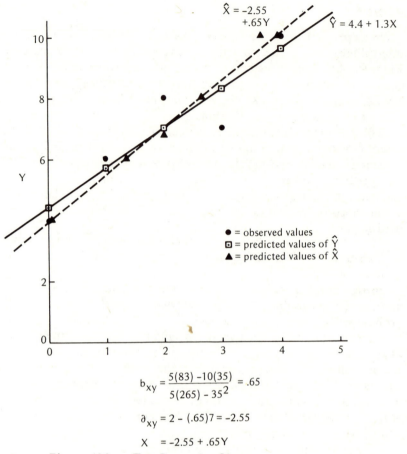

$$\hat{X} = -2.55 + .65Y$$

$$\hat{Y} = 4.4 + 1.3X$$

● = observed values
□ = predicted values of $\hat{Y}$
▲ = predicted values of $\hat{X}$

$$b_{xy} = \frac{5(83) - 10(35)}{5(265) - 35^2} = .65$$

$$\partial_{xy} = 2 - (.65)7 = -2.55$$

$$X = -2.55 + .65Y$$

Figure 10.8   *Two Regression Lines*

and

Formula 10.7,

$$r^2_{yx} = \frac{\Sigma \hat{y}^2}{\Sigma y^2} \quad \text{becomes} \quad r^2_{xy} = \frac{\Sigma \hat{x}^2}{\Sigma x^2}$$

measuring curvilinear correlation: eta-square

We mentioned above that one of the necessary preconditions for calculation of the Pearson r or r^2 is that the data must tend to fall along a
straight line. When there are marked departures from the assumption
of rectilinearity, the Pearson r is inappropriate as a measure of associa-

tion. Figure 10.6(c) and (d) showed two instances where a strong relationship exists between two variables, but for which the computed value of r would not accurately reflect the strength of the relationship. For these data, it is obvious that a *curved* line would offer a better prediction model than would any straight line.

Eta-square (η^2) is an asymmetric measure of one-way association for curvilinear data. Because it is asymmetric, we can compute two values, η^2_{yx} and $\eta^2_{xy}{}'$ for any set of two variables. In most respects η^2 is interpreted as r^2.

A noteworthy distinction between η^2 and r^2 is that the former requires only that the dependent variable be measured at the interval level; the independent variable may be at the interval level, but it may also be at the ordinal or nominal level of measurement. Mathematically, η^2 differs from r^2 in that the calculation of η^2 involves "breaking up the data" into segments (Figure 10.9) and, for each segment, predicting a Y-value on the basis of the mean of Y *within* each segment, rather than on the basis of the regression line (as in the case with r^2). The segments, or

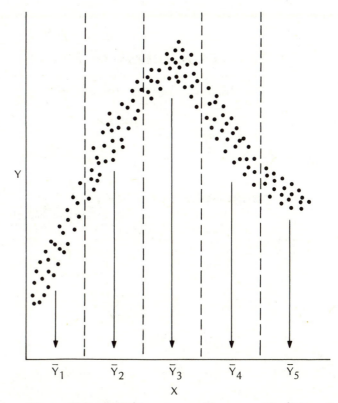

Figure 10.9   *Within-category Means as a Prediction Rule*

class intervals, are somewhat arbitrarily selected, so care should be taken to ensure that they accurately reflect the nature of the distribution.

Eta-square has a PRE interpretation. In terms of the PRE logic, the first prediction rule for η^2 is the same as for r^2.

Prediction Rule 1 (η^2): To predict Y, use the mean of Y.

E_1 is defined similarly as for r^2. Prediction rule 2, however, differs from that for r^2.

Prediction Rule 2 (η^2): To predict Y, in any given category of X use the within-category mean of Y.

E_2 is defined as the sum of squared deviations of the within-category means from the grand mean.

Procedures for calculating eta-square will not be described here. The interested student can consult Mueller, Schuessler and Costner (1970) for a procedure for grouped data, and Freeman (1965) for a simple procedure for ungrouped data.

important terms to know
Pearson product-moment correlation coefficient (r)
The coefficient of determination (r^2)
Regression line
Three assumptions for r
Eta-square (η^2)

suggested readings
Blalock (1972: 361–393); Mueller, Schuessler and Costner (1970: 195–341); Runyon and Haber (1976: 146–162).

essential statistics for social research

answer section

QUICK QUIZ 10.1 $\Sigma X = 9$ $\Sigma Y = 21$ $\Sigma XY = 64$ $\Sigma X^2 = 29$
$\overline{X} = 3$ $\overline{Y} = 7$

$$b_{yx} = \frac{3(64) - 9(21)}{3(29) - 9^2} = \frac{192 - 189}{87 - 81} = \frac{3}{6}$$

$$= 0.5$$

$$a_{yx} = 7 - 0.5(3) = 7 - 1.5 = 5.5$$

QUICK QUIZ 10.2

X	Y	X²	Y²	XY	x	y	x²	y²	xy
2	5	4	25	10	−2	3	4	9	−6
3	2	9	4	6	−1	0	1	0	0
4	3	16	9	12	0	1	0	1	0
7	−2	49	4	−14	3	−4	9	16	−12
16	8	78	42	14	0	0	14	26	−18

$\overline{X} = 4$ $\overline{Y} = 2$

Using Formula 10.10

$$r = \frac{-18}{\sqrt{14(26)}} = \frac{-18}{\sqrt{364}} = \frac{-18}{19.08}$$

$$= -.94$$

Using Formula 10.11

$$r = \frac{4(14) - 16(8)}{\sqrt{[4(78) - 16^2][4(42) - 8^2]}}$$

$$= \frac{56 - 128}{\sqrt{(312) - (256)(168 - 64)}} = \frac{-72}{\sqrt{(56)(104)}}$$

$$= \frac{-72}{\sqrt{5824}} = \frac{-72}{76.32}$$

$$= -.94$$

$$r^2 = .88$$

analysis of three or more variables

In Chapters 2, 3 and 4 we examined some common statistical techniques which are used to describe a single variable, and in Chapters 8, 9 and 10 we described techniques which are used to analyze the relationship between two variables. While one- and two-variable analyses are undoubtedly common and valuable in sociological research, the inescapable fact remains that most problems with which we deal are not univariate or even bivariate, but *multi*variate in nature. We may describe suicide rates (a single variable), and we might show that married persons have lower suicide rates than single persons (two variables), but we also should be able to say something about the suicide rates of married persons who are Catholic, as opposed to those who are Protestant (three variables: suicide, marital status and religion). And, of course, we could add a fourth variable, and a fifth and so on, until we reach the point where adding another variable brings nothing more to our explanation of suicide.

In this chapter we shall examine four ways of analyzing multivariate data sets: elaboration, multiple correlation, partial correlation and analysis of variance. We will focus on three-variable problems, but you should note that the principles involved in the analysis of three variables can readily be extended to the analysis of four or more variables.

elaboration: tabular analysis of percentage differences

One of the simplest ways of mathematically analyzing more than two variables at a time is *elaboration*. Simply put, the logic of elaboration is as follows. We begin by noting a relationship between two variables. We then select a third variable, called a *control variable*, or *test factor* and examine the original relationship as it exists under different control or

11

test conditions. In some instances, an originally strong relationship will weaken or disappear; in others, a relationship which originally seemed to be virtually nonexistent will emerge; or, a strong relationship may be shown to exist under one test condition but not under another. Let us illustrate this point with several examples.

Suppose we examine two hundred geographical areas. In each area we obtain a measure of the birth rate and of the number of storks. We are interested in determining whether a relationship exists between the number of storks in an area and the birth rate. Our simple research hypothesis is that as the number of storks increases, the birth rate increases. The null hypothesis is that there is no association between storks and babies. After collecting our data, we arrange the findings in a conventional 2×2 table (and perhaps compute some measure of association). The data of Table 11.1 appear to confirm the research hypothesis, and the statistical test leads to a rejection of the null hypothesis. But now common sense enters the scene. Someone points out that there is no plausible reason for associating storks and babies, and also notes that both storks and babies might be a function of whether the geographical area under scrutiny is rural or urban. Therefore, we decide to introduce as a test factor the variable rural-urban. In so doing we organize the original data into a *conditional table* (Table 11.2). In this elaborated table we see that, under the rural condition, the original relationship is greatly changed. We see this in two ways. (1) In Table 11.1, the original percentage difference, across columns, was thirty (the difference between seventy and forty, or between thirty and sixty). In the conditional table, the rural percentage difference is two (the difference between forty and forty-two or between sixty and fifty-eight). (2) Even more striking, the zero-order Gamma, which was $+0.56$ ($p <$ .01) has now become, under the rural condition, -0.04. This originally strong and positive relationship has become, with the introduction of the control variable, weak and negative. Under the urban condition we do not observe this drastic change of direction, but we do see that the originally strong relationship is considerably weakened; the value of Gamma has dropped from .56 to .20.

table 11.1 **storks and babies**

		NO. OF STORKS IN AREA			
		FEW		MANY	
		%	(N)	%	(N)
BIRTH RATE	Low	70	(70)	40	(40)
	High	30	(30)	60	(60)
	Totals	100	(100)	100	(100)

$$G = +0.56$$
$$p < .01$$

table 11.2   storks and babies by type of area

		RURAL				URBAN			
		TYPE OF AREA							
		NO. OF STORKS							
		Few		Many		Few		Many	
		%	(N)	%	(N)	%	(N)	%	(N)
BIRTH RATE	Low	40	(6)	42	(36)	69	(59)	60	(9)
	High	60	(9)	58	(49)	31	(26)	40	(6)
	Totals	100	(15)	100	(85)	100	(85)	100	(15)

G = −.04   G = .20

p = NS   p = NS

What shall we make of this? (1) We can first note that the original relationship is *spurious*. That is, a relationship does exist between storks and babies, but this relationship is not direct and not causal. The relationship exists because both of the variables, storks and babies, are related to a third variable. Stated differently, a relationship is said to be spurious if the introduction of a test factor reduces the original relationship to zero (or near zero). (2) The example illustrates the *importance of models and theory*. In the first instance we had a very simple two-variable model:

Model A:

Storks ————————————→Babies
(Independent Variable, X)   (Dependent Variable, Y)

This model was supported by our original examination of the data. But then someone questioned the model, perhaps because of previous research, a theoretical proposition, or common sense, or perhaps on a hunch. The questioner wondered if the relationship might not be better explained by an alternative model, a three-variable model:

Model B:

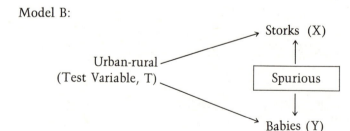

essential statistics for social research

The new model, by introducing the test variable T, postulated that X and Y were not related in any causal sequence. Examination of the conditional tables confirmed this.

The pattern of spuriousness is not the only pattern which can be detected by elaboration. Introduction of a control variable may reveal a pattern of *specification*. For example, suppose that in a study of political behavior a researcher found that a greater proportion of Republicans voted in a certain election (Table 11.3). The researcher then recalled studies which showed that Republicans tended to come from higher socioeconomic classes than did Democrats and, therefore, decided to develop conditional tables, using social class as a test factor. The results obtained might be similar to those in Table 11.4 (p. 188). This table specifies the condition under which the original relationship holds. In this case, the original finding that Republicans vote in greater number than Democrats is found to hold under the condition of relatively lower social class. However, under the condition of high social class, there is virtually no difference in the proportion of Republicans and Democrats who vote.

In some instances, the zero-order association may be at or near zero, but when a test factor is introduced, a relationship may suddenly appear. Such a pattern is called *suppression* because, until identified, the test factor suppresses the underlying relationship. As an example, suppose we begin with the data of Table 11.5 (p. 188), which suggest that there is no relationship between social class and attitudes toward abortion. Then, because attitudes toward abortion are theoretically linked to religious beliefs, we introduce as a test variable a measure of religious liberalism/ conservatism. We then obtain results as in Table 11.6 (p. 188). The conditional tables reveal two opposite patterns. For persons who are religiously liberal, there is a tendency to become less tolerant as social class increases. For persons who are religiously conservative, the pattern is just the opposite.

table 11.3   party and voting

| | PARTY AFFILIATION | | | |
| | DEMOCRAT | | REPUBLICAN | |
	%	(N)	%	(N)
VOTED	60	(36)	72	(36)
DID NOT VOTE	40	(24)	28	(14)
Totals	100	(60)	100	(50)

table 11.4 party and voting, by social class

	SOCIAL CLASS							
	LOWER				HIGHER			
	PARTY AFFILIATION							
	DEMOCRAT		REPUBLICAN		DEMOCRAT		REPUBLICAN	
	%	(N)	%	(N)	%	(N)	%	(N)
VOTED	50	(15)	72	(18)	70	(21)	72	(18)
DID NOT VOTE	50	(15)	28	(7)	30	(9)	28	(7)
Totals	100	(30)	100	(25)	100	(10)	100	(25)

table 11.5 social class and attitude toward abortion

	SOCIAL CLASS					
	LOW		MEDIUM		HIGH	
	%	(N)	%	(N)	%	(N)
LESS TOLERANT	52	(26)	54	(54)	55	(22)
MORE TOLERANT	48	(24)	46	(46)	45	(18)
Totals	100	(50)	100	(100)	100	(40)

$$G = -.04$$

table 11.6 social class and attitude toward abortion, by religious liberalism

	RELIGIOUS TYPE											
	LIBERAL						CONSERVATIVE				
					SOCIAL CLASS							
	LOW		MEDIUM		HIGH		LOW		MEDIUM		HIGH	
	%	(N)	%	(N)	%	(N)	%	(N)	%	(N)	%	(N)
LESS TOLERANT	40	(8)	50	(25)	60	(9)	67	(20)	56	(28)	48	(12)
MORE TOLERANT	60	(12)	50	(25)	40	(6)	33	(10)	44	(22)	52	(13)
	100	(20)	100	(50)	100	(15)	100	(30)	100	(50)	100	(25)

$$G = -.23 \qquad\qquad\qquad G = +.23$$

The process of *elaboration* involves the re-analysis of a two-variable relationship by the introduction of a third variable, a *test factor* or *control variable*. This process breaks an original pattern of association called *zero-order association*, into two or more *conditional* associations. In other words, the original relationship is analyzed under various conditions of the test factor. The purpose of elaboration is to determine whether the zero-order association is as it seems to be. A more complete discussion of the techniques of elaboration can be found in Rosenberg (1968) or Zeisel (1957).

SUMMARY

essential statistics for social research

partial correlation

Elaboration of tabular differences involves a considerable exercise in analyzing the logical relationships among variables. It requires that we look at a relationship between two variables under different conditions of a third variable. In this section we take a slightly different approach to the problem of analyzing three variables. Using diagrams to illustrate what is involved, let us visualize the relationship between the number of storks and the number of babies as a pair of overlapping circles (Figure 11.1). The area of overlap (shaded) represents the statistical relationship between the two variables. If a relationship is perfect, the two circles will be congruent as in Figure 11.2(a) and a zero relationship will be illustrated by two circles which do not overlap at all as in Figure 11.2(b). These diagrams, of course, give an oversimplified view of reality, for two variables rarely coexist in total isolation from other variables. For example, we earlier saw that some rural-urban dimension might be related to both storks and babies. Thus Figure 11.3 gives a more accurate picture of the "real world." But this picture also shows us that a measurement of the relationship between X (storks) and Y (babies) is "contaminated" by Z (rural-urban factor). We might ask: What will happen if we pull (or, technically, if we *partial*) Z out of the relationship between X and Y? Will X and Y remain as strongly associated as they originally appeared to be in Figure 11.1? Or is Z so involved with X and with Y that partialling out Z will eliminate some or even all of the overlap between X and Y?

THE PARTIAL R
The partial correlation coefficient provides us with answers to these questions. (Actually, there are several different partial coefficients, as we shall see below. But unless one of the others is directly specified, a reference to a partial coefficient will usually mean a reference to the partial r.) If we have three variables, X, Y and Z, we can compute a Pearson r for the relationship between X and Y, between X and Z and between

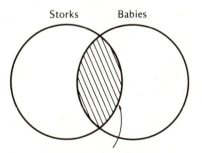

Relationship between
Storks and Babies

Figure 11.1 *Storks and Babies*

analysis of three or more variables 189

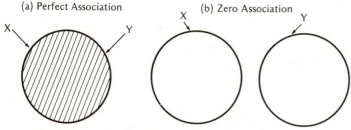

Figure 11.2   *Perfect and Zero Association*

Y and Z. These zero-order coefficients can then be statistically manipulated to reveal the "true" relationship between any two variables with the effect of the third variable "partialled out." Without going into the complex mathematics underlying this procedure, we present a simple formula for computing partial r.

$$r_{xy.z} = \frac{r_{xy} - r_{xz}r_{yz}}{\sqrt{(1 - r_{xz}^2)(1 - r_{yz}^2)}}$$ (*Formula 11.1*)

The notation, $r_{xy.z}$, indicates that we are interested in the relationship between X and Y, with Z partialled out. We could also compute $r_{xz.y}$ or $r_{yz.x}$ by simply rearranging the values of Formula 11.1. (As a memory aid note that, in the formula, the variable being partialled appears in every subscript except the first term of the numerator.)

We can illustrate the application of this formula with a simple example. Suppose we obtained interval level measures on the age (X), weight (Y) and some test score (Z) for a group of school children. We then calculate the Pearson r for each pair of variables and obtain

$$r_{xy} = .80 \qquad r_{xz} = .60 \qquad r_{yz} = .50$$

Looking at these data, we might be puzzled by the moderately strong

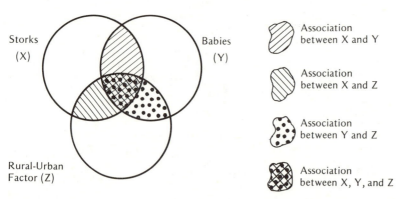

Figure 11.3   *Storks, Babies and Rural-Urban Areas*

essential statistics for social research

relationship between weight and test score, r_{yz}. Why should a person's weight be related to test score? Is this relationship at all meaningful, or is it perhaps spurious? Since we have data on a third variable, age, which might be related to both weight and test score (older children weigh more than younger children, and older children may do better on the test than younger children), we can reexamine the original weight-test score relationship by statistically removing the effect of age:

$$r_{yz.x} = \frac{r_{yz} - r_{yx}r_{xz}}{\sqrt{(1 - r_{yx}^2)(1 - r_{xz}^2)}}$$

$$= \frac{.50 \quad (.00)(.60)}{\sqrt{(1 - .80^2)(1 - .60^2)}}$$

$$= \frac{.50 - .48}{\sqrt{(.36)(.64)}}$$

$$= \frac{.02}{.48}$$

$$= .04$$

The partial correlation coefficient, $r_{yz.x}$, reveals that the association between Y and Z "shrinks" from .50 to .04 when X is partialled out. Stated differently, the YZ relationship is shown to be spurious when X is removed.

quick quiz
11.1

For the above data, compute $r_{xy.z}$.

It is a simple matter to extend Formula 11.1 so that we can partial out yet another, and another, variable. For example, if we have four variables, we can determine the relationship between any two of them with the effects of the remaining two variables partialled out by

(Formula 11.2)

$$r_{12.34} = \frac{r_{12.3} - r_{14.3}r_{24.3}}{\sqrt{(1 - r_{14.3}^2)(1 - r_{24.3}^2)}}$$

We can do the same with five variables (three being partialled out):

(Formula 11.3)

$$r_{12.345} = \frac{r_{12.34} - r_{15.34}r_{25.34}}{\sqrt{(1 - r_{15.34}^2)(1 - r_{15.34}^2)}}$$

We could, in principle, add variables indefinitely, but there is usually little to be gained by going beyond a four or five variable partialling.

The partial r is similar in meaning and interpretation to the simple Pearson r. It varies in magnitude from $+1.00$ to -1.00. The partial r may be squared and given an interpretation analogous to that of r^2.

The ordinal level measure of association, Kendall's Tau, is subject to the same partialling procedure as r. Using a different set of subscripts (not because they have any inherent meaning, but because you should get used to seeing different notations), the computing formula for partial Tau is

PARTIAL TAU

$$\tau_{ab.c} = \frac{\tau_{ab} - \tau_{ab}\tau_{bc}}{\sqrt{(1 - \tau_{ac}^2)(1 - \tau_{bc}^2)}}$$ (Formula 11.4)

Because the formula and procedures for partial Tau are the same as for partial r, we will not discuss this statistic in detail.

The procedures involved in computing a partial Gamma can be extended to any of the measures of association based on pair-by-pair comparison. The procedure calls for the categorization of any two variable relationship under different conditions of the control variable. The values of n_s and n_d are then computed for *each* of the two or more conditional tables; these values are then summed across tables, and the partial Gamma is defined as

PARTIAL GAMMA

$$G_p = \frac{\Sigma(n_s - n_d)}{\Sigma(n_s + n_d)}$$ (Formula 11.5)

For example, consider again the data from Tables 11.1 and 11.2. In 11.1 the value of Gamma is $+0.56$, indicating a strong relationship between the number of storks (X) and babies (Y). In 11.2 the original two variable relationship has been categorized into two conditions of a rural-urban factor (Z). For each of these conditional tables we then compute n_s and n_d:

	n_s	n_d	$(n_s - n_d)$	$(n_s + n_d)$
Rural:	250	350	-100	600
Urban:	300	250	50	550
SUM:			-50	1150

With the sums of the last two columns we can compute the partial Gamma:

$$G_{xy.z} = \frac{-50}{1150}$$

$$= -.04$$

essential statistics for social research

Thus we see that when the rural-urban factor is partialled out of the relationship between storks and babies, the value of Gamma "shrinks" from +.56 to −.04. The partial Gamma has statistically removed the effects of the test variable and given us a more refined measure of the true relationship between the number of storks and babies.

The value of a partial Gamma is an overall measure of association; as such, it has certain advantages and disadvantages when compared to simple tabular differences. An obvious advantage is simplicity: a single figure conveys accurate information about a relatively complex set of variables. The disadvantage is that the partial coefficient does not have the capacity to point out some of the more interesting patterns of elaboration which can be revealed in tabular analysis.

quick quiz
11.2

Using the data from Table 11.6, compute a partial Gamma which shows the relationship between social class and attitudes toward abortion with the effects of religious liberalism/conservatism removed.

multiple correlation

In a certain sense, multiple correlation is the opposite of partial correlation. Whereas the partial r tells us the relationship between two variables with the effect of a third variable removed, multiple R (the capital R is frequently used to distinguish multiple correlation from other types of correlation) tells us the relationship between one variable, the dependent variable, and the *combined effects* of two or more variables.

Let us use circle diagrams to illustrate this basic concept. A dependent variable, X, may be related to two independent variables, Y and Z, as in Figure 11.4. Furthermore, Y and Z may also be related to each other. In each case, the shaded area represents the simple correlation between two variables. But what kind of picture will we get if we recognize the fact that all three variables are interrelated? This "real world" probably looks something like Figure 11.5. In visual terms, how can we assess this multiple relationship? We can "see" the relationship between X and Y (Figure 11.4), and we can statistically measure this relationship by using the Pearson r. But if we now try to add the X-Z relationship to the X Y relationship, we will be adding in a portion (the double-hatched area) which has already been accounted for by X-Y. So to add the effects of Z to X-Y we must first partial out the Y variable from the X-Z relationship. But this is further complicated by the fact that some of Z's influence on X is inextricably bound up with Y, and partialling Y does not

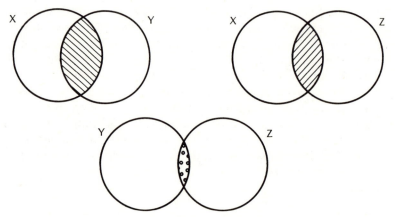

Figure 11.4   *Simple Relationships Among Three Variables*

give us a completely accurate picture of Z's influence. (The reasons for this are complicated, and will not be discussed here.) This means that we cannot simply add the XY value and the XZ.Y value to obtain the multiple correlation coefficient. The actual mathematical relationship is:

$$R_{x.yz} = \sqrt{r_{xy}^2 + r_{xz.y}^2(1 - r_{xy}^2)}$$ (*Formula 11.6*)

(This formula also permits us to calculate $R_{x.yz}^2$ by simply removing the square root sign from the right-hand side of the equation.)

Let us look at another way of conceptualizing multiple correlation. In Chapter 10 we began our discussion of the Pearson r with the straight line equation

$$Y = a + bX$$

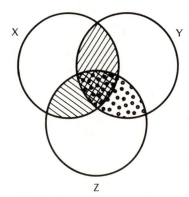

Figure 11.5 *Relationships Among Three Variables*

essential statistics for social research

Now, if we have not one independent variable, but two, this equation can be simply extended to

$$Y = a + b_1X_1 + b_2X_2$$

and for three independent variables

$$y = a + b_1X_1 + b_2X_2 = b_3X_3$$

This process can be extended indefinitely, depending only on the number of independent variables. The mathematical solution of these multivariate equations is beyond the scope of this book, but the logic of the approach should be easily grasped.

The most frequently used computational formula for determining multiple R for two independent variables uses the zero-order correlation coefficients. The formula may appear a bit awesome, but it is actually quite easy to use.

(*Formula 11.7*)
$$R_{x.yz} = \sqrt{\frac{r_{xy}^2 + r_{xz}^2 - 2r_{xy}r_{xz}r_{yz}}{1 - r_{yz}^2}}$$

To illustrate the application of this formula, let us suppose we have three interval level variables, age (X), income (Y), and education (Z). These variables are related to each other as follows:

$$r_{xy} = .70 \qquad r_{xz} = -.20 \qquad r_{yz} = .50$$

If we wish to examine the effect on income, as a dependent variable, of the combined effects of age and education, we can use Formula 11.7.

$$R_{y.xz} = \sqrt{\frac{r_{yx}^2 + r_{yz}^2 - 2r_{yx}r_{yz}r_{xz}}{1 - r_{xz}^2}}$$

$$= \sqrt{\frac{.70^2 + .50^2 - 2(.70)(.50)(-.20)}{1 - (-.20^2)}}$$

$$= \sqrt{\frac{.49 + .25 - (-.14)}{1 - .04}}$$

$$= \sqrt{\frac{.88}{.96}}$$

$$= \sqrt{.9167}$$

$$= .96$$

The logical interpretation of $R_{y.xz} = .96$ is complicated, but the interpretation of $R_{y.x_z}^2 = .92$ is straightforward: it is the same as that given to the simple r^2 in Chapter 10. That is, 92 percent of the variance in income (Y) can be explained by age and education. Whereas age alone explains 49 percent of the variance in income, and education alone explains 25 percent of the variance in income, the two together combine to give a much more powerful explanation of the dependent variable. The interpretation of R^2 is also similar to the interpretation of r^2 in that both may vary from 0.00 to $+1.00$, with a value of unity indicating that the independent variables perfectly predict the dependent variable and a value of zero indicating that the dependent variable bears no linear relationship to the combined independent variables.

The extension of multiple correlations to three or more independent variables is accomplished by a manipulation of Formula 11.6. With three independent variables, the formula becomes: **THREE OR MORE INDEPENDENT VARIABLES**

$$R_{1.234} = \sqrt{R_{1.23}{}^2 + r_{14.23}{}^2(1 - R_{1.23}{}^2)}$$

and for the general case of k independent variables

$$R_{1.23\ldots k} = \sqrt{R_{1.23\ldots(k-1)}{}^2 + r_{1k.23\ldots(k-1)}{}^2(1 - R_{1.23\ldots(k-1)}{}^2)}$$ (*Formula 11.8*)

To put Formula 11.8 into words, if we have k variables, we first compute a multiple R for $(k - 1)$ variables; we then compute a partial r which gives the relationship between the dependent variable and the k-th variable (this is then multiplied by $(1 - R^2)$); finally, we extract the square root.

If the above formulas (11.6, 11.7 or 11.8) are used on population data, the computed values of R will be accurate. However, if sample data are used, the computed value of R will be an overestimate. This bias can be corrected by the following formula: **CORRECTION FOR SAMPLING ERROR**

$$R_c = \sqrt{1 - \frac{n-1}{n-k}(1 - R^2)}$$ (*Formula 11.9*)

where R_c is the corrected value; n is the sample size; and k is the number of independent variables. In most instances, the corrected value will not differ greatly from the original value, unless n is relatively small or k is relatively large.

important terms to know

Control variable   **Zero-order association**
Test factor   **Partial correlation**
Spurious relationship   **Multiple correlation**

suggested reading

Blalock (1972: 429–464); Rosenberg (1968); Zeisel (1957).

answer section

QUICK QUIZ 11.1

$$r_{xy.z} = \frac{r_{xy} - r_{xz}r_{yz}}{\sqrt{(1 - r_{xz}^2)(1 - r_{yz}^2)}}$$

$$= \frac{.80 - (.60)(.50)}{\sqrt{(1 - .60^2)(1 - .50^2)}}$$

$$= \frac{.80 - .30}{\sqrt{(.64)(.75)}}$$

$$= \frac{.50}{.69}$$

$$= .72$$

QUICK QUIZ 11.2

	n_s	n_d	$(n_s - n_d)$	$(n_s + n_d)$
Liberal:	398	633	-235	1031
Conservative:	1064	664	400	1728
SUM:			165	2759

$$G_p = \frac{165}{2759} = .06$$

QUICK QUIZ 11.3 First compute the partial r:

$$r_{yz.x} = \frac{r_{yz} - r_{xy}r_{xz}}{\sqrt{(1 - r_{xy}^2)(1 - r_{xz}^2)}}$$

$$= \frac{.50 - (.70)(-.20)}{\sqrt{(1 - .70^2)(1 - (-.20^2))}}$$

$$= \frac{.64}{\sqrt{(.51)(.96)}} \quad = \frac{.64}{.70}$$

$$= .91$$

Then, using Formula 11.6

$$R_{y.xz} = \sqrt{.70^2 + .91^2(1 - .70^2)}$$

$$= \sqrt{.49 + .83(.51)}$$

$$= \sqrt{.49 + .4233} \quad = \sqrt{.9133}$$

$$= .96$$

appendix

How to use this table: Each page of the table contains two sets of three columns each. The first column contains the number whose square or square root is being sought. The second column contains the *square* of the number in the first column. The third column contains the *square root* of the number in the first column.

Examples: The square of 58 is 3364; the square root of 58 is 7.616. The square of 312 is 97,344; the square root of 312 is 17.664.

If you are comfortable with mathematics, you will find it useful to determine square roots of numbers not found in the table by using the relationships

$$10^k \sqrt{N} = \sqrt{10^{2k}(N)}$$

Thus, $10\sqrt{150}$ yields the square root of 15,000, and $\frac{1}{100}\sqrt{150}$ yields the square root of .015.

If you are not comfortable using this method, you will find the following paragraphs a bit more tedious, but if you understand them, you will obtain satisfactory results. Please use the examples to make certain that you understand the procedures.

squares and square roots of decimal numbers and numbers greater than 1,000.

(a) *To find the approximate square root of numbers larger than 1,000:* (1) Find, in column 2 of the Table, the number nearest in value to the number in question. (2) Read the approximate square root from column 1. *Examples:*

N	$\sqrt{N}$ (approx.)	$\sqrt{N}$ (actual)
115,600	340	340
27,532	166	165.928
9,868	99	99.338

(b) *To find the approximate square root of decimal numbers:* (1) First make certain that the number is expressed as having an *even* number of digits to the right of the decimal point.* Thus, if the number in question 1.637, it is expressed as 1.6370. (2) Now shift the decimal point to the *right*, until the decimal is cleared. Thus, 1.6370 becomes 16.370 (3) From column 2 find the nearest value to the adjusted number. In our example, that value is 16384. (4) Read the corresponding value from column 1. In this case, that value is 128. (5) Finally, for every *two*

---

*If the resulting value is between 1 and 1,000, the square root can be read directly from the table, but the value read must be adjusted by moving the decimal point of the number from column 3 *one place to the left* for every two places that it was previously moved right. Thus, $\sqrt{.65} = .8062$; $\sqrt{.0139} = .1179$; and $\sqrt{7.3} = 2.7019$.

places that the decimal was moved to the *right* in step (2), move the decimal point one place to the left. In our example, since we moved four places to the right in step (2), we now move two places to the left. Our final answer is thus $\sqrt{1.637} = 1.28$. (The actual value of $\sqrt{1.637}$ is 1.279.) Other examples:

N	approx. $\sqrt{N}$	actual $\sqrt{N}$
0.93	0.9644	0.9644
17.6	4.22	4.1952
0.003	0.0548	0.0548
0.751	0.87	0.8666
0.9108	0.95	0.9544

(c) *To find the approximate square of numbers larger than 1,000:* (1) Move the decimal point an *even* number of places to the *left* until the number is between 1 and 1,000. (2) From column 1, find the nearest value to the adjusted number. (3) Read the corresponding square from column 1, but move the decimal *two places to the right* for every *one* place moved *left* in step (1). Some examples:

N	approx N^2	actual N^2
2,000	4,000,000	4,000,000
75,638	5,715,360,000	5,721,107,000
4,567	21,160,000	20,857,489

(d) *To find the approximate square of a decimal number:* If N is greater than 1,000, use the procedures described in paragraph c. If 1.000 $\leq$ N $\leq$ 31.632, find the nearest corresponding value in column 3 and read the approximate square from column 1. If 31.633 $\leq$ N $\leq$ 1,000; find the nearest corresponding value in column 1 and read the square from column 2. If N < 1.000, as above, (1) first make certain that the number is expressed as having an *even* number of digits to the right of the decimal point. (2) Next, clear the decimal point by moving it to the *right*. (3) From column 1, find the corresponding nearest value. (If this value is greater than 1,000, use the procedures in paragraph c.) (4) Read the corresponding value from column 2. (5) Finally, for *two* places that the decimal was moved *right* in step 2, now move *four places left* the decimal point of the value obtained from step 4. Some examples:

N	approx N^2	actual N^2
0.93	0.8649	0.8649
17.6	310.0	309.76
0.003	0.000009	0.000009
0.751	0.5625	0.5640

table A   squares and square roots of the numbers from 1 to 1,000

Number	Square	Square Root	Number	Square	Square Root
1	1	1.000	41	16 81	6.403
2	4	1.414	42	17 64	6.481
3	9	1.732	43	18 49	6.557
4	16	2.000	44	19 36	6.633
5	25	2.236	45	20 25	6.708
6	36	2.449	46	21 16	6.782
7	49	2.646	47	22 09	6.856
8	64	2.828	48	23 04	6.928
9	81	3.000	49	24 01	7.000
10	1 00	3.162	50	25 00·	7.071
11	1 21	3.317	51	26 01	7.141
12	1 44	3.464	52	27 04	7.211
13	1 69	3.606	53	28 09	7.280
14	1 96	3.742	54	29 16	7.348
15	2 25	3.873	55	30 25	7.416
16	2 56	4.000	56	31 36	7.483
17	2 89	4.123	57	32 49	7.550
18	3 24	4.243	58	33 64	7.616
19	3 61	4.359	59	34 81	7.681
20	4 00	4.472	60	36 00	7.746
21	4 41	4.583	61	37 21	7.810
22	4 84	4.690	62	38 44	7 874
23	5 29	4.796	63	39 69	7.937
24	5 76	4.899	64	40 96	8.000
25	6 25	5.000	65	42 25	8.062
26	6 76	5.099	66	43 56	8.124
27	7 29	5.196	67	44 89	8.185
28	7 84	5.292	68	46 24	8.246
29	8 41	5.385	69	47 61	8.307
30	9 00	5.477	70	49 00	8.367
31	9 61	5.568	71	50 41	8.426
32	10 24	5.657	72	51 84	8.485
33	10 89	5.745	73	53 29	8.544
34	11 56	5.831	74	54 76	8.602
35	12 25	5.916	75	56 25	8.660
36	12 96	6.000	76	57 76	8.718
37	13 69	6.083	77	59 29	8.775
38	14 44	6.164	78	60 84	8.832
39	15 21	6.245	79	62 41	8.888
40	16 00	6.325	80	64 00	8.944

table A squares and square roots of the numbers from 1 to 1,000

Number	Square	Square Root	Number	Square	Square Root
81	65 61	9.000	121	1 46 41	11.000
82	67 24	9.055	122	1 48 84	11.045
83	68 89	9.110	123	1 51 29	11.091
84	70 56	9.165	124	1 53 76	11.136
85	72 25	9.220	125	1 56 25	11.180
86	73 96	9.274	126	1 58 76	11.225
87	75 69	9.327	127	1 61 29	11.269
88	77 44	9.381	128	1 63 84	11.314
89	79 21	9.434	129	1 66 41	11.358
90	81 00	9.487	130	1 69 00	11.402
91	82 81	9.539	131	1 71 61	11.446
92	84 64	9.592	132	1 74 24	11.489
93	86 49	9.644	133	1 76 89	11.533
94	88 36	9.695	134	1 79 56	11.576
95	90 25	9.747	135	1 82 25	11.619
96	92 16	9.798	136	1 84 96	11.662
97	94 09	9.849	137	1 87 69	11.705
98	96 04	9.899	138	1 90 44	11.747
99	98 01	9.950	139	1 93 21	11.790
100	1 00 00	10.000	140	1 96 00	11.832
101	1 02 01	10.050	141	1 98 81	11.874
102	1 04 04	10.100	142	2 01 64	11.916
103	1 06 09	10.149	143	2 04 49	11.958
104	1 08 16	10.198	144	2 07 36	12.000
105	1 10 25	10.247	145	2 10 25	12.042
106	1 12 36	10.296	146	2 13 16	12.083
107	1 14 49	10.344	147	2 16 09	12.124
108	1 16 64	10.392	148	2 19 04	12.166
109	1 18 81	10.440	149	2 22 01	12.207
110	1 21 00	10.488	150	2 25 00	12.247
111	1 23 21	10.536	151	2 28 01	12.288
112	1 25 44	10.583	152	2 31 04	12.329
113	1 27 69	10.630	153	2 34 09	12.369
114	1 29 96	10.677	154	2 37 16	12.410
115	1 32 25	10.724	155	2 40 25	12.450
116	1 34 56	10.770	156	2 43 36	12.490
117	1 36 89	10.817	157	2 46 49	12.530
118	1 39 24	10.863	158	2 49 64	12.570
119	1 41 61	10.909	159	2 52 81	12.610
120	1 44 00	10.954	160	2 56 00	12.649

essential statistics for social research

table A   squares and square roots of the numbers from 1 to 1,000

Number	Square	Square Root	Number	Square	Square Root
161	2 59 21	12.689	201	4 04 01	14.177
162	2 62 44	12.728	202	4 08 04	14.213
163	2 65 69	12.767	203	4 12 09	14.248
164	2 68 96	12.806	204	4 16 16	14.283
165	2 72 25	12.845	205	4 20 25	14.318
166	2 75 56	12.884	206	4 24 36	14.353
167	2 78 89	12.923	207	4 28 49	14.387
168	2 82 24	12.961	208	4 32 64	14.422
169	2 85 61	13.000	209	4 36 81	14.457
170	2 89 00	13.038	210	4 41 00	14.491
171	2 92 41	13.077	211	4 45 21	14.526
172	2 95 84	13.115	212	4 49 44	14.560
173	2 99 29	13.153	213	4 53 69	14.595
174	3 02 76	13.191	214	4 57 96	14.629
175	3 06 25	13.229	215	4 62 25	14.663
176	3 09 76	13.266	216	4 66 56	14.697
177	3 13 29	13.304	217	4 70 89	14.731
178	3 16 84	13.342	218	4 75 24	14.765
179	3 20 41	13.379	219	4 79 61	14.799
180	3 24 00	13.416	220	4 84 00	14.832
181	3 27 61	13.454	221	4 88 41	14.866
182	3 31 24	13.491	222	4 92 84	14.900
183	3 34 89	13.528	223	4 97 29	14.933
184	3 38 56	13.565	224	5 01 76	14.967
185	3 42 25	13.601	225	5 06 25	15.000
186	3 45 96	13.638	226	5 10 76	15.033
187	3 49 69	13.675	227	5 15 29	15.067
188	3 53 44	13.711	228	5 19 84	15.100
189	3 57 21	13.748	229	5 24 41	15.133
190	3 61 00	13.784	230	5 29 00	15.166
191	3 64 81	13.820	231	5 33 61	15.199
192	3 68 64	13.856	232	5 38 24	15.232
193	3 72 49	13.892	233	5 42 89	15.264
194	3 76 36	13.928	234	5 47 56	15.297
195	3 80 25	13.964	235	5 52 25	15.330
196	3 84 16	14.000	236	5 56 96	15.362
197	3 88 09	14.036	237	5 61 69	15.395
198	3 92 04	14.071	238	5 66 44	15.427
199	3 96 01	14.107	239	5 71 21	15.460
200	4 00 00	14.142	240	5 76 00	15.492

Number	Square	Square Root	Number	Square	Square Root
241	5 80 81	15.524	281	7 89 61	16.763
242	5 85 64	15.556	282	7 95 24	16.793
243	5 90 49	15.588	283	8 00 89	16.823
244	5 95 36	15.620	284	8 06 56	16.852
245	6 00 25	15.652	285	8 12 25	16.882
246	6 05 16	15.684	286	8 17 96	16.912
247	6 10 09	15.716	287	8 23 69	16.941
248	6 15 04	15.748	288	8 29 44	16.971
249	6 20 01	15.780	289	8 35 21	17.000
250	6 25 00	15.811	290	8 41 00	17.029
251	6 30 01	15.843	291	8 46 81	17.059
252	6 35 04	15.875	292	8 52 64	17.088
253	6 40 09	15.906	293	8 58 49	17.117
254	6 45 16	15.937	294	8 64 36	17.146
255	6 50 25	15.969	295	8 70 25	17.176
256	6 55 36	16.000	296	8 76 16	17.205
257	6 60 49	16.031	297	8 82 09	17.234
258	6 65 64	16.062	298	8 88 04	17.263
259	6 70 81	16.093	299	8 94 01	17.292
260	6 76 00	16.125	300	9 00 00	17.321
261	6 81 21	16.155	301	9 06 01	17.349
262	6 86 44	16.186	302	9 12 04	17.378
263	6 91 69	16.217	303	9 18 09	17.407
264	6 96 96	16.248	304	9 24 16	17.436
265	7 02 25	16.279	305	9 30 25	17.464
266	7 07 56	16.310	306	9 36 36	17.493
267	7 12 89	16.340	307	9 42 49	17.521
268	7 18 24	16.371	308	9 48 64	17.550
269	3 23 61	16.401	309	9 54 81	17.578
270	7 29 00	16.432	310	9 61 00	17.607
271	7 34 41	16.462	311	9 67 21	17.635
272	7 39 84	16.492	312	9 73 44	17.664
273	7 45 29	16.523	313	9 79 69	17.692
274	7 50 76	16.553	314	9 85 96	17.720
275	7 56 25	16.583	315	9 92 25	17.748
276	7 61 76	16.613	316	9 98 56	17.776
277	7 67 29	16.643	317	10 04 89	17.804
278	7 72 84	16.673	318	10 11 24	17.833
279	7 78 41	16.703	319	10 17 61	17.861
280	7 84 00	16.733	320	10 24 00	17.889

Number	Square	Square Root	Number	Square	Square Root
321	10 30 41	17.916	361	13 03 21	19.000
322	10 36 84	17.944	362	13 10 44	19.026
323	10 43 29	17.972	363	13 17 69	19.053
324	10 49 76	18.000	364	13 24 96	19.079
325	10 56 25	18.028	365	13 32 25	19.105
326	10 62 76	18.055	366	13 39 56	19.131
327	10 69 29	18.083	367	13 46 89	19.157
328	10 75 84	18.111	368	13 54 24	19.183
329	10 82 41	18.138	369	13 61 61	19.209
330	10 89 00	18.166	370	13 69 00	19.235
331	10 95 61	18.193	371	13 76 41	19.261
332	11 02 24	18.221	372	13 83 84	19.287
333	11 08 89	18.248	373	13 91 29	19.313
334	11 15 56	18.276	374	13 98 76	19.339
335	11 22 25	18.303	375	14 06 25	19.363
336	11 28 96	18.330	376	14 13 76	19.391
337	11 35 69	18.358	377	14 21 29	19.416
338	11 42 44	18.385	378	14 28 84	19.442
339	11 49 21	18.412	379	14 36 41	19.468
340	11 56 00	18.439	380	14 44 00	19.494
341	11 62 81	18.466	381	14 51 61	19.519
342	11 69 64	18.493	382	14 59 24	19.545
343	11 76 49	18.520	383	14 66 89	19.570
344	11 83 36	18.547	384	14 74 56	19.596
345	11 90 25	18.574	385	14 82 25	19.621
346	11 97 16	18.601	386	14 89 96	19.647
347	12 04 09	18.628	387	14 97 69	19.672
348	12 11 04	18.655	388	15 05 44	19.698
349	12 18 01	18.682	389	15 13 21	19.723
350	12 25 00	18.708	390	15 21 00	19.748
351	12 32 01	18.735	391	15 28 81	19.774
352	12 39 04	18.762	392	15 36 64	19.799
353	12 46 09	18.788	393	15 44 49	19.824
354	12 53 16	18.815	394	15 52 36	19.849
355	12 60 25	18.841	395	15 60 25	19.875
356	12 67 36	18.868	396	15 68 16	19.900
357	12 74 49	18.894	397	15 76 09	19.925
358	12 81 64	18.921	398	15 84 04	19.950
359	12 88 81	18.947	399	15 92 01	19.975
360	12 96 00	18.974	400	16 00 00	20.000

table A   squares and square roots of the numbers from 1 to 1,000

Number	Square	Square Root	Number	Square	Square Root
401	16 08 01	20.025	441	19 44 81	21.000
402	16 16 04	20.050	442	19 53 64	21.024
403	16 24 09	20.075	443	19 62 49	21.048
404	16 32 16	20.100	444	19 71 36	21.071
405	16 40 25	20.125	445	19 80 25	21.095
406	16 48 36	20.149	446	19 89 16	21.119
407	16 56 49	20.174	447	19 98 09	21.142
408	16 64 64	20.199	448	20 07 04	21.166
409	16 72 81	20.224	449	20 16 01	21.190
410	16 81 00	20.248	450	20 25 00	21.213
411	16 89 21	20.273	451	20 34 01	21.237
412	16 97 44	20.298	452	20 43 04	21.260
413	17 05 69	20.322	453	20 52 09	21.284
414	17 13 96	20.347	454	20 61 16	21.307
415	17 22 25	20.372	455	20 70 25	21.331
416	17 30 56	20.396	456	20 79 36	21.354
417	17 38 89	20.421	457	20 88 49	21.378
418	17 47 24	20.445	458	20 97 64	21.401
419	17 55 61	20.469	459	21 06 81	21.424
420	17 64 00	20.494	460	21 16 00	21.448
421	17 72 41	20.518	461	21 25 21	21.471
422	17 80 84	20.543	462	21 34 44	21.494
423	17 89 29	20.567	463	21 43 69	21.517
424	17 97 76	20.591	464	21 52 96	21.541
425	18 06 25	20.616	465	21 62 25	21.564
426	18 14 76	20.640	466	21 71 56	21.587
427	18 23 29	20.664	467	21 80 89	21.610
428	18 31 84	20.688	468	21 90 24	21.633
429	18 40 41	20.712	469	21 99 61	21.656
430	18 49 00	20.736	470	22 09 00	21.679
431	18 57 61	20.761	471	22 18 41	21.703
432	18 66 24	20.785	472	22 27 84	21.726
433	18 74 89	20.809	473	22 37 29	21.749
434	18 83 56	20.833	474	22 46 76	21.772
435	18 92 25	20.857	475	22 56 25	21.794
436	19 00 96	20.881	476	22 65 76	21.817
437	19 09 69	20.905	477	22 75 29	21.840
438	19 18 44	20.928	478	22 84 84	21.863
439	19 27 21	20.952	479	22 94 41	21.886
440	19 36 00	20.976	480	23 04 00	21.909

essential statistics for social research

table A   squares and square roots of the numbers from 1 to 1,000

Number	Square	Square Root	Number	Square	Square Root
481	23 13 61	21.932	521	27 14 41	22.825
482	23 23 24	21.954	522	27 24 84	22.847
483	23 32 89	21.977	523	27 35 29	22.869
484	23 42 56	22.000	524	27 45 76	22.891
485	23 52 25	22.023	525	27 56 25	22.913
486	23 61 96	22.045	526	27 66 76	22.935
487	23 71 69	22.068	527	27 77 29	22.956
488	23 81 44	22.091	528	27 87 84	22.978
489	23 91 21	22.113	529	27 98 41	23.000
490	24 01 00	22.136	530	28 09 00	23.022
491	24 10 81	22.159	531	28 19 61	23.043
492	24 20 64	22.181	532	28 30 24	23.065
493	24 30 49	22.204	533	28 40 89	23.087
494	24 40 36	22.226	534	28 51 56	23.108
495	24 50 25	22.249	535	28 62 25	23.130
496	24 60 16	22.271	536	28 72 96	23.152
497	24 70 09	22.293	537	28 83 69	23.173
498	24 80 04	22.316	538	28 94 44	23.195
499	24 90 01	22.338	539	29 05 21	23.216
500	25 00 00	22.361	540	29 16 00	23.238
501	25 10 01	22.383	541	29 26 81	23.259
502	25 20 04	22.405	542	29 37 64	23.281
503	25 30 09	22.428	543	29 48 49	23.302
504	25 40 16	22.450	544	29 59 36	23.324
505	25 50 25	22.472	545	29 70 25	23.345
506	25 60 36	22.494	546	29 81 16	23.367
507	25 70 49	22.517	547	29 92 09	23.388
508	25 80 64	22.539	548	30 03 04	23.409
509	25 90 81	22.561	549	30 14 01	23.431
510	26 01 00	22.583	550	30 25 00	23.452
511	26 11 21	22.605	551	30 36 01	23.473
512	26 21 44	22.627	552	30 47 04	23.495
513	26 31 69	22.650	553	30 58 09	23.516
514	26 41 96	22.672	554	30 69 16	23.537
515	26 52 25	22.694	555	30 80 25	23.558
516	26 62 56	22.716	556	30 91 36	23.580
577	26 72 89	22.738	557	31 02 49	23.601
518	26 83 24	22.760	558	31 13 64	23.622
519	26 93 61	22.782	559	31 24 81	23.643
520	27 04 00	22.804	560	31 36 00	23.664

table A   squares and square roots of the numbers from 1 to 1,000

Number	Square	Square Root	Number	Square	Square Root
561	31 47 21	23.685	601	36 12 01	24.515
562	31 58 44	23.707	602	36 24 04	24.536
563	31 69 69	23.728	603	36 36 09	24.556
564	31 80 96	23.749	604	36 48 16	24.576
565	31 92 25	23.770	605	36 60 25	24.597
566	32 03 56	23.791	606	36 72 36	24.617
567	32 14 89	23.812	607	36 84 49	24.637
568	32 26 24	23.833	608	36 96 64	24.658
569	32 37 61	23.854	609	37 08 81	24.678
570	32 49 00	23.875	610	37 21 00	24.698
571	32 60 41	23.896	611	37 33 21	24.718
572	32 71 84	23.917	612	37 45 44	24.739
573	32 83 29	23.937	613	37 57 69	24.759
574	32 94 76	23.958	614	37 69 96	24.779
575	33 06 25	23.979	615	37 82 25	24.799
576	33 17 76	24.000	616	37 94 56	24.819
577	33 29 29	24.021	617	38 06 89	24.839
578	33 40 84	24.042	618	38 19 24	24.860
579	33 52 41	24.062	619	38 31 61	24.880
580	33 64 00	24.083	620	38 44 00	24.900
581	33 75 61	24.104	621	38 56 41	24.920
582	33 87 24	24.125	622	38 68 84	24.940
583	33 98 89	24.145	623	38 81 29	24.960
584	34 10 56	24.166	624	38 93 76	24.980
585	34 22 25	24.187	625	39 06 25	25.000
586	34 33 96	24.207	626	39 18 76	25.020
587	34 45 69	24.228	627	39 31 29	25.040
588	34 57 44	24.249	628	39 43 84	25.060
589	34 69 21	24.269	629	39 56 41	25.080
590	34 81 00	24.290	630	39 69 00	25.100
591	34 92 81	24.310	631	39 81 61	25.120
592	35 04 64	24.331	632	39 94 24	25.140
593	35 16 49	24.352	633	40 06 89	25.159
594	35 28 36	24.372	634	40 19 56	25.179
595	35 40 25	24.393	635	40 32 25	25.199
596	35 52 16	24.413	636	40 44 96	25.219
597	35 64 09	24.434	637	40 57 69	25.239
598	35 76 04	24.454	638	40 70 44	25.259
599	35 88 01	24.474	639	40 83 21	25.278
600	36 00 00	24.495	640	40 96 00	25.298

table A   squares and square roots of the numbers from 1 to 1,000

Number	Square	Square Root	Number	Square	Square Root
641	41 08 81	25.318	681	46 37 61	26.096
642	41 21 64	25.338	682	46 51 24	26.115
643	41 34 49	25.357	683	46 64 89	26.134
644	41 47 36	25.377	684	46 78 56	26.153
645	41 60 25	25.397	685	46 92 25	26.173
646	41 73 16	25.417	686	47 05 96	26.192
647	41 86 09	25.436	687	47 19 69	26.211
648	41 99 04	25.456	688	47 33 44	26.230
649	42 12 01	25.475	689	47 47 21	26.249
650	42 25 00	25.495	690	47 61 00	26.268
651	42 38 01	25.515	691	47 74 81	26.287
652	42 51 04	25.534	692	47 88 64	26.306
653	42 64 09	25.554	693	48 02 49	26.325
654	42 77 16	25.573	694	48 16 36	26.344
655	42 90 25	25.593	695	48 30 25	26.363
656	43 03 36	25.612	696	48 44 16	26.382
657	43 16 49	25.632	697	48 58 09	26.401
658	43 29 64	25.652	698	48 72 04	26.420
659	43 42 81	25.671	699	48 86 01	26.439
660	43 56 00	25.690	700	49 00 00	26.458
661	43 69 21	25.710	701	49 14 01	26.476
662	43 82 44	25.729	702	49 28 04	26.495
663	43 95 69	25.749	703	49 42 09	26.514
664	44 08 96	25.768	704	49 56 16	26.533
665	44 22 25	25.788	705	49 70 25	26.552
666	44 35 56	25.807	706	49 84 36	26.571
667	44 48 89	25.826	707	49 98 49	26.589
668	44 62 24	25.846	708	50 12 64	26.608
669	44 75 61	25.865	709	50 26 81	26.627
670	44 89 00	25.884	710	50 41 00	26.646
671	45 02 41	25.904	711	50 55 21	26.665
672	45 15 84	25.923	712	50 69 44	26.683
673	45 29 29	25.942	713	50 83 69	26.702
674	45 42 76	25.962	714	50 97 96	26.721
675	45 56 25	25.981	715	51 12 25	26.739
676	45 69 76	26.000	716	51 26 56	26.758
677	45 83 29	26.019	717	51 40 89	26.777
678	45 96 84	26.038	718	51 55 24	26.796
679	46 10 41	26.058	719	51 69 61	26.814
680	46 24 00	26.077	720	51 84 00	26.833

table A   squares and square roots of the numbers from 1 to 1,000

Number	Square	Square Root	Number	Square	Square Root
721	51 98 41	26.851	761	57 91 21	27.586
722	52 12 84	26.870	762	58 06 44	27.604
723	52 27 29	26.889	763	58 21 69	27.622
724	52 41 76	26.907	764	58 36 96	27.641
725	52 56 25	26.926	765	58 52 25	27.659
726	52 70 76	26.944	766	58 67 56	27.677
727	52 85 29	26.963	767	58 82 89	27.695
728	52 99 84	26.981	768	58 98 24	27.713
729	53 14 41	27.000	769	59 13 61	27.731
730	53 29 00	27.019	770	59 29 00	27.749
731	53 43 61	27.037	771	59 44 41	27.767
732	53 58 24	27.055	772	59 59 84	27.785
733	53 72 89	27.074	773	59 75 29	27.803
734	53 87 56	27.092	774	59 90 76	27.821
735	54 02 25	27.111	775	60 06 25	27.839
736	54 16 96	27.129	776	60 21 76	27.857
737	54 31 69	27.148	777	60 37 29	27.875
738	54 46 44	27.166	778	60 52 84	27.893
739	54 61 21	27.185	779	60 68 41	27.911
740	54 76 00	27.203	780	60 84 00	27.928
741	54 90 81	27.221	781	60 99 61	27.946
742	55 05 64	27.240	782	61 15 24	27.964
743	55 20 49	27.258	783	61 30 89	27.982
744	55 35 36	27.276	784	61 46 56	28.000
745	55 50 25	27.295	785	61 62 25	28.018
746	55 65 16	27.313	786	61 77 96	28.036
747	55 80 09	27.331	787	61 93 69	28.054
748	55 95 04	27.350	788	62 09 44	28.071
749	56 10 01	27.368	789	62 25 21	28.089
750	56 25 00	27.386	790	62 41 00	28.107
751	56 40 01	27.404	791	62 56 81	28.125
752	56 55 04	27.423	792	62 72 64	28.142
753	56 70 09	27.441	793	62 88 49	28.160
754	56 85 16	27.459	794	63 04 36	28.178
755	57 00 25	27.477	795	63 20 25	28.196
756	57 15 36	27.495	796	63 36 16	28.213
757	57 30 49	27.514	797	63 52 09	28.231
758	57 45 64	27.532	798	63 68 04	28.249
759	57 60 81	27.550	799	63 84 01	28.267
760	57 76 00	27.568	800	64 00 00	28.284

Number	Square	Square Root	Number	Square	Square Root
881	77 61 61	29.682	921	84 82 41	30.348
882	77 79 24	29.698	922	85 00 84	30.364
883	77 96 89	29.715	923	85 19 29	30.381
884	78 14 56	29.732	924	85 37 76	30.397
885	78 32 25	29.749	925	85 56 25	30.414
886	78 49 96	29.766	926	85 74 76	30.430
887	78 67 69	29.783	927	85 93 29	30.447
888	78 85 44	29.799	928	86 11 84	30.463
889	79 03 21	29.816	929	86 30 41	30.480
890	79 21 00	29.833	930	86 49 00	30.496
891	79 38 81	29.850	931	86 67 61	30.512
892	79 56 64	29.866	932	86 86 24	30.529
893	79 74 49	29.883	933	87 04 89	30.545
894	79 92 36	29.900	934	87 23 56	30.561
895	80 10 25	29.916	935	87 42 25	30.578
896	80 28 16	29.933	936	87 60 96	30.594
897	80 46 09	29.950	937	87 79 69	30.610
898	80 64 04	29.967	938	87 98 44	30.627
899	80 82 01	29.983	939	88 17 21	30.643
900	81 00 00	30.000	940	88 36 00	30.659
901	81 80 01	30.017	941	88 54 81	30.676
902	81 36 04	30.033	942	88 73 64	30.692
903	81 54 09	30.050	943	88 92 49	30.708
904	81 72 16	30.067	944	89 11 36	30.725
905	81 90 25	30.083	945	89 30 25	30.741
906	82 08 36	30.100	946	89 49 16	30.757
907	82 26 49	30.116	947	89 68 09	30.773
908	82 44 64	30.133	948	89 87 04	30.790
909	82 62 81	30.150	949	90 06 01	30.806
910	82 81 00	30.166	950	90 25 00	30.822
911	82 99 21	30.183	951	90 44 01	30.838
912	83 17 44	30.199	952	90 63 04	30.854
913	83 35 69	30.216	953	90 82 09	30.871
914	83 53 96	30.232	954	91 01 16	30.887
915	83 72 25	30.249	955	91 20 25	30.903
916	83 90 56	30.265	956	91 39 36	30.919
917	84 08 89	30.282	957	91 58 49	30.935
918	84 27 24	30.299	958	91 77 64	30.952
919	84 45 61	30.315	959	91 96 81	30.968
920	84 64 00	30.332	960	92 16 00	30.984

table A   squares and square roots of the numbers from 1 to 1,000

Number	Square	Square Root	Number	Square	Square Root
801	64 16 01	28.302	841	70 72 81	29.000
802	64 32 04	28.320	842	70 89 64	29.017
803	64 48 09	28.337	843	71 06 49	29.034
804	64 64 16	28.355	844	71 23 36	29.052
805	64 80 25	28.373	845	71 40 25	29.069
806	64 96 36	28.390	846	71 57 16	29.086
807	65 12 49	28.408	847	71 74 09	29.103
808	65 28 64	28.425	848	71 91 04	29.120
809	65 44 81	28.443	849	72 08 01	29.138
810	65 61 00	28.460	850	72 25 00	29.155
811	65 77 21	28.478	851	72 42 01	29.172
812	65 93 44	28.496	852	72 59 04	29.189
813	66 09 69	28.513	853	72 76 09	29.206
814	66 25 96	28.531	854	72 93 16	29.223
815	66 42 25	28.548	855	73 10 25	29.240
816	66 58 56	28.566	856	73 27 36	29.257
817	66 74 89	28.583	857	73 44 49	29.275
818	66 91 24	28.601	858	73 61 64	29.292
819	67 07 61	28.618	859	73 78 81	29.309
820	67 24 00	28.636	860	73 96 00	29.326
821	67 40 41	28.653	861	74 13 21	29.343
822	67 56 84	28.671	862	74 30 44	29.360
823	67 73 29	28.688	863	74 47 69	29.377
824	67 89 76	28.705	864	74 64 96	29.394
825	68 06 25	28.723	865	74 82 25	29.411
826	68 22 76	28.740	866	74 99 56	29.428
827	68 39 29	28.758	867	75 16 89	29.445
828	68 55 84	28.775	868	75 34 24	29.462
829	68 72 41	28.792	869	75 51 61	29.479
830	68 89 00	28.810	870	75 69 00	29.496
831	69 05 61	28.827	871	75 86 41	29.513
832	69 22 24	28.844	872	76 03 84	29.530
833	69 38 89	28.862	873	76 21 29	29.547
834	69 55 56	28.879	874	76 38 76	29.563
835	69 72 25	28.896	875	76 56 25	29.580
836	69 88 96	28.914	876	76 73 76	29.597
837	70 05 69	28.931	877	76 91 29	29.614
838	70 22 44	28.948	878	77 08 84	29.631
839	70 39 21	28.965	879	77 26 41	29.648
840	70 56 00	28.983	880	77 44 00	29.665

table A squares and square roots of the numbers from 1 to 1,000

Number	Square	Square Root	Number	Square	Square Root
961	92 35 21	31.000	981	96 23 61	31.321
962	92 54 44	31.016	982	96 43 24	31.337
963	92 73 69	31.032	983	96 62 89	31.353
964	92 92 96	31.048	984	96 82 56	31.369
965	93 12 25	31.064	985	97 02 25	31.385
966	93 31 56	31.081	986	97 21 96	31.401
967	93 50 89	31.097	987	97 41 69	31.417
968	93 70 24	31.113	988	97 61 44	31.432
969	93 89 61	31.129	989	97 81 21	31.448
970	94 09 00	31.145	990	98 01 00	31.464
971	94 28 41	31.161	991	98 20 81	31.480
972	94 47 84	31.177	992	98 40 64	31.496
973	94 67 29	31.193	993	98 60 49	31.512
974	94 86 76	31.209	994	98 80 36	31.528
975	95 06 25	31.225	995	99 00 25	31.544
976	95 25 76	31.241	996	99 20 16	31.559
977	95 45 29	31.257	997	99 40 09	31.575
978	95 64 84	31.273	998	99 60 04	31.591
979	95 84 41	31.289	999	99 80 01	31.607
980	96 04 00	31.305	1000	100 00 00	31.623

How to use this table: The values in Table B represent proportions of the area under the standard normal curve. This curve has a mean of 0.00, a standard deviation of 1.00 and a total area of 1.00. Because the normal curve is symmetrical, the areas corresponding to negative z-scores are identical to the areas corresponding to positive z-scores. Thus, in using the table, areas corresponding to −z will be the same as those of +z.

Values of z are given in column A. Column B contains the corresponding area between the mean and z.

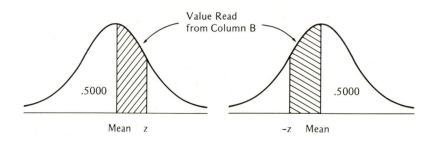

Column C contains the area beyond z.

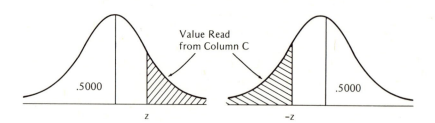

Since the curve is symmetric, each half of the curve contains .5000 of the total area. This fact, plus the values from the table, enable us to calculate any area under the curve in terms of a z-score or z-scores.

(A) z	(B) area between mean and z	(C) area beyond z	(A) z	(B) area between mean and z	(C) area beyond z	(A) z	(B) area between mean and z	(C) area beyond z
0.00	.0000	.5000	0.55	.2088	.2912	1.10	.3643	.1357
0.01	.0040	.4960	0.56	.2123	.2877	1.11	.3665	.1335
0.02	.0080	.4920	0.57	.2157	.2843	1.12	.3686	.1314
0.03	.0120	.4880	0.58	.2190	.2810	1.13	.3708	.1292
0.04	.0160	.4840	0.59	.2224	.2776	1.14	.3729	.1271
0.05	.0199	.4801	0.60	.2257	.2743	1.15	.3749	.1251
0.06	.0239	.4761	0.61	.2291	.2709	1.16	.3770	.1230
0.07	.0279	.4721	0.62	.2324	.2676	1.17	.3790	.1210
0.08	.0319	.4681	0.63	.2357	.2643	1.18	.3810	.1190
0.09	.0359	.4641	0.64	.2389	.2611	1.19	.3830	.1170
0.10	.0398	.4602	0.65	.2422	.2578	1.20	.3849	.1151
0.11	.0438	.4562	0.66	.2454	.2546	1.21	.3869	.1131
0.12	.0478	.4522	0.67	.2486	.2514	1.22	.3888	.1112
0.13	.0517	.4483	0.68	.2517	.2483	1.23	.3907	.1093
0.14	.0557	.4443	0.69	.2549	.2451	1.24	.3925	.1075
0.15	.0596	.4404	0.70	.2580	.2420	1.25	.3944	.1056
0.16	.0636	.4364	0.71	.2611	.2389	1.26	.3962	.1038
0.17	.0675	.4325	0.72	.2642	.2358	1.27	.3980	.1020
0.18	.0714	.4286	0.73	.2673	.2327	1.28	.3997	.1003
0.19	.0753	.4247	0.74	.2704	.2296	1.29	.4015	.0985
0.20	.0793	.4207	0.75	.2734	.2266	1.30	.4032	.0968
0.21	.0832	.4168	0.76	.2764	.2236	1.31	.4049	.0951
0.22	.0871	.4129	0.77	.2794	.2206	1.32	.4066	.0934
0.23	.0910	.4090	0.78	.2823	.2177	1.33	.4082	.0918
0.24	.0948	.4052	0.79	.2852	.2148	1.34	.4099	.0901
0.25	.0987	.4013	0.80	.2881	.2119	1.35	.4115	.0885
0.26	.1026	.3974	0.81	.2910	.2090	1.36	.4131	.0869
0.27	.1064	.3936	0.82	.2939	.2061	1.37	.4147	.0853
0.28	.1103	.3897	0.83	.2967	.2033	1.38	.4162	.0838
0.29	.1141	.3859	0.84	.2995	.2005	1.39	.4177	.0823
0.30	.1179	.3821	0.85	.3023	.1977	1.40	.4192	.0808
0.31	.1217	.3783	0.86	.3051	.1949	1.41	.4207	.0793
0.32	.1255	.3745	0.87	.3078	.1922	1.42	.4222	.0778
0.33	.1293	.3707	0.88	.3106	.1894	1.43	.4236	.0764
0.34	.1331	.3669	0.89	.3133	.1867	1.44	.4251	.0749
0.35	.1368	.3632	0.90	.3159	.1841	1.45	.4265	.0735
0.36	.1406	.3594	0.91	.3186	.1814	1.46	.4279	.0721
0.37	.1443	.3557	0.92	.3212	.1788	1.47	.4292	.0708
0.38	.1480	.3520	0.93	.3238	.1762	1.48	.4306	.0694
0.39	.1517	.3483	0.94	.3264	.1736	1.49	.4319	.0681
0.40	.1554	.3446	0.95	.3289	.1711	1.50	.4332	.0668
0.41	.1591	.3409	0.96	.3315	.1685	1.51	.4345	.0655
0.42	.1628	.3372	0.97	.3340	.1660	1.52	.4357	.0643
0.43	.1664	.3336	0.98	.3365	.1635	1.53	.4370	.0630
0.44	.1700	.3300	0.99	.3389	.1611	1.54	.4382	.0618
0.45	.1736	.3264	1.00	.3413	.1587	1.55	.4394	.0606
0.46	.1772	.3228	1.01	.3438	.1562	1.56	.4406	.0594
0.47	.1808	.3192	1.02	.3461	.1539	1.57	.4418	.0582
0.48	.1844	.3156	1.03	.3485	.1515	1.58	.4429	.0571
0.49	.1879	.3121	1.04	.3508	.1492	1.59	.4441	.0559
0.50	.1915	.3085	1.05	.3531	.1469	1.60	.4452	.0548
0.51	.1950	.3050	1.06	.3554	.1446	1.61	.4463	.0537
0.52	.1985	.3015	1.07	.3577	.1423	1.62	.4474	.0526
0.53	.2019	.2981	1.08	.3599	.1401	1.63	.4484	.0516
0.54	.2054	.2946	1.09	.3621	.1379	1.64	.4495	.0505

table B   proportions of area under the normal curve

(A) z	(B) area between mean and z	(C) area beyond z	(A) z	(B) area between mean and z	(C) area beyond z	(A) z	(B) area between mean and z	(C) area beyond z
1.65	.4505	.0495	2.22	.4868	.0132	2.79	.4974	.0026
1.66	.4515	.0485	2.23	.4871	.0129	2.80	.4974	.0026
1.67	.4525	.0475	2.24	.4875	.0125	2.81	.4975	.0025
1.68	.4535	.0465	2.25	.4878	.0122	2.82	.4976	.0024
1.69	.4545	.0455	2.26	.4881	.0119	2.83	.4977	.0023
1.70	.4554	.0446	2.27	.4884	.0116	2.84	.4977	.0023
1.71	.4564	.0436	2.28	.4887	.0113	2.85	.4978	.0022
1.72	.4573	.0427	2.29	.4890	.0110	2.86	.4979	.0021
1.73	.4582	.0418	2.30	.4893	.0107	2.87	.4979	.0021
1.74	.4591	.0409	2.31	.4896	.0104	2.88	.4980	.0020
1.75	.4599	.0401	2.32	.4898	.0102	2.89	.4981	.0019
1.76	.4608	.0392	2.33	.4901	.0099	2.90	.4981	.0019
1.77	.4616	.0384	2.34	.4904	.0096	2.91	.4982	.0018
1.78	.4625	.0375	2.35	.4906	.0094	2.92	.4982	.0018
1.79	.4633	.0367	2.36	.4909	.0091	2.93	.4983	.0017
1.80	.4641	.0359	2.37	.4911	.0089	2.94	.4984	.0016
1.81	.4649	.0351	2.38	.4913	.0087	2.95	.4984	.0016
1.82	.4656	.0344	2.39	.4916	.0084	2.96	.4985	.0015
1.83	.4664	.0336	2.40	.4918	.0082	2.97	.4985	.0015
1.84	.4671	.0329	2.41	.4920	.0080	2.98	.4986	.0014
1.85	.4678	.0322	2.42	.4922	.0078	2.99	.4986	.0014
1.86	.4686	.0314	2.43	.4925	.0075	3.00	.4987	.0013
1.87	.4693	.0307	2.44	.4927	.0073	3.01	.4987	.0013
1.88	.4699	.0301	2.45	.4929	.0071	3.02	.4987	.0013
1.89	.4706	.0294	2.46	.4931	.0069	3.03	.4988	.0012
1.90	.4713	.0287	2.47	.4932	.0068	3.04	.4988	.0012
1.91	.4719	.0281	2.48	.4934	.0066	3.05	.4989	.0011
1.92	.4726	.0274	2.49	.4936	.0064	3.06	.4989	.0011
1.93	.4732	.0268	2.50	.4938	.0062	3.07	.4989	.0011
1.94	.4738	.0262	2.51	.4940	.0060	3.08	.4990	.0010
1.95	.4744	.0256	2.52	.4941	.0059	3.09	.4990	.0010
1.96	.4750	.0250	2.53	.4943	.0057	3.10	.4990	.0010
1.97	.4756	.0244	2.54	.4945	.0055	3.11	.4991	.0009
1.98	.4761	.0239	2.55	.4946	.0054	3.12	.4991	.0009
1.99	.4767	.0233	2.56	.4948	.0052	3.13	.4991	.0009
2.00	.4772	.0228	2.57	.4949	.0051	3.14	.4992	.0008
2.01	.4778	.0222	2.58	.4951	.0049	3.15	.4992	.0008
2.02	.4783	.0217	2.59	.4952	.0048	3.16	.4992	.0008
2.03	.4788	.0212	2.60	.4953	.0047	3.17	.4992	.0008
2.04	.4793	.0207	2.61	.4955	.0045	3.18	.4993	.0007
2.05	.4798	.0202	2.62	.4956	.0044	3.19	.4993	.0007
2.06	.4803	.0197	2.63	.4957	.0043	3.20	.4993	.0007
2.07	.4808	.0192	2.64	.4959	.0041	3.21	.4993	.0007
2.08	.4812	.0188	2.65	.4960	.0040	3.22	.4994	.0006
2.09	.4817	.0183	2.66	.4961	.0039	3.23	.4994	.0006
2.10	.4821	.0179	2.67	.4962	.0038	3.24	.4994	.0006
2.11	.4826	.0174	2.68	.4963	.0037	3.25	.4994	.0006
2.12	.4830	.0170	2.69	.4964	.0036	3.30	.4995	.0005
2.13	.4834	.0166	2.70	.4965	.0035	3.35	.4996	.0004
2.14	.4838	.0162	2.71	.4966	.0034	3.40	.4997	.0003
2.15	.4842	.0158	2.72	.4967	.0033	3.45	.4997	.0003
2.16	.4846	.0154	2.73	.4968	.0032	3.50	.4998	.0002
2.17	.4850	.0150	2.74	.4969	.0031	3.60	.4998	.0002
2.18	.4854	.0146	2.75	.4970	.0030	3.70	.4999	.0001
2.19	.4857	.0143	2.76	.4971	.0029	3.80	.4999	.0001
2.20	.4861	.0139	2.77	.4972	.0028	3.90	.49995	.00005
2.21	.4864	.0136	2.78	.4973	.0027	4.00	.49997	.00003

From Richard P. Runyon and Audrey Haber, *Fundamentals of Behavioral Statistics*, 2nd edition. Reading, Mass.: Addison-Wesley, 1971, pp. 290–291. Reprinted by permission of the authors and the publisher.

essential statistics for social research

TABLE C.
CRITICAL VALUES
OF STUDENT'S T

How to use this table: The first two rows of figures in the table indicate the level of significance (α) for one- and two-tail tests, respectively. The first *column* of figures indicates the degrees of freedom for the test. Remember:

a. when the data are not matched (that is, for the large sample and the small sample t-test), df $= n_1 + n_2 - 2$. For all practical purposes, however, the df for the large sample t-test may be assumed to be infinite (∞).

b. when the data are correlated, or matched, df $= n - 1$, where n is the *number of pairs.*

Once df has been determined and the level of significance has been chosen, simply locate the critical value of t from the corresponding row and column. If the computed value of t equals or exceeds the critical value obtained from the table, reject the null hypothesis. If the observed value of t is less than the critical value, do not reject the null hypothesis.

Example: For a set of uncorrelated data, where $n_1 = 20$ and $n_2 = 16$, a value of t $= 1.92$ was computed. For a one-tail test with $= .05$, this observed value exceeds the critical value (which is 1.697); therefore, reject the null hypothesis.

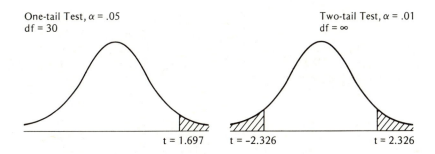

One-tail Test, $\alpha = .05$
df = 30

Two-tail Test, $\alpha = .01$
df = ∞

t = 1.697   t = –2.326   t = 2.326

table C   distribution of t

df	Level of significance for one-tailed test					
	.10	.05	.025	.01	.005	.0005
	Level of significance for two-tailed test					
	.20	.10	.05	.02	.01	.001
1	3.078	6.314	12.706	31.821	63.657	636.619
2	1.886	2.920	4.303	6.965	9.925	31.598
3	1.638	2.353	3.182	4.541	5.841	12.941
4	1.533	2.132	2.776	3.747	4.604	8.610
5	1.476	2.015	2.571	3.365	4.032	6.859
6	1.440	1.943	2.447	3.143	3.707	5.959
7	1.415	1.895	2.365	2.998	3.499	5.405
8	1.397	1.860	2.306	2.896	3.355	5.041
9	1.383	1.833	2.262	2.821	3.250	4.781
10	1.372	1.812	2.228	2.764	3.169	4.587
11	1.363	1.796	2.201	2.718	3.106	4.437
12	1.356	1.782	2.179	2.681	3.055	4.318
13	1.350	1.771	2.160	2.650	3.012	4.221
14	1.345	1.761	2.145	2.624	2.977	4.140
15	1.341	1.753	2.131	2.602	2.947	4.073
16	1.337	1.746	2.120	2.583	2.921	4.015
17	1.333	1.740	2.110	2.567	2.898	3.965
18	1.330	1.734	2.101	2.552	2.878	3.922
19	1.328	1.729	2.093	2.539	2.861	3.883
20	1.325	1.725	2.086	2.528	2.845	3.850
21	1.323	1.721	2.080	2.518	2.831	3.819
22	1.321	1.717	2.074	2.508	2.819	3.792
23	1.319	1.714	2.069	2.500	2.807	3.767
24	1.318	1.711	2.064	2.492	2.797	3.745
25	1.316	1.708	2.060	2.485	2.787	3.725
26	1.315	1.706	2.056	2.479	2.779	3.707
27	1.314	1.703	2.052	2.473	2.771	3.690
28	1.313	1.701	2.048	2.467	2.763	3.674
29	1.311	1.699	2.045	2.462	2.756	3.659
30	1.310	1.697	2.042	2.457	2.750	3.646
40	1.303	1.684	2.021	2.423	2.704	3.551
60	1.296	1.671	2.000	2.390	2.660	3.460
120	1.289	1.658	1.980	2.358	2.617	3.373
∞	1.282	1.645	1.960	2.326	2.576	3.291

Abridged from R. A. Fisher and F. Yates, *Statistical Tables for Biological, Agricultural and Medical Research*, 6th edition. London: Longman Group Ltd., 1974, Table III, p. 46. (Previously published by Oliver & Boyd, Edinburgh.) Reprinted by permission of the authors and publishers.

essential statistics for social research

How to use this table: This table is read exactly as Table C *except* that the statistic A is significant at a given level of alpha if it is equal to or *less than* the table value.

Example: If df = 25, α = .05, two-tail test, and the computed value of A is 0.22, A is significant since this value is less than the table value of 0.265. In other words, this would lead us to reject the null hypothesis. If the computed value of A is greater than the table value, we would not reject the null hypothesis.

table D critical values of A

For any given value of n − 1, the table shows the values of A corresponding to various levels of probability. A is significant at a given level if it is equal to or *less than* the value shown in the table.

n − 1*	Level of significance for one-tailed test					n − 1*
	.05	.025	.01	.005	.0005	
	Level of significance for two-tailed test					
	.10	.05	.02	.01	.001	
1	0.5125	0.5031	0.50049	0.50012	0.5000012	1
2	0.412	0.369	0.347	0.340	0.334	2
3	0.385	0.324	0.286	0.272	0.254	3
4	0.376	0.304	0.257	0.238	0.211	4
5	0.372	0.293	0.240	0.218	0.184	5
6	0.370	0.286	0.230	0.205	0.167	6
7	0.369	0.281	0.222	0.196	0.155	7
8	0.368	0.278	0.217	0.190	0.146	8
9	0.368	0.276	0.213	0.185	0.139	9
10	0.368	0.274	0.210	0.181	0.134	10
11	0.368	0.273	0.207	0.178	0.130	11
12	0.368	0.271	0.205	0.176	0.126	12
13	0.368	0.270	0.204	0.174	0.124	13
14	0.368	0.270	0.202	0.172	0.121	14
15	0.368	0.269	0.201	0.170	0.119	15
16	0.368	0.268	0.200	0.169	0.117	16
17	0.368	0.268	0.199	0.168	0.116	17
18	0.368	0.267	0.198	0.167	0.114	18
19	0.368	0.267	0.197	0.166	0.113	19
20	0.368	0.266	0.197	0.165	0.112	20
21	0.368	0.266	0.196	0.165	0.111	21
22	0.368	0.266	0.196	0.164	0.110	22
23	0.368	0.266	0.195	0.163	0.109	23
24	0.368	0.265	0.195	0.163	0.108	24
25	0.368	0.265	0.194	0.162	0.108	25
26	0.368	0.265	0.194	0.162	0.107	26
27	0.360	0.265	0.193	0.161	0.107	27
28	0.368	0.265	0.193	0.161	0.106	28
29	0.368	0.264	0.193	0.161	0.106	29
30	0.368	0.264	0.193	0.160	0.105	30
40	0.368	0.263	0.191	0.158	0.102	40
60	0.369	0.262	0.189	0.155	0.099	60
120	0.369	0.261	0.187	0.153	0.095	120
∞	0.370	0.260	0.185	0.151	0.092	∞

*n = number of pairs

Joseph Sadler, "A Test of Significance of the Difference between Means of Correlated Measures, Based on a Simplification of Student's t." *British Journal of Psychology* 46 (1955), p. 226. Reprinted by permission of the author and publisher.

How to use this table: The first two pages of this table are used when $\alpha = .05$; the second two pages are used when $\alpha = .01$.

The first row of figures indicates the degrees of freedom associated with the *larger* mean square; the first column indicates the degrees of freedom associated with the *lesser* mean square. The body of the table contains the critical values of F. If a computed value of F equals or exceeds the critical value, reject the null hypothesis. If the computed value is less than the critical value, do not reject the null hypothesis.

The F-test is nondirectional, so no distinction is made between one- and two-tail tests.

Example: A value of F = 3.26 is computed; with $df_1 = 6$ and $df_2 = 16$, this value is significant at the .05 level, because it exceeds the critical value of 2.74. F = 3.26 is not significant at the .01 level, however, since it does not exceed the critical value of 4.20.

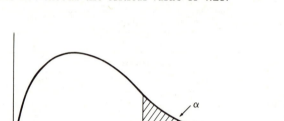

essential statistics for social research

table E   distribution of F; Pr = 0.05

df_2 \ df_1	1	2	3	4	5	6	8	10
1	161.4	199.5	215.7	224.6	230.2	234.0	238.9	241.9
2	18.51	19.00	19.16	19.25	19.30	19.33	19.37	19.40
3	10.13	9.55	9.28	9.12	9.01	8.94	8.85	8.79
4	7.71	6.94	6.59	6.39	6.26	6.16	6.04	5.96
5	6.61	5.79	5.41	5.19	5.05	4.95	4.82	4.74
6	5.99	5.14	4.76	4.53	4.39	4.28	4.15	4.06
7	5.59	4.74	4.35	4.12	3.97	3.87	3.73	3.64
8	5.32	4.46	4.07	3.84	3.69	3.58	3.44	3.35
9	5.12	4.20	3.86	3.63	3.48	3.37	3.23	3.14
10	4.96	4.10	3.71	3.48	3.33	3.22	3.07	2.98
11	4.84	3.98	3.59	3.36	3.20	3.09	2.95	2.85
12	4.75	3.89	3.49	3.26	3.11	3.00	2.85	2.75
13	4.67	3.81	3.41	3.18	3.03	2.92	2.77	2.67
14	4.60	3.74	3.34	3.11	2.96	2.85	2.70	2.60
15	4.54	3.68	3.29	3.06	2.90	2.79	2.64	2.54
16	4.49	3.63	3.24	3.01	2.85	2.74	2.59	2.49
17	4.45	3.59	3.20	2.96	2.81	2.70	2.55	2.45
18	4.41	3.55	3.16	2.93	2.77	2.66	2.51	2.41
19	4.38	3.52	3.13	2.90	2.74	2.63	2.48	2.38
20	4.35	3.49	3.10	2.87	2.71	2.60	2.45	2.35
21	4.32	3.47	3.07	2.84	2.68	2.57	2.42	2.32
22	4.30	3.44	3.05	2.82	2.66	2.55	2.40	2.30
23	4.28	3.42	3.03	2.80	2.64	2.53	2.37	2.27
24	4.26	3.40	3.01	2.78	2.62	2.51	2.36	2.25
25	4.24	3.39	2.99	2.76	2.60	2.49	2.34	2.24
26	4.23	3.37	2.98	2.74	2.59	2.47	2.32	2.22
27	4.21	3.35	2.96	2.73	2.57	2.46	2.31	2.20
28	4.20	3.34	2.95	2.71	2.56	2.45	2.29	2.19
29	4.18	3.33	2.93	2.70	2.55	2.43	2.28	2.18
30	4.17	3.32	2.92	2.69	2.53	2.42	2.27	2.16
40	4.08	3.23	2.84	2.61	2.45	2.34	2.18	2.08
60	4.00	3.15	2.76	2.53	2.37	2.25	2.10	1.99
80	3.96	3.11	2.72	2.48	2.33	2.21	2.05	1.95
120	3.92	3.07	2.68	2.45	2.29	2.17	2.02	1.91
∞	3.84	3.00	2.60	2.37	2.21	2.10	1.94	1.83

table E   distribution of F; Pr = 0.05

df_1 / df_2	12	15	20	30	40	60	120	∞
1	243.9	245.9	248.0	250.1	251.1	252.2	253.3	254.3
2	19.41	19.43	19.45	19.46	19.47	19.48	19.49	19.50
3	8.74	8.70	8.66	8.62	8.59	8.57	8.55	8.53
4	5.91	5.86	5.80	5.75	5.72	5.69	5.66	5.63
5	4.68	4.62	4.56	4.50	4.46	4.43	4.40	4.36
6	4.00	3.94	3.87	3.81	3.77	3.74	3.70	3.67
7	3.57	3.51	3.44	3.38	3.34	3.30	3.27	3.23
8	3.28	3.22	3.15	3.08	3.04	3.01	2.97	2.93
9	3.07	3.01	2.94	2.86	2.83	2.79	2.75	2.71
10	2.91	2.85	2.77	2.70	2.66	2.62	2.58	2.54
11	2.79	2.72	2.65	2.57	2.53	2.49	2.45	2.40
12	2.69	2.62	2.54	2.47	2.43	2.38	2.34	2.30
13	2.60	2.53	2.46	2.38	2.34	2.30	2.25	2.21
14	2.53	2.46	2.39	2.31	2.27	2.22	2.18	2.13
15	2.48	2.40	2.33	2.25	2.20	2.16	2.11	2.07
16	2.42	2.35	2.28	2.19	2.15	2.11	2.06	2.01
17	2.38	2.31	2.23	2.15	2.10	2.06	2.01	1.96
18	2.34	2.27	2.19	2.11	2.06	2.02	1.97	1.92
19	2.31	2.23	2.16	2.07	2.03	1.98	1.93	1.88
20	2.28	2.20	2.12	2.04	1.99	1.95	1.90	1.84
21	2.25	2.18	2.10	2.01	1.96	1.92	1.87	1.81
22	2.23	2.15	2.07	1.98	1.94	1.89	1.84	1.78
23	2.20	2.13	2.05	1.96	1.91	1.86	1.81	1.76
24	2.18	2.11	2.03	1.94	1.89	1.84	1.79	1.73
25	2.16	2.09	2.01	1.92	1.87	1.82	1.77	1.71
26	2.15	2.07	1.99	1.90	1.85	1.80	1.75	1.69
27	2.13	2.06	1.97	1.88	1.84	1.79	1.73	1.67
28	2.12	2.04	1.96	1.87	1.82	1.77	1.71	1.65
29	2.10	2.03	1.94	1.85	1.81	1.75	1.70	1.64
30	2.09	2.01	1.93	1.84	1.79	1.74	1.68	1.62
40	2.00	1.92	1.84	1.74	1.69	1.64	1.58	1.51
60	1.92	1.84	1.75	1.65	1.59	1.53	1.47	1.39
80	1.88	1.80	1.70	1.60	1.54	1.49	1.41	1.32
120	1.83	1.75	1.66	1.55	1.50	1.43	1.35	1.25
∞	1.75	1.67	1.57	1.46	1.39	1.32	1.22	1.00

essential statistics for social research

table E   distribution of F; Pr = 0.01

df_1 / df_2	12	15	20	30	40	60	120	∞
1	6106	6157	6209	6261	6287	6313	6339	6366
2	99.42	99.43	99.45	99.47	99.47	99.48	99.49	99.50
3	27.05	26.87	26.69	26.50	26.41	26.32	26.22	26.13
4	14.37	14.20	14.02	13.84	13.75	13.65	13.56	13.46
5	9.89	9.72	9.55	9.38	9.29	9.20	9.11	9.02
6	7.72	7.56	7.40	7.23	7.14	7.06	6.97	6.88
7	6.47	6.31	6.16	5.99	5.91	5.82	5.74	5.65
8	5.67	5.52	5.36	5.20	5.12	5.03	4.95	4.86
9	5.11	4.96	4.81	4.65	4.57	4.48	4.40	4.31
10	4.71	4.50	4.41	4.25	4.17	4.08	4.00	3.91
11	4.40	4.25	4.10	3.94	3.86	3.78	3.69	3.60
12	4.16	4.01	3.86	3.70	3.62	3.54	3.45	3.36
13	3.96	3.82	3.66	3.51	3.43	3.34	3.25	3.17
14	3.80	3.66	3.51	3.35	3.27	3.18	3.09	3.00
15	3.67	3.52	3.37	3.21	3.13	3.05	2.96	2.87
16	3.55	3.41	3.26	3.10	3.02	2.93	2.84	2.75
17	3.46	3.31	3.16	3.00	2.92	2.83	2.75	2.65
18	3.37	3.23	3.08	2.92	2.84	2.75	2.66	2.57
19	3.30	3.15	3.00	2.84	2.76	2.67	2.58	2.49
20	3.23	3.09	2.94	2.78	2.69	2.61	2.52	2.42
21	3.17	3.03	2.88	2.72	2.64	2.55	2.46	2.36
22	3.12	2.98	2.83	2.67	2.58	2.50	2.40	2.31
23	3.07	2.93	2.78	2.62	2.54	2.45	2.35	2.26
24	3.03	2.89	2.74	2.58	2.49	2.40	2.31	2.21
25	2.99	2.85	2.70	2.54	2.45	2.36	2.27	2.17
26	2.96	2.81	2.66	2.50	2.42	2.33	2.23	2.13
27	2.93	2.78	2.63	2.47	2.38	2.29	2.20	2.10
28	2.90	2.75	2.60	2.44	2.35	2.26	2.17	2.06
29	2.87	2.73	2.57	2.41	2.33	2.23	2.14	2.03
30	2.84	2.70	2.55	2.39	2.30	2.21	2.11	2.01
40	2.66	2.52	2.37	2.20	2.11	2.02	1.92	1.80
60	2.50	2.35	2.20	2.03	1.94	1.84	1.73	1.60
80	2.41	2.28	2.11	1.94	1.84	1.75	1.63	1.49
120	2.34	2.19	2.03	1.86	1.76	1.66	1.53	1.38
∞	2.18	2.04	1.88	1.70	1.59	1.47	1.32	1.00

table E   *distribution of F; Pr = 0.01*

df_1 / df_2	1	2	3	4	5	6	8	10
1	4052	4999.5	5403	5625	5764	5859	5982	6056
2	98.50	99.00	99.17	99.25	99.30	99.33	99.37	99.40
3	34.12	30.82	29.46	28.71	28.24	27.91	27.49	27.23
4	21.20	18.00	16.69	15.98	15.52	15.21	14.80	14.55
5	16.26	13.27	12.06	11.39	10.97	10.67	10.29	10.05
6	13.75	10.92	9.78	9.15	8.75	8.47	8.10	7.87
7	12.25	9.55	8.45	7.85	7.46	7.19	6.84	6.62
8	11.26	8.65	7.59	7.01	6.63	6.37	6.03	5.81
9	10.56	8.02	6.99	6.42	6.06	5.80	5.47	5.26
10	10.04	7.56	6.55	5.99	5.64	5.39	5.06	4.85
11	9.65	7.21	6.22	5.67	5.32	5.07	4.74	4.54
12	9.33	6.93	5.95	5.41	5.06	4.82	4.50	4.30
13	9.07	6.70	5.74	5.21	4.86	4.62	4.30	4.10
14	8.86	6.51	5.56	5.04	4.69	4.46	4.14	3.94
15	8.68	6.36	5.42	4.89	4.56	4.32	4.00	3.80
16	8.53	6.23	5.29	4.77	4.44	4.20	3.89	3.69
17	8.40	6.11	5.18	4.67	4.34	4.10	3.79	3.59
18	8.29	6.01	5.09	4.58	4.25	4.01	3.71	3.51
19	8.18	5.93	5.01	4.50	4.17	3.94	3.63	3.43
20	8.10	5.85	4.94	4.43	4.10	3.87	3.56	3.37
21	8.02	5.78	4.87	4.37	4.04	3.81	3.51	3.31
22	7.95	5.72	4.82	4.31	3.99	3.76	3.45	3.26
23	7.88	5.66	4.76	4.26	3.94	3.71	3.41	3.21
24	7.82	5.61	4.72	4.22	3.90	3.67	3.36	3.17
25	7.77	5.57	4.68	4.18	3.85	3.63	3.32	3.13
26	7.72	5.53	4.64	4.14	3.82	3.59	3.29	3.09
27	7.68	5.49	4.60	4.11	3.78	3.56	3.26	3.06
28	7.64	5.45	4.57	4.07	3.75	3.53	3.23	3.03
29	7.60	5.42	4.54	4.04	3.73	3.50	3.20	3.00
30	7.56	5.39	4.51	4.02	3.70	3.47	3.17	2.98
40	7.31	5.18	4.31	3.83	3.51	3.29	2.99	2.80
60	7.08	4.98	4.13	3.65	3.34	3.12	2.82	2.63
80	6.96	4.88	4.04	3.56	3.25	3.04	2.74	2.55
120	6.85	4.79	3.95	3.48	3.17	2.96	2.66	2.47
∞	6.63	4.61	3.78	3.32	3.02	2.80	2.51	2.32

Abridged from R. A. Fisher and F. Yates, *Statistical Tables for Biological, Agricultural and Medical Research*, 6th Edition. London: Longman Group Ltd., 1974, Table V, p. 57. (Previously published by Oliver & Boyd, Edinburgh.) Reprinted by permission of the authors and publishers.

TABLE F.
CRITICAL VALUES
OF CHI-SQUARE

How to use this table: The first row of this table lists the probabilities, or levels of significance, of observing given values of Chi-square. The first column of figures indicates the degrees of freedom. For the Chi-square statistic,

$$df = (r - 1)(c - 1)$$

where r and c are the number of rows and columns, respectively, in the data table. A computed value of Chi-square is significant at a given level if it is equal to or greater than the critical value in the table.

Example: If df = 4, a computed value of Chi-square = 10.03 is significant at the .05 level, since the computed value exceeds the table value of 9.488. This observation would lead us to reject the null hypothesis; in other words, we would reject the model of statistical independence. If the observed value was less than the table value, we would not reject the null hypothesis, and we could assume that the model of statistical independence was valid.

Note: With Chi-square, all tests of significance are essentially one-tail tests. This is because the Chi-square test is nondirectional. The test simply determines whether there is any departure from the chance model.

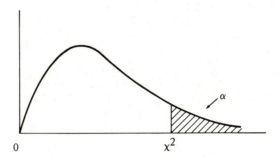

table F   chi square distribution

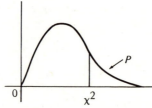

VALUES OF χ^2 FOR VARIOUS VALUES OF P
AND DEGREES OF FREEDOM n

	P			
Degrees of Freedom n	0.10	0.05	0.02	0.01
1	2.706	3.841	5.412	6.635
2	4.605	5.991	7.824	9.210
3	6.251	7.815	9.837	11.341
4	7.779	9.488	11.668	13.277
5	9.236	11.070	13.388	15.086
6	10.645	12.592	15.033	16.812
7	12.017	14.067	16.622	18.475
8	13.362	15.507	18.168	20.090
9	14.684	16.919	19.679	21.666
10	15.987	18.307	21.161	23.209
11	17.275	19.675	22.618	24.725
12	18.549	21.026	24.054	26.217
13	19.812	22.362	25.472	27.688
14	21.064	23.685	26.873	29.141
15	22.307	24.996	28.259	30.578
16	23.542	26.296	29.633	32.000
17	24.769	27.587	30.995	33.409
18	25.989	28.869	32.346	34.805
19	27.204	30.144	33.687	36.191
20	28.412	31.410	35.020	37.566
21	29.615	32.671	36.343	38.932
22	30.813	33.924	37.659	40.289
23	32.007	35.172	38.968	41.638
24	33.196	36.415	40.270	42.980
25	34.382	37.652	41.566	44.314
26	35.563	36.885	42.856	45.642
27	36.741	40.113	44.140	46.963
28	37.916	41.337	45.419	48.278
29	39.087	42.557	46.693	49.588
30	40.256	43.773	47.962	50.892

Abridged from R. A. Fisher and F. Yates, *Statistical Tables for Biological, Agricultural and Medical Research*, 6th edition. London: Longman Group Ltd., 1974, Table IV, p. 47. (Previously published by Oliver & Boyd, Edinburgh.) Reprinted by permission of the authors and publishers.

essential statistics for social research

TABLE G.
PROBABILITY
THAT S (FOR
KENDALL'S TAU,
GOODMAN AND
KRUSKAL'S
GAMMA, AND
SOMERS' D)
ATTAINS OR
EXCEEDS A
SPECIFIC VALUE

How to use this table: This table is used when n ≤ 10. After S is computed as $n_s - n_d$, enter the table for the corresponding values of S and n. The table value is the exact probability of observing a given value of S under sample size n.

The table is constructed for a one-tail test. For a two-tail test, simply *double* the values in the body of the table. For example, for a two-tail test, n = 7, a value of S = 15 was computed. The table value for these data is .015; doubling this gives us a probability of .03. In other words, under a two-tail test, there is only a 3 percent chance of observing a value of S ≥ 15.

The table lists only positive values of S. However, since the distribution of S is symmetric, the probabilities of negative values of S are the same as the corresponding positive values.

table G — probability that S attains or exceeds a specified value. (shown only for positive values. negative values obtainable by symmetry)

S	4	5	8	9
0	0·625	0·592	0·548	0·540
2	0·375	0·408	0·452	0·460
4	0·167	0·242	0·360	0·381
6	0·042	0·117	0·274	0·306
8		0·042	0·199	0·238
10		$0·0^283$	0·138	0·179
12			0·089	0·130
14			0·054	0·090
16			0·031	0·060
18			0·016	0·038
20			$0·0^271$	0·022
22			$0·0^228$	0·012
24			$0·0^387$	$0·0^263$
26			$0·0^319$	$0·0^229$
28			$0·0^425$	$0·0^212$
30				$0·0^343$
32				$0·0^312$
34				$0·0^425$
36				$0·0^528$

S	6	7	10
1	0·500	0·500	0·500
3	0·360	0·386	0·431
5	0·235	0·281	0·364
7	0·136	0·191	0·300
9	0·068	0·119	0·242
11	0·028	0·068	0·190
13	$0·0^283$	0·035	0·146
15	$0·0^214$	0·015	0·108
17		$0·0^254$	0·078
19		$0·0^214$	0·054
21		$0·0^320$	0·036
23			0·023
25			0·014
27			$0·0^283$
29			$0·0^246$
31			$0·0^223$
33			$0·0^211$
35			$0·0^347$
37			$0·0^318$
39			$0·0^458$
41			$0·0^415$
43			$0·0^528$
45			$0·0^628$

Note.—Repeated zeros are indicated by powers, *e.g.* $0·0^347$ stands for $0·00047$.

How to use this table: The first two rows give the levels of significance (α) for one- and two-tail tests. In the first column is the number of pairs (n) which are ranked. The body of the table contains the critical values. If a computed value of rho equals or excees the table value, reject the null hypothesis. If the computed value of rho is less than the Table value, do not reject the null hypothesis.

Example: A value of rho = .66 was computed from a set of data; with n = 20, α = .01, and a one-tail test, we would reject the null hypothesis since the computed value is greater than the table value of .534. (If the computed value was less than .534, we would not reject the null hypothesis.)

For Rho, df = n − 2, where n is the number of pairs.

**TABLE H.
CRITICAL VALUES
OF RHO
(SPEARMAN'S
RANK-ORDER
CORRELATION
COEFFICIENT)**

table H   critical value of rho (rank-order correlation coefficient)

	Level of significance for one-tailed test			
	.05	.025	.01	.005
	Level of significance for two-tailed test			
n*	.10	.05	.02	.01
5	.900	1.000	1.000	--
6	.829	.886	.943	1.000
7	.714	.786	.893	.929
8	.643	.738	.833	.881
9	.600	.683	.783	.833
10	.564	.648	.746	.794
12	.506	.591	.712	.777
14	.456	.544	.645	.715
16	.425	.506	.601	.665
18	.399	.475	.564	.625
20	.377	.450	.534	.591
22	.359	.428	.508	.562
24	.343	.409	.485	.537
26	.329	.392	.465	.515
28	.317	.377	.448	.496
30	.306	.364	.432	.478

*n = number of pairs

Adapted from E. G. Olds, *Annals of Mathematical Statistics*, Vol. 9 (1938), pp. 133–148 and Vol. 20 (1949), pp. 117–118. Reprinted by permission.

How to use this table: For r, df = N − 2. The critical value of r is determined by df, the level of alpha, and the use of a one- or two-tail test. If a computed value of r equals or exceeds the table value, the null hypothesis r = 0.0 is rejected. If the computed value is less than the Table value, the null hypothesis is not rejected.

Example: With df = 15, α = .01, and a two tail test, any value of r equal to or greater than .606 would lead us to reject the null hypothesis; values of r less than .606 would not enable us to reject the null hypothesis. In other words, with df = 15 and a two-tail test, a computed value of r as large or larger than .606 would occur by chance only one time in a hundred.

**TABLE I.
CRITICAL VALUES
OF THE
PEARSON R**

table I significant values of r for testing H_0.

df	Two-Tailed Test $\alpha = .05$	Two-Tailed Test $\alpha = .01$	One-Tailed Test $\alpha = .05$	One-Tailed Test $\alpha = .01$
1	.997	.9999	.988	.9995
2	.950	.990	.900	.980
3	.878	.959	.805	.934
4	.811	.917	.729	.882
5	.754	.874	.669	.833
6	.707	.834	.622	.789
7	.666	.798	.582	.750
8	.632	.765	.549	.716
9	.602	.735	.521	.685
10	.576	.708	.497	.658
11	.553	.684	.476	.634
12	.532	.661	.458	.612
13	.514	.641	.441	.592
14	.497	.623	.426	.574
15	.482	.606	.412	.558
16	.468	.590	.400	.542
17	.456	.575	.389	.528
18	.444	.561	.378	.516
19	.433	.549	.369	.503
20	.423	.537	.360	.492
21	.413	.526	.352	.482
22	.404	.515	.344	.472
23	.396	.505	.337	.462
24	.388	.496	.330	.453
25	.381	.487	.323	.445
26	.374	.479	.317	.437
27	.367	.471	.311	.430
28	.361	.463	.306	.423
29	.355	.456	.301	.416
30	.349	.449	.296	.409
35	.325	.418	.275	.381
40	.304	.393	.257	.358
45	.288	.372	.243	.338
50	.273	.354	.231	.322
60	.250	.325	.211	.295
70	.232	.303	.195	.274
80	.217	.283	.183	.256
90	.205	.267	.173	.242
100	.195	.254	.164	.230

R. A. Fisher and F. Yates, *Statistical Tables for Biological, Agricultural and Medical Research*, 6th edition. London: Longman Group Ltd., 1974, Table VII, p. 61. (Previously published by Oliver & Boyd, Edinburgh.) Reprinted by permission of the authors and publishers.

Anderson, Theodore R. and Morris Zelditch, Jr.
    1975   A Basic Course in Statistics. Third edition. New York: Holt, Rinehart and Winston.

Blalock, Hubert M., Jr.
    1972   Social Statistics. Second edition. New York: McGraw-Hill.

Costner, Herbert L.
    1965   Criteria for measures of association. American Sociological Review. 30 (June): 341–353.

Davis, James A.
    1967   A partial coefficient for Goodman and Kruskal's Gamma. Journal of the American Statistical Association. 62: 189–193.

Edwards, Allen L.
    1974   Statistical Analysis. Fourth edition. New York: Holt, Rinehart and Winston.

Freeman, Linton C.
    1965   Elementary Applied Statistics. New York: John Wiley and Sons.

Freund, John E.
    1973   Modern Elementary Statistics. Fourth edition. Englewood Cliffs, N.J.: Prentice-Hall.

Goodman, Leo A. and William H. Kruskal
    1954   Measures of association for cross classification. Journal of the American Statistical Association. 49 (December): 732–764.

    ———
    1959   Measures of association for cross classifications. II: Further discussion and references. Journal of the American Statistical Association. 54 (March): 123–163.

    ———
    1963   Measures of association for cross classifications. III: Approximate sampling theory. Journal of the American Statistical Association. 58 (June): 310–364.

Huff, Darrel
    1954   How to Lie with Statistics. New York: Norton & Co.

Kendall, Maurice G.
    1962   Rank Correlation Methods. Third edition. London: Charles Griffin.

Kendall, Maurice G. and A. Stuart
    1961   The Advanced Theory of Statistics. Volume two. London: Charles Griffin.

    ———
    1963   The Advanced Theory of Statistics. Volume one. London: Charles Griffin.

Kolstoe, Ralph H.
    1973   Introduction to Statistics for the Behavioral Sciences. Revised edition. Homewood, Ill.: The Dorsey Press.

Loether, Herman J. and Donald G. McTavish
    1974a Descriptive Statistics for Sociologists. Boston: Allyn and Bacon.

    ———
    1974b Inferential Statistics for Sociologists. Boston: Allyn and Bacon.

Mendenhall, William, Lyman Ott and Richard F. Larson
    1974   Statistics. North Scituate, Mass.: Duxbury Press.
Mueller, John H., Karl F. Schuessler and Herbert L. Costner
    1970   Statistical Reasoning in Sociology. Second edition. Boston: Houghton Mifflin.
Phillips, John L., Jr.
    1973   Statistical Thinking. San Francisco: W. H. Freeman.
Rosenberg, Morris
    1968   The Logic of Survey Analysis. New York: Basic Books.
Runyon, Richard P. and Audrey Haber
    1976   Fundamentals of Behavioral Statistics. Third edition. Reading, Mass.: Addison-Wesley.
Sandler, Joseph
    1965   A test of significance of the difference between the means of correlated measures, based on a simplification of Student's t. British Journal of Psychology. 46 (August): 225–226.
Siegel, Sidney
    1956   Nonparametric Statistics. New York: McGraw-Hill.
Slonim, Morris J.
    1960   Sampling. New York: Simon and Schuster.
Somers, Robert H.
    1962   A new asymmetric measure of association for ordinal variables. American Sociological Review. 27 (December): 799–811.
Steven, S. S.
    1946   On the theory of scales of measurement. Science. 103 (June 7): 677–680.
U.S. Bureau of the Census
    1974   Statistical Abstract of the United States. 95th edition. Washington, D.C.: U.S. Government Printing Office.
Weiss, Robert S.
    1968   Statistics in Social Research. New York: John Wiley and Sons.
Wilson, T. P.
    1969   A proportional-reduction-in-error interpretation for Kendall's tau-b. Social Forces. 47 (March): 340–342.
Winer, B. J.
    1962   Statistical Principles in Experimental Design. New York: McGraw-Hill.
Zeisel, Hans
    1957   Say It With Figures. Revised, fourth edition. New York: Harper & Row.
Zeller, Richard A.
    1974   On teaching correlation and regression. Teaching Sociology. 1 (April): 224–241.

index

A. *See* Sandler's A.
Absolute value, 46, 120
Alpha, 69
Analysis of variance (ANOV), 99–106
  between sum of squares in, 104
  degrees of freedom for, 103–105
  F-ratio in, 102
  total sum of squares in, 104
  within sum of squares in, 105
Association. *See also* Correlation.
  defined, 108–111
  direction of, 110
  interval measures of, 161–182
  nominal measures of, 121–134
  ordinal measures of, 137–158
  and PRE logic, 129–130
  types of, 126–128
Asymmetric measure, 126–128
Average, *See also* Mean; Median; Mode.
  comparison of, 38.
Average deviation, 45–47

Between groups sum of squares, 104
Binomial distribution, 64
Boundaries, 15

C. *See* Contingency coefficient.
Causation, 109–110
Centile, 30
Central tendency, 4–5, 21, 29–30, 38–40.
  See also Mean; Median; Mode.
Chance, 61
Chi-square
  cell collapsing, 120–121
  computation of, 114–116
  degrees of freedom for, 116–118
  expected frequencies for, 112–114
  Fisher's exact test for, 120

related measures and, 121
  Yates' correction for, 120
Class boundaries. *See* Boundaries.
Coded data, 34–35
Conditional association, 187
Conditional table, 185
Confidence interval, 82–85, 91–92
Contigency coefficient (C), 123
Continuous distribution, 68
Control variable, 185
Correlation. *See also* Association.
  curvilinear, 180–182
  linear, 162–180
  multiple, 193–197
  partial, 189–193
  rank-order, 154
  zero-order, 187
Correlated samples, 97
Cramer's V, 123
Criterion variable, 12

d (Somers'). *See* Somer's d.
Decile, 30
Degrees of freedom
  discussed, 95–96
  for Chi-square, 117
  for F-test, 103–105
  for r, 178
  for Rho, 158
  for t-test, 96–97
Descriptive statistics, 4
Deviation
  mean, 31–33
  measures of, 45–55
Discrete distribution, 67
Dispersion, 5, 42–55
Dissimilar pairs, 139

Elaboration, 184–188
Empirical probability, 59
Error, proportional reduction in,
   for Gamma, 145–146
   for Lambda, 124
   for r^2, 163, 166
   for Rho-square, 156–157
   for Tau, Goodman, and Kruskal's, 132
Estimation, 80–87
   and sample size, 85–87
   from finite populations, 87
   interval, 82–85
   point, 82
Eta-square, 180–182
Event, 62. *See also* Outcome.
Expected values for Chi-square, 112–114

F-test, 102
Fisher's exact test, 120
Frequency curve, 17
Frequency distribution, 12–15
   continuous (infinite), 68
   discrete (finite), 67
   rules for construction of, 13–14
Frequency polygon, 15

Gamma
   discussed, 137–141
   for grouped data, 142–144
   PRE interpretation of, 144–146
   tied ranks and, 141
   significance test for, 152–154
   and Yule's Q, 146
Goodman, Leo, 131, 137
Goodman's tau, 131–134
Gossett, W. S. ("Student"), 92–93
Guessed mean, 33–34

Histogram, 15
Homoscedasticity, 174, 177
Hypothesis. *See* Null hypothesis.
Hypothesis testing, 70–71. *See also*
   Significance test.

Independence, 109, 112
Inferential statistics, 4, 58
Interaction of variables, 99
Interdecile range, 44
Interquartile range, 44
Interval. *See* Association; Measurement.
Interval estimate, 82

Kendall, M. G., 147
Kendall's tau, 152–154
   significance test for, 152–154
Kruskal, William H., 131, 137
Kruskal's tau, 131–134

Lambda
   interpretation of, 125–126
   prediction rules for, 125–126
   symmetric, 128–129
Least squares, principle of, 47
Levels of measurement. *See* Measurement.
Limits. *See* Boundaries.

Marginal values, 113
Matched samples, 97
Mean
   defined, 3, 31
   deviations from, 31–32
   for grouped data, 33–36
   guessed, 33–34
   weighted, 37
Mean square, 48, 106
Measurement, 6
   interval level, 9–11
   nominal level, 7–8, 11
   ordinal level, 8–9, 11
   ratio level, 9–11
Median
   defined, 24
   for grouped data, 26–28
Modal category, 23
Mode
   defined, 22
   for grouped data, 22
   for ungrouped data, 23
   within category (lambda), 124, 126
Multiple correlation, 193–197
Mutual association, 126–128

Nominal. *See* Association; Measurement.
Normal distribution, 52
   and binomial probability, 64–68
   and standard deviation, 50–55
Norming variable, 12
Null hypothesis, 69

One-tail test, 70
One-way association, 126–128
Ordinal. *See* Association; Measurement.
Outcome, 59. *See also* Event.

Parameter, 95
Partial correlation
   for gamma, 192–193
   for r, 189–192
   for tau, 192
Pearson r
   assumptions for, 175
   as computation for grouped data,
      172–180
   as computation for ungrouped data,
      170–172
   as a PRE measure, 162–169
   reversibility of, 179

essential statistics for social research

significance test for, 178
and standard scores, 169–170
Percentage difference, 111, 184–189
Phi coefficient, 121–123
Phi-square, 122
Point estimate, 82
Population, 76
Probability, 58
   and hypothesis testing, 68–72
   basic rules of, 62–63
   binomial, 64–68
   empirical, 59
   event, 62
   outcome, 59
Proportional reduction in error (PRE)
   errors in prediction, 130
   explained, 129–131
   prediction rules for, 129–130

Q. See Yule's Q.
Quartile, 29

r. See Pearson r.
Range, 43
   extreme scores, influence of, 43
   interdecile, 44
   interquartile, 44
Rate, 11–12
Ratio, 12. See also Measurement.
Regression line, 164, 169
Rejection, region of. See Alpha.
Rho. See Spearman rank-order correlation
   coefficient.

S, 141
   significance test for, 152–154
Samples, types of, 77–78
Sampling distribution, 79–80
Sampling error, 80
Sandler's A-statistic, 98–99
Scales. See Measurement.
Scatterplot, 173
Significance tests
   for A, 98–99
   for Chi-square, 118–119
   for F, 103
   for Gamma, 152–154
   for r, 178
   for Rho, 158
   for S, 152–154
   for t, 93
Similar pairs, 138
Skewness, 38
Slope of a line, 164
Somer's d, 149–152
   significance test for, 152–154

Somers, R., 149
Spearman rank-order correlation
   coefficient (Rho)
   defined, 154
   Rho-squared, 156–158
   significance test for, 158
   tied ranks and, 155–156
Specification, 187
Spurious relationship, 186
Standard deviation, 47–55
   and normal distribution, 50–55
   for grouped data, 50
   for ungrouped data, 49
Standard error, 81–87
   and sample size, 85–87
   of the difference between means, 93
Standard score, 5, 52–55
Statistics
   descriptive, 4
   inferential, 4
Student's t. See t-test.
Sum of squares, 47–48, 84, 104–105
Suppression, 187
Symmetric measure, 126–128

t-test, 90–99
   defined, 93
   degrees of freedom for, 95
   for correlated samples, 97–98
   for small samples, 94–97
Tau. See Goodman's tau; Kendall's tau;
   Kruskal's tau.
Test factor, 185
Total sum of squares, ANOV, 104
True limits, 15
Two-tail test, 70
Type I Error, 69–70
Type II Error, 69–70

V. See Cramer's V.
Variability. See Dispersion.
Variance, 48–50. See also Analysis of
   variance.
Variation, 5, 42–55, 168

Weighted mean, 37
Weiss, Robert, 108, 110–111
Within groups sum of squares, 105

Y-intercept, 164
Yates' correction, 120
Yule's Q, 146

z-score, 52–55
Zero-order association, 187